DANCE TO FREEDOM

FROM GHUNGROOS TO GUNPOWDER

A.K. GANDHI

FINGERPRINT!

Published by

FiNGERPRINT!

An imprint of Prakash Books India Pvt. Ltd

113/A, Darya Ganj,
New Delhi-110 002
Email: info@prakashbooks.com/sales@prakashbooks.com

Fingerprint Publishing
@FingerprintP
@fingerprintpublishingbooks
www.fingerprintpublishing.com

ISBN: 978 93 5856 962 9

CONTENTS

Part V : Begum Hazrat Mahal

Part VI : Dharman Bibi

Preface

Dance in India has a rich heritage spanning centuries, evolving into a unique art form that has gracefully adapted and transformed, showcasing a myriad of vibrant hues over time. The *tawaifs* have contributed greatly to its evolution and transformation, and in many cases, they have been at the forefront of developing the Hindustani variety of dance and music that has kept the audience hooked to it over centuries and continues to enthrall them even today.

The term 'tawaif' once denoted a noble, exalted, elite, and dignified woman, but with the massive political changes taking place in the country, its meaning deteriorated, as did the attitude with which people looked at the ladies belonging to this class. While they flourished during the Muslim period with some roadblocks under some rulers like Aurangzeb, the rule of the British did them the greatest harm as they bracketed the practitioners of these fine arts with prostitutes, which brought them a bad name and social censure. Over centuries, tawaifs experienced a stark societal shift—from a period when nobles and the wealthy felt proud on being seen in their company, even sending their children for etiquette training, to a time when they were looked at as a blot on the society.

This is a complex journey over centuries in which the tawaifs saw their trade touch the zenith of popularity and then fall to irredeemable depths.

The tawaifs, however, were very ingenious as they adapted to the new environs developing around them while simultaneously guarding their traditional form by standing up to face the challenges that the British Raj threw at them. There are scores of them who confronted and did their bit in the fight against the foreign masters. Some of them are very popular to the extent that people do not accept them as tawaifs at all, as is the case with Begum Hazrat Mahal.

However, the contribution of most of them has been vastly overlooked. They have been reduced to mere footnotes, while many others are not considered worthy enough for even this. We also have a third category of these tawaifs whose contribution to the freedom struggle has survived only in folktales at the local level without any substantial evidence.

In this book, I have included the tawaifs belonging to all three categories who stood up against the British boldly. The sacrifices of these tawaifs, although varying, are exemplary example of unprecedented courage. Some of them died fighting or faced death penalties, while others suffered horrible injustice at the hands of the mighty and resourceful imperialists.

It was an enduring and adventurous journey of research that included diving into the annals of history to locate the nuggets of information because, in most cases, the records were either not created or were wiped out. This was especially the case when a nautch girl was linked to a person who had earned a worthy place in our history, as people thought that they could be a blot on the exalted name of the freedom fighter. One can find solace in the fact that, in some cases, their stories have filtered down to generations in the form of folktales, folksongs, and legends. Due

to limited resources, I have penned down their stories in the form of 'soft' history without deviating from 'hard' facts that could be corroborated by the confirmed sources. This style has allowed me to narrate their lives in an interesting way that would capture a common reader without losing sight of the facts.

Acknowledgment

The research for the book took me to several states several times over a period of two years, with much of the distance being covered by self-driving in company of my eternal source of motivation: Alka, my better half, who would read out books while I drove and pointed out facts that could be of interest to me. Alka also played a pivotal role in recording numerous conversations and was instrumental in engaging individuals who might not have otherwise participated. Her immense dedication has made a significant contribution to this endeavor. I am also sincerely grateful to a large number of historians, professors, journalists, writers, and common people who have helped me in diverse ways. While I can't list them all, there are some names I would certainly like to mention.

Firstly, let me name the stalwarts who have been a perennial source of inspiration to me and are ever willing to engage in lively discussions whenever I am in the process of starting a new book—Dr. K.D. Sharma, Dr. Amit Pathak, Dr. K.K. Sharma, Dr. Vignesh Tyagi, Pankaj Chaturvedi—all of them are historians and writers of repute. In addition to these, there were many who went out of their

way to help me, and these include—Rajiv Edgar (Kanpur), Dr. Ram Sharma (Ballia), Dr. Pravesh Bhardwaj (BHU, Banaras), Dr. Vinod Kumar Jaiswal (BHU, Banaras), and Kunwar Virbhadra Singh (ninth-generation descendant of Babu Kunwar Singh, Jagdishpur).

I would also like to thank the writers and professors who have been kind enough to make their books and papers available. In addition, there were several other people from across different states of India who helped me in a variety of ways, of whom I would like to name a few: Dr. Subodh Garg, Dr. R.K. Bhatnagar, Tribhuvan Singh, Umakant Dixit, (sadly, Late) P.K. Maurya, Manoj Gautam Manu, Vinay Mohan, Vivek Rao, Deepak Bhardwaj, Ashok Shukla, A.K. Mishra, Gaurav Dixit, Raj Gopal Singh Verma, Raj Kishore Sharma Raje, Dr. Suman Jain, Dr. Jyoti Sinha, Ram Dheeraj, Shivdutt Mishra, Ramesh Ojha, Prof Kusum Kedia, Alok Singh, Sunil Sahasrabuddhi, Dr. Snehvir Pundeer, Samuel Elbert, Maulana Shamsudin, Anupam Bajpai, Anil Mishra Bhaig, Manish Awasthy, Ram Kishor Bajpayee, Saket Sahay, among others. The list is not at all exhaustive.

I would like to extend my heartfelt gratitude to all those ladies who requested not to record, name, or quote them in the book but helped me learn invaluable facets of the lives of tawaifs and other people associated with the trade.

Prashant Agarwal has been associated with me for over two decades and helps resolve technical glitches. In the book, he helped me sketch the two maps.

I would like to thank my younger son, Sanchit Gandhi, a research scholar, who read parts of my manuscript despite paucity of time and contributed useful insights and suggestions.

In the end, I should make it a point to thank Suhail Mathur of *The Book Bakers* for his services as a literary agent. His insightful observations have helped me up the ante. As an author, I wish to express my gratitude to Fingerprint Publishing for presenting my

work to the public. I am appreciative of the steadfast belief in my work provided by Shantanu Duttagupta, the Executive Publisher at Fingerprint. I had a great experience working with Shruti Tiwari, the editor at Fingerprint. I truly appreciate her hard work and the instructive insights she provided in the book.

Part
I

Fall of the Nautch Girl

1

The Nautch Girls and Their Rise

Dance is one of the most noble sentiments and fine arts, and ranks high among the performing arts. It is an integral part of the tradition and culture of India. Together with music, it is considered of divine origin.

Dancers have been held in high esteem since time immemorial. We find mention of dance and dancers even in the ancient Hindu mythological texts, which delineate the *apsaras* or nymphs giving live performances in the royal court of Indra. These apsaras were created by Lord Brahma to undertake the delicate *lasya* dance. They danced to the music of the *Gandharvas*, the mythological divine singers. The Puranas mention a number of apsaras, including Rambha, Ambika, Manorama, Alka, and others.

Apart from dancing, these divine damsels helped the gods in their endeavors. For instance, whenever Lord Indra felt his throne threatened by the earthlings' hard penance, he would take the help of the *apsaras* to break their penance. One renowned example of

the same is when Indra asked Menaka to break the penance being undertaken by Sage Vishwamitra.

The *Vedas* mention the word *nritya* in several places and talk about women dancers giving public performances in the company of instrument players, and talk about how they enjoyed a high status in society. The *Upanishads* and other Vedic scriptures describe dance and music vividly, and it was at this stage that different classical dance forms started to take shape. At this time, dance was associated with a noble, spiritual value and was also seen as a form of yogic exercise to strengthen the mental state and physical capabilities. The Puranas in particular speak of dance as an exalted form of skill and the presence of a dancer on a festive occasion as auspicious.

Subsequently, the tradition of having dancers in the royal courts was prevalent in the ancient period as well, and dance performances were common during festivals too. Different popular dance forms accompanied drama, singing, acting, and emotions to match the occasion and theme of the dance. The great epics *The Ramayana* and *The Mahabharata* too mention it at different instances. When the Pandavas were in exile, Arjuna learned dancing from Urvashi, a heavenly nymph, and used this skill during the one-year-long incognito period of the exile. Moreover, Lord Krishna himself is said to be a master at dancing. Talking about the *Ramayana*, on their return from the exile, Ram and Sita were welcomed by a grand dance performance by the *ganikas* of the kingdom.

Historians have even found a dancing figurine belonging to the Indus Valley civilization at Mohenjo Daro and the temples of the ancient India are decorated with dance figurines all around—this speaks of the importance of this form of fine art and the status that the dancers enjoyed during this era. Another evidence of the same is the *Kamasutra.* Written around the 2nd–3rd century BC by Vatsayana, it, among other topics, talks about how courtesans could extract favors or gifts from the clients.

In the ancient period, there is a mention of ganikas or courtesans accomplished in sixty-four *kalas* (arts or skills). Also called *devadasis*, they were married to the deity of the temple and spent their lives in the service of the deity. When Urvashi, the apsara, imparted the divine knowledge of dance to human beings, the devadasis were the first recipients, and this introduced the tradition of dance to the temples. Their presence in domestic festive and marriage occasions was considered auspicious, and they were also deputed to lead the marriage processions. In different regions, they were known by different names, such as *mahari* in Odisha.

Amrapali, also known as Ambapalika, Ambapali, or Amra, was a celebrated courtesan in about 500 BC who finds mention in the old Pali texts and Buddhist traditions. She lived in Vaishali, the capital city of the Lacchavi tribe, whose eight clans formed the Vajji (Vajjian) confederacy, the oldest republic in the world. The extremely beautiful Amrapali became a courtesan and an accomplished dancer. She rose to be the *rajnartaki,* or the royal dancer and came to be associated with Bimbisara and Ajatashatru and later embraced Buddhism. She also undertook welfare measures like constructing roads, schools, temples, and other institutions.

Over time, they performed in the royal courts, had intimate relationship with the royalty, and could be seen in the company of nobles, high officers, and literati. The subjects of dance-drama gradually deviated from religion to other worldly topics, including heroes, kings, legends, historical/holy places, and so on. Those who performed in the royal courts came to be called *rajnartakis*, and those who also gave performances for the elite classes came to be called *nagarvadhus*. These ganikas participated in the scholarly and poetic assemblies, and were treated on par with men. There is a mention of one Bindumati who sang so passionately that the Ganga water started to flow upstream, astounding the Mauryan emperor Ashoka the Great.

Royal patronage ensured that these ganikas enjoyed high status and political influence. We find mention of these girls donating to the temples for their upkeep as well as for the education of the children, as the temples were more like community centers.

The text *Nrityashastra*, written during the 3rd century AD, talks about how dance and music were also crucial elements of worship and speaks of the third element of *abhinaya*, or acting, which helped to depict stories through song and/or dance. During the Gupta period, these fine arts developed further. We see that Emperor Samudragupta is embossed on coins with a *Veena,* and the texts by the great dramatist and poet, Kalidasa, clearly show the importance of these art forms. Moreover, the importance of the dancers sustained during the Buddhist period, and the texts mention their presence. The exchange of dancers between temples and royal courts became an established practice. In the seventh century, Banabhatta, in his *Harsha Charita*, described dancers and their performances in the court vividly.

Toward the close of the ancient period, the Rajput kings have been described to have a penchant for music and dance as they had for warfare. The very term 'rajnartaki' is a symbol of nobility and power. Al-Baruni has also said that there was a tradition of temples having devadasis, who sang and danced—this brought additional revenues to the temples and ultimately to the royal coffers. In addition to this, the celebrated Chinese pilgrim Xuan Zang (Huein Tsang), who visited India in the 7th century, has written about temple dancers in Multan (now in Pakistan). We also find mention of them in the writings of Al-Beruni (*Tarikh al-Hind*), Kalhana (*Rajatrangini*), and others.

By this time, courtesans grew professional and started to seek clients from across wide social classes, but they mostly eyed the wealthy and the powerful. These women started to adopt some unethical tricks to extort money, so the non-institutional

courtesans came to be called *kutani,* or mysterious, and the Hindi term *koot* (cipher) might have been derived from this term. Things went awry to such an extent that in the eighth century, Damodar Gupta, Chief Minister of Kashmir's ruler Jayapida, wrote a poetic treatise called *Kuttanimatam.* It describes several cunning tricks employed by the *kutanis*, as advised by a procuress. Similarly, in *Kathasaritsagara*, a large 11th century work compiled by Shaivite Somadeva, at least one story deals with the tricks employed by the courtesans to lure clients.

The courtesans had earned great prestige for themselves as they were seen in the company of the high and the powerful, and vice versa, as the elite felt a sense of pride when seen in their company. Often, the rich vied with each other to win their favors. This was the age when the sphere of influence of these women, known for their physical charm and manners, widened. All those rulers and chieftains who could afford it maintained a glorious troupe of dancers. Often, the singers and dancers performed while the court proceedings were in progress, and the festivities continued late into the night. Thus, it was a major source of indoor entertainment in those times.

2

Nartaki to Tawaif

The tradition of dance and dancers continued in the courts in the medieval period. With the advent of the Muslim rulers in a large part of India, the dancers got a boost as they too were great patrons of fine art. The women in the royal *harem* practiced several fine arts including singing and dancing.

Their arrival, however, had an adverse effect on north Indian dance traditions with which the devadasi system declined; though, South India remained largely immune from the Islamic effect.

The Delhi sultans were a mixture of fundamentalists and art patrons—some of them supported the arts, including dance and music, while others found them anti-Islamic. There is a mention of Ala-ud-din Khalji having held a grand function, on the occasion of his son Khizra Khan's marriage in which well-known courtesans from all over India were invited. Sultan Balban also patronized them.

The *Ain-e-Akbari* mentions that some women took up the profession of dancing, and Akbar called them *Kinchani.* These women

performed on the occasion of festivals and other special occasions. Competitions were also held among them and maid-servants of the elite class were taught singing and dancing. Abul Fazl has written that some women sang *Sohal* and *Dhrupad* with clapping and beating of the drums.

Many of the dancers have grown quite well-known, right from Anarkali in Akbar's court to Rai Praveen in the Orchha court in the 16th century, where a special stage was raised on which the favorite dancer gave a live performance every evening in the presence of the ruler, his family members, and important guests.

Ibn-Batuta has written in his text, *Kitaburrehla,* that women-slaves were trained in singing and dancing. They were often gifted to other rulers. He cites an example from the Delhi Sultanate period, when Muhammad Tughluq gifted 100 men and 100 women slaves proficient in singing and dancing. His predecessor, Ghiyas-ud-din Tughluq, had prohibited music, but he was opposed, he did not live long after passing this dictum.

Dr. UN Ghoshal has written in his book, *Delhi Sultanate,* that the Muslims felt proud of enslaving Hindu women, who also comprised of princesses, and they were forced to dance in the court and gatherings of the elite. Nizamuddin Ahmed too has, in the *Tabakate Akbari*, written about similar instances. Additionally, several writers have mentioned that there were men and women who sold themselves as slaves out of some compulsion and worked as singers or dancers.

During the rule of the first five Mughal rulers, musicians were patronized. Babur himself was a singer and composer. Humayun loved music and classified musicians as *Ahl-e-Murad.* Akbar paid attention to the development of music and patronized a number of Hindu, Turrani, Iranian, and Kashmiri men and women and divided musicians into seven categories who performed on a fixed day of the week. The legendary Tansen thrived during Akbar's time.

Interestingly, Akbar is said to have a very pretty courtesan, Nadira Begum, on whom he bestowed the title of Anarkali—a name that is immemorial in history. Legend has it that he found her extending pangs of love with Prince Salim (later Jahangir). Abul Fazl has written that once Salim was caught entering into the place she was kept. Infuriated at this, Akbar got her buried between two walls, and it is said that she shrieked out the name of her lover when the last brick was laid.

This tradition continued with Jahangir and Shah Jahan as well. William Foster, in his book *Early Travels*, writes that hundreds of women singers and dancers performed in court and were rewarded adequately. The courtesans enjoyed the best-ever status during the Mughal period and were considered part of the nobility. Jahangir, in his book *Tuzuk-e-Jahangiri*, has praised the Indian style of *ghazal,* and Shah Jahan's son, Dara Shikoh, was married to a courtesan named Rana Dil. Historically, the chief courtesan was called *Deredar Tawaif*, but the meaning of this term underwent a change with the passage of time.

It was during the Mughal period that new dance styles and costumes began to develop and the *Dhrupad* and *Dhamar* styles of singing originated during this period. At the same time, the spiritual element of the ancient period gradually vanished, and dance came to be known as a source of entertainment and pleasure by the time the last of the Mughals were staring at their squeezing fortunes desperately. The Mughal court seemed to indulge itself in a last spell of pleasure with decorated halls, courtesans, and *mushairas* (poetic symposia) in the lamp-light. This change in attitude also brought into existence some unsophisticated forms.

The dance girls grew so influential with the rulers that they held sway over several aspects of life, including political decisions. The rulers got built beautiful palaces in their honor, such as for Rai Praveen in the Orchha Fort by Raja Indrajit Singh.

Interestingly, as noted by Pt. Rakesh Ayachi in his Hindi book on the history of Orchha, Rai Praveen was gifted out to the Mughal emperor, but when she did not like the atmosphere in the Mughal court, she wished to be sent back, and her wish was honored. This also shows the clout the dance girls enjoyed in that era. There exists a Praveen Mahal in the Orchha Fort, adorned with some murals dedicated to her.

When Aurangzeb came to power in 1658, he prohibited music and dance programs. from being held in the court, as noted by VD Mahajan in his book, *History of Modern India.* He allowed his family women to use music and dance for entertainment and his own daughter, Zeb-un-Nissa, is said to possess command over singing and composing poetry.

In 1739, when the barbaric Nadir Shah went back from Delhi, he is said to be so impressed by the performance by one courtesan named Nur Bai that he ordered her to be paid four thousand guineas and be taken to Persia. She somehow managed to decline the offer.

In Bundelkhand, there is a popular legend about the dancer Mastani, who adorned the court of Chhatrasal, a Bundela king, and even got a palace built in her honor in Dhubela. Later, he presented her to Baji Rao as a token of gratitude for his help in the battle against the Mughals, with a promise that he would marry her. So, she became Baji Rao's second wife. Sunk in her beauty, he neglected his state duties and indulged himself in hedonistic activities such as drinking and meat-eating that were prohibited in the orthodox Brahmin family. She was kidnapped and imprisoned, but Baji Rao could not tolerate the pangs of separation from her and fell seriously ill. Learning of this, Mastani managed to escape from prison, but he had died before she reached him. She too committed *Sati* (self-immolation) to join her lover in the heavens.

In comparison, South India continued with its classical forms replete with spirituality, and dance continued to adorn the temple festivals. The Hindu kings patronized the dancers and also bequeathed villages to support the dancers and musicians in opening schools. Krishnadeva Raya, the well-known ruler of the Vijayanagara empire in the sixteenth century, established the town of Ganika Nagar for the dancers. Almost all ruling dynasties in South India supported the dancers and musicians linked with the temple and court traditions. Those who performed in the temples were called *devadasis*, while those who performed on other occasions were called *nartakis*. A distinction was made between the secular dancers who performed in court or other state functions and those who performed to entertain guests—the former were the rajnartakis, while the latter were *alankardasis*.

3

From Tawaif to Nautch Girl

With the six great Mughals gone by 1707, the later Mughals proved to be incompetent rulers who saw their territories terribly shrink, and by the time of the last Mughal, Bahadur Shah Zafar, their territory was just around Delhi. However, this never meant that they did not patronize musicians and dancers. The last Mughal had several of them, despite his empty coffers.

During this period, native dancers thrived in Indian dance and song traditions, while the Mughals, having emerged from their Persian traditions recently, were more inclined to listen to Persian renderings. They also commissioned dancing girls from there. Thus, two distinct styles got an opportunity to blend, and this glorious fusion led to the evolution of Hindustani music and dance, at the head of which was *Kathak*. With the rulers taking active interest, it attained a more developed form of entertainment. Originally, Kathak was performed by male Brahmin story tellers to introduce an element of drama in their stories, which evolved into

a dance, and later it came to be associated with the tawaifs, who made it popular.

Living closer to the patron rulers for the greater part, the courtesans enjoyed an elevated status, and many of them actually became queens, as it had happened with Lal Kunwar, whom Jahandar Shah married and conferred on her the title of Imtiaz Mahal. Similarly, Mohammad Shah Rangila married a dancing girl, Uttambai, who came to be known as Qudsia Begum. This period was a paradox—the courtesans prospered and flourished while the rulers gradually declined in power and prestige, which led to the emergence of the Nawabs.

The Nawabs continued to patronize the dancers and several new styles were introduced into the classical Kathak, a form of dance-drama. It was at this time that the term 'tawaif' was used popularly to describe the dancers. The Awadhi term tawaif, borrowed from the Persian *tawaaf*, signifies a highly skilled courtesan. It was associated with a dancer and singer who was considered to be the epitome of good taste and high fashion. At this time, the Muslim culture influenced not only dance and music but also other aspects related to them, especially *adab*, *tehzeeb,* and *nafasat* (manners, etiquette, and disposition).

Among the rulers, Wajid Ali Shah of Awadh led the rest as far as patronage was concerned, and this drew courtesans to Lucknow from all around the land. He himself was a keen singer and dancer and established the *Parikhana,* where young girls were trained in dance and music.

At this time, the rulers were not the only patrons—a class of wealthy people had also emerged that was equally fascinated by dancers. These people included courtiers, government officials, and rich merchants. A new class adding to this list was that of the zamindars, or estate-holders, also called *Babus* or *Rajahs*, who were bestowed large tracts of land by rulers to charge revenue

from peasants. Often, these people held dance performances in their mansions called *havelis*, and the occasions for these were festivals or weddings. Those who could afford it did this to show off their extravagance, luxury, wealth, and power, as many landlords were not too rich to afford them, as the courtesans charged a hefty fee. It was utterly impossible for common people to have this luxury.

On other occasions, the courtesans ran their shows at their own places, called *kotha*, a word which etymologically signifies 'the first floor', where these places were generally located. The place was open to all those who could pay, though there were certain others who reserved the right of admission to only a select few, like the nobility or the chieftains. The audience was expected to rain money on the dancer when she performed a delicate, supple, sensual movement. A courtesan could also be *paband* (restricted) to one patron, and she performed for others only with his consent, as he looked after all her needs of money, jewellery, clothing and living. In return, she remained 'virtuous' to him.

We should not deny the fact that the courtesans were quite pretentious too, as they had learned and mastered all the tricks to coax money. The patrons, in their allure, paid them heftily in terms of money, jewellery, and property. It was like a child's play for a courtesan to bring dishonor to a patron, as they could start gossip that would be the talk of a town in hours.

They would often pretend that the patron was the master, but the fact was often the other way round, it was the 'matron' who had absolute control over him. This led to several of them becoming powerful enough to have the power to interfere in the administration. For instance, Hakim Mahdi is alleged to have become the *Vazir* (or chief minister) of Awadh through the efforts of a courtesan named Piyaro.

Once you think of a tawaif, fancy notions instead of the truth envelop the mind. The first thing that comes to mind must be a

scene from blockbuster films like *Pakeezah*, *Devdas*, *Umrao Jaan*, *Sadhana*, *Anarkali*, *Mughal-e-Azam,* and more, in which the dancers present live performances in a hall surrounded by admirers or clients. All these are instances of Muslim influence on professional dance of the period.

Clearly, the medieval period had a great impact on this profession, though its quality had started to wane gradually. During this period, there was a significant increase in the number of courtesans and prostitutes. This was owing to the fact that whenever the Muslim invaders won a battle, the troops were set free to plunder the place for a few days, and during this period, they abducted and raped women too. Many of these women were abandoned by their families, and finding no other shelter, they turned to kothas or brothels. Many girls and women who got trapped in pretense of love also landed in these places.

In South India, on the other hand, the devadasi tradition continued, but the increasing influence of the Muslims as well as the British led to the decline of the Hindu kingdoms, and with this, the revenues of the temples decreased. Until now, the devadasis had restricted themselves to the temples, and their secular counterparts to the nobility, but now they were forced to seek patronage from other elite classes, like landlords, and chieftains.

The rulers in other parts of India patronized dancers and singers to a greater or lesser extent, as in the Punjab where Maharaja Ranjit Singh is said to have a troupe of over 150 dancers, which included native, Persian, and Kashmiri girls. The most celebrated of these was one Padma, who was received by him as a tribute from the ruler of Kashmir.

Then dawned the period this book is more concerned with—the European or the British period. Dance at this time branched out in two distinct directions—one was classical and spiritual,

limited to families or traditions (schools), and the other was the one performed by the tawaifs for entertainment.

The arrival of the Europeans brought about a vital change in the dance form, as it started to lose its identity as a classic form of art and entertainment and got restricted to pleasure and sexuality. This form was entering the phase from which it would find itself irredeemable.

4

Nautch Girls in Pre-steamship Period

The British Raj period can be divided into pre-steamship and post-steamship periods.

At the beginning of the British period, courtesans were seen as the most educated women. Many of them composed texts and verses with the purpose of giving stunning performances before their patrons; unfortunately, this literature has not survived. The legendary writer, poet and, playwright Bhartendu Harishchandra has admitted that he used to visit tawaifs to cultivate an understanding of arts and traditions.

As the Europeans grew influential and later became the masters of territories, the courtesans were forced to look for newer patrons, which they found in the Europeans or the *Sahibs*. The native rulers and chieftains invited them to live performances, and notably, this form of entertainment was quite different from what they were habituated to back at home. The sahibs found this

mode of entertainment quite a pastime, as they were here mostly without families. Travel from Europe to India took a long time and involved exorbitant cost, so hardly any women came to India. At the end of the eighteenth century, there were only 250 women against 4000 men in Calcutta. Being small in numbers, these European women too attended these performances. Many of the men became so infatuated with this native trend that they too had one or more courtesans under their own patronage. They found the native courtesans 'shapely in form, with delicate limbs and lovely features.' They even found them prettier than their 'western sisters'. Many of them wrote even poetry in their praise. The lavish lifestyle of the European merchants drew the 'dusky girls' to them, who formed part of the *zenana* (seraglio). Any entertainment for the Europeans was not considered complete without a nautch. The nautch girls often accompanied the marching British army to entertain the troops. This attracted more and more nautch girls to the British garrison towns. Many Europeans gifted the figurines of their favorite nautch girls to the guests. Thus, this period witnessed great European support for the nautch and nautch girls.

Some of them also kept courtesans as temporary wives called *Bibis*, normally on the condition that they would not bear children. How popular these courtesans grew can be gauged from the fact that several of them emerged on matchbox covers in several countries, including Sweden and Czechoslovakia. This is a testimonial to their commercial appeal among the population.

Organization of *mehfils* or assemblies in private places like havelis was a very formal occasion, and decorum was maintained. The halls were decorated following Mughal aesthetics, with a tent overhead. In the middle of the hall was placed the soft silken *masnad* (mat/low bed) with a large bolster, over which was hung a decorative chandelier alive with the candles. This was meant for the most important patron or client. If the guest was European,

a chair would be arranged, as they found sitting down on the mat quite uncomfortable. One side was occupied by the musicians, with the senior-most or the most popular occupying the center. The entire hall was also decorated with a scent pot, *paan dan* (betel leaf box), spittoon, flower basket, and a hookah too. Keeping with the occasion or festival, other things were also arranged, such as colors on Holi. There was also a fashion for hanging birdcages. The passage of time in the night was described as 'the night growing young'. In such an environment, a courtesan sang. The clients would sway their heads in joy while their hands would be ever-busy showering notes and guineas. There were observed rules even regarding where to put off shoes and where to wash or wipe feet, but the Europeans seldom removed shoes in these mehfils. Large mehfils often involved performances by several tawaifs belonging to different *deras* (camps or schools). They were richly clad in silk and jewellery, and apart from their face, hands, and feet, no part of the body was visible. Their hands and feet were tinted with henna, and their head was covered with a dupatta, which was considered a mark of honor.

The main dance form was Kathak in Uttar Pradesh, though other dance forms from across India were over time incorporated, such as Manipuri, Bharatnatyam, and Jhumar. Kathak was performed to the singing of *thumris*, specifically written to accompany *abhinaya*, or acting. The Persian ghazals were also sung, but they gradually inclined towards Hindustani. Often, the mehfils started with fun songs, but as the night grew young and the assembly thinned with only serious music lovers remaining, classical songs and dances took the center stage. The most famous singer or dancer took the stage at last. When this tradition gradually ceased, the zenith of etiquette too gradually vanished, and superficiality replaced it. The Europeans have also written about the role of *massaulchis* (torch-bearers) in a dance performance, as they would

bring the burning torches near the courtesan's face to lay emphasis on the expressions.

It was at this stage that the north Indian classical Kathak and south Indian Sadir came together to be called 'nautch' and their performers as 'nautch girls', and gradually, these terms came to be employed for all types of dances and dancers across the land.

At this point of time, the nobility and the elite classes were facing pressure from the East India Company's policies. For the British officers, it was more important to carry wealth abroad than to do good to people here. In such conditions, only they could hope to survive who towed their line. Traditional economy was in a shambles, as the Company was expanding its base of influence over newer territories and classes of people. Interestingly, the Europeans coming to India grew rich quickly and when they returned home, they lived a lavish lifestyle, imitating the Nawabs, and came to be called *Nabobs*.

One very well-known example of the nautch in religious festivals and before the Europeans, was the one conducted on the occasion of Durga Puja after the battle of Plassey (1757). It was celebrated at Shobhabazar (also called Sova Bazar) Rajbari (Royal Palace) in Calcutta by Nabakrishna Deb, an ally of the Company who was later given the title of Rajah, to which Robert Clive and his wife Margaret were also invited. Two distinct features of this Puja were the lavish nautch performances and abundant serving of wines, both of which were considered taboos in those times. The celebration was followed by a ball, which continued until the wee hours of the following morning. This Durga Puja came to be called Company Puja.

One high feature of this celebration was that the nautch girls could draw outlines of images on the floor with flower petals or colored powders with their toes. This tradition continued for another century. One tradition that also continued was the placing

of two mirrors on each side of the goddess's idol—one engraved with the image of Lord Clive and the other with that of his wife Margaret's. This celebration also marked the beginning of a competition among different Puja Pandals, as they used to invite the British to seek favors. This tradition of competition, too, has survived till today, though for a different purpose.

However, when the circumstances of the Nawabs and other higher classes changed, they could no longer patronize the tawaifs, and this marked the beginning of their decline.

5

Tides of Change: Post-steamship Period

The mid-nineteenth century is marked by several incidences that transformed how the nautch and nautch girls came to be seen by the Europeans. Of the two major events, the first was the introduction of steamships, which reduced the travel time from Europe to India, and this encouraged families to sail together with their men. This helped them create a cultural and social atmosphere here much similar to what they had back in Europe. The second was the breakout of the 1857 Uprising, which changed the relationship between the British and the Indians like never before. The British now started to look at themselves as masters and looked down upon the Indians and their culture as backward; this also changed their attitude towards the nautch girls, as they had their institutions set up here, which they found to their liking.

The Europeans looked at the tawaifs as if they were mere prostitutes who also sang and danced. They failed to distinguish

between the traditional tawaifs, whose primary concern was song and dance and were the epitome of etiquette, and the ordinary prostitutes. They employed the common term 'nautch girls' for both, while officially, they created an occupational category of 'dancing and singing girls'. In her paper "Lifestyle as Resistance: The Case of the Courtesans of Lucknow", Veena Talwar Oldenburg writes that the courtesans were in the highest individual tax-payer category. They possessed property including houses, orchards, manufacturing, and retail establishments for food and luxury items, which were confiscated by the British for anti-British activities during the 1857 Uprising. The charges against them on this count were instigation, pecuniary assistance to rebels, though they themselves essentially remained non-combatants. Talwar lists several items confiscated from them in Lucknow, and these include "gold and silver ornaments studded with precious stones, embroidered cashmere wool and brocade shawls, bejeweled caps and shoes, silver-, gold-, jade- and amber-handled fly whisks, silver cutlery, jade goblets, plates, spittoons, hookah and silver utensils for serving and storing food and drink, and valuable furnishings", all valued at about four million rupees, which in today's terms equals to more than 160 million rupees.

Meanwhile, European women had two distinct perspectives on how they looked at the nautch girls. Many of them found nautch a native tradition for the entertainment of men and took it in stride. They praised this skill, saying that they could convey the meaning of what they were singing through their gestures even when their words were unintelligible to them. In contrast, the other group looked at Indian women in general and these courtesans in particular from the Victorian viewpoint—in which women were seen as idealistic. As a result, they created a reformist discourse about the cultural heritage of these nautch girls looking through the glasses of British racial, moralistic, Victorian and middle-

class inclination. Even the Church contributed to the anti-nautch movement when the Christian Society, Madras, in 1893, issued an appeal to the English ladies not to attend any nautch performance and also requested that they keep their husbands away from any such program. It came like a shock for the courtesans, but they were powerless to do anything about it.

The middle class was still influential owing to its command over trade. It had earlier served the rulers and Nawabs and was the first to embrace new professions that came their way because of western education, opening new vistas for them. However, this class had its own limitations in social terms.

With the ever-expanding resources at their disposal, the middle class could now look for such means of entertainment that were mostly out of their reach until now. They also looked at the kothas and tawaifs with awe and admiration but could not confront the social milieu in which they had grown. Womanhood was still perceived in the 'ideal form', in which purity was the highest ideal for a woman. On the other hand, with the shrinking influence of the elite classes, the tawaifs were forced to look for new clients from the middle class. This change was sure to adversely affect the quality, as only delicacy, etiquette, and good manners could not keep the new clients hooked to them. There was more demand for sensuality and pleasure.

While several men from the middle class became their regular clients, a social conflict arose in society. Most men still looked down upon them, at least publicly. Whether a kotha-goer or not, they all tried to safeguard their girls and women from evil eyes, as the number of kothas grew in towns. Several cities emerged as important centers for tawaifs, which included Lahore, Amritsar, Banaras, Kanpur, Lucknow, Calcutta, and others.

The women, in turn, tried to keep their men away from these 'wicked' places and opposed whenever their men tried to hold a tawaif's performance in the household. It was due to the conviction

of these domestic women that the Puritan movement run by the Brahmo Samaj could thrive, as they dictated that acts like drinking alcohol, going to prostitutes, and watching theatre could not be tolerated. The social reformers, influenced by western education, worked for the betterment of women through education, and eradication of evils like Sati custom, female infanticide, and child marriage; they also joined the anti-nautch movement without distinguishing between the traditional art and prostitution.

Paradoxically, the very social reformers who helped a woman come out of the house cage to get education branded the tawaif and her arts as immoral and obscene and described her as a threat to the society. Keshub Chandra Sen of the Brahmo Samaj went to the extent of describing nautch girl as a hideous woman. Later, the Arya Samaj too joined in the anti-nautch movement. The British often held nautch programs in several official functions, but in 1905, the persistent efforts of the social reformers prevailed upon the government to decide not to hold a nautch entertainment in the honor of the visiting Prince of Wales in Madras. The social reformers did not stop at this—they pressurized the owners to evict tawaifs from their properties in the wake of public morality and succeeded to a great extent.

Evidently, the tawaifs were excluded from the sphere of women's reform, and were bracketed in morality, law and order, public health, and even sanitation. Earlier, the tawaifs, whether Hindu or Muslim, were seen as a community and had their own law of inheritance, but as mentioned earlier, the British made no distinction between tawaifs and prostitutes and did not acknowledge them as a community to have personal inheritance rights. They merely saw them as either Hindu or Muslim. This too had an adverse impact on their property rights and adoption rights. This opened a plethora of court cases against them, as male members of their families could now claim a share in the property.

The British government was not very sincere when it came to social reforms. Whatever steps it took were either cosmetic or taken under pressure. However, a large number of social reformers worked to eradicate this problem, and many of them did good work in this field as they trained them in other crafts. Unfortunately, most social reformers were more interested in removing these 'blots' from the public eye, rather than undertaking a substantial step by which these women could lead a respectable life. Some of them established some ashrams or orphanages for them, but over time, these places turned into 'secret brothels' where the inmates' condition worsened further. The donors, too, had their selfish interests. This was one reason that several courtesans resisted against institutions.

Gandhiji too joined the fray when he asked the tawaifs to jettison the profession and take up the *charkha* (spinning wheel). As a result of his call, the Tawaif Sabha was formed in Banaras, under the aegis of which they joined the national movement. His social reform in respect of the tawaifs was, however, partial, as he looked at them from an impractical idealistic perspective where a woman was supposed to be dignified and pure; he opined that they were not essential for the society, even in those early times when there were hardly any means of entertainment. He wanted them to take up the charkha for both livelihood and purification but was comfortably non-committal about the minimum income to them. He even refused to accept the cause of the courtesans at par with that of the Harijans.

A case in point is that of the courtesans of Barisal (now in Bangladesh) in 1921. Responding to a call from Gandhiji, 350 courtesans became members of the Congress party by paying a fee of 14 annas each; they had also contributed to the Tilak Swaraj Fund, founded by him to gather funds for social amelioration. These courtesans sought to become officials in the Congress, but

Gandhi objected, saying that none could officiate 'who did not approach it with pure hands and a pure heart'. He advised them to take up the charkha, and give up their profession completely, and join the freedom struggle through singing nationalistic songs.

Maybe, Gandhi's views had been shaped because of his interactions with the prostitutes as he has admitted in his autobiography. He wrote an article titled "For Fallen Humanity" in *Young India* on September 11, 1924. He begins the article thus: "It was at Barisal that I had the privilege of meeting our fallen sisters, victims of our lust, now nearly three years ago. Some of them said, 'We earn from two to three rupees per day. You must give us some occupation that would give us as much.' For a moment, I sank within me but immediately came to myself and said, 'No, my dear sisters, I cannot suggest anything that would give you two to three rupees per day but I must ask you to give up your calling even though you have to starve. There is the spinning wheel however. If you take it, it will be your salvation.'"

The establishment of the Kashi Tawaif Sabha came about because of his direct motivation. Despite a favorable reaction to his call by tawaifs, he remained reluctant to engage with them, and thus his steps and suggestions for their amelioration were seen as only cosmetic, which forced several women back into the trade. Moreover, in 1925, he did not hesitate to call the profession 'obscene', and looked at a tawaif as 'an impure, always an impure'. He even saw their musical training as a tool to strengthen their manipulative capabilities. On April 16, 1925, in his article "Our Unfortunate Sisters," he concludes by alluding to this profession in negative terms again: "I cannot write all I have learnt about this social disease, this moral leprosy."

With this view, it was certain that social reform could not meet its purpose, especially when he did not intend to bar the

industrialists who were harming the interests of those who spun cotton on *charkhas*.

This opposition was felt in South India too, where dedicating women to the temples was opposed, and in some cases, even the dance performances by girls were opposed. In fact, the anti-nautch movement found its roots in Madras province around 1892–93. This did a great disservice to them, as earlier they were viewed as belonging to diverse classes as devadasis, while nautch girls and prostitutes were classified into several sub-categories; but now all of them were included in one broad homogenous group of nautch girls—a group which formed their identity as prostitutes.

Yet another factor that contributed to the declining status of the tawaifs was the entry of a larger number of women into the profession. Until this time, the courtesans trained for years before they gave their first performance. But due to the Company's biased policies, the financial condition of the poor worsened, and many women looked to the kothas as the likely source of income. But, most of them were not accomplished singers or dancers, nor did they possess the delicate etiquettes which characterized the earlier tawaifs. Now, popular cultural forms were mixed with the licentious and voluptuous tastes of the vulgar, and the trade was gradually slumping into prostitution.

The tawaifs declined towards the middle of the twentieth century, but a revival of classical music and dance took place.

6

The Many Faces of Tawaifs

The classification of tawaifs is quite interesting and deserves a mention when dwelling on their history. The two main categories of the above are *Deredar* Tawaifs and other Tawaifs.

The former claimed to have descended from high castes across both religions, Islam and Hinduism. In the Mughal period, they performed in the royal courts. They succeeded in maintaining the dignity of their profession through etiquette as well as the quality of singing and dancing to a great extent and served only one or a few patrons. They were very proud of their matrilineal clan and ancestry and maintained purity of conduct in the sense that they remained loyal to their patron(s), and although the children born from tawaifs lived with the mother and not the father, they were raised in the faith of the latter. As for the daughter, she was basically trained in singing and dancing, was taught to read and write, and undertook domestic duties like cooking and tailoring. Some of them were also trained in higher

skills like horse riding and chess. This was done so that they could be later assigned to some elite landlord or ruler. Normally, the girl stayed with whom she was assigned, and in the event of his death, she lived the life of a widow while continuing to get maintenance from his offspring.

With the dawn of the twentieth century, an awakening had come about among them. Now, they sent their sons and daughters to schools, and encouraged them to adopt other professions. Despite being assigned to a patron, the tawaifs never refused to take part in concerts, *mehfils,* or *muzras* (dance concerts), as it remained their primary profession; even the courtesans assigned to rulers were no exception. So, they had to specifically learn the tactics of evading sexual invitations. Most of them avoided attending the programs held by the so-called lower caste people. These tawaifs claimed to belong to clans like Kanchan, Buxariye, Katesar, Bangarahe, Radhe, etc., most of which signify the places or villages they originated in, such as Baxariye which originated in Buxar.

On the other hand, the ordinary tawaifs were categorized as *Nauchi* and *Kasbia.* They held muzras in places wherever they were invited on payment, and were often invited to perform in marriages and other assemblies. As they lacked in skill as well as beauty, they would often rely more on their cheap manners, glances, and expressions, trying to flaunt their physiques, and were seldom paband (restricted or dedicated) to one or a few patrons.

Socially, as a group, all courtesans were classified into two or three types: *Gandharva*, *Ramjani,* and *Gaunharin*, but this categorization is not universally accepted.

In earlier times, they mostly sang songs of classical variety, called *pucca gayaki* but as the quality of the patrons waned, light (*kutcha* or *halka-fulka*) songs started to become prominent in the performances. The clients started to demand more film or ghazal variety.

This tawaif was not so lucky as she was susceptible to exploitation, and often landed in brothels located in areas called red-light areas. She might not ever become a wife, yet when she was offered to a patron for sex services for the first time, a ceremony was observed called *nath utarana* (opening nose pin). Until this occasion, a young one wore only a *nath* (nose-pin) in the nose, and the patron replaced it with a *keel* (nose pin resembling a nail). On this occasion, he also brought sweets, fruits, gifts, ornaments, etc., most of which were distributed among other tawaifs of the clan. In many instances, the patron was the highest bidder amongst the competitors. The tawaifs of this class sought to employ pimps who lured clients. In some tribes, this custom has survived to this date.

There is an interesting anecdote concerning the legendary revolutionary, Sukhdev, who made the supreme sacrifice along with Bhagat Singh and Rajguru. Once, in the company of Bhagat Singh and Jaidev, he was passing through a red-light area near Chawri Bazar in Delhi. Sukhdev often dressed funnily, and so a prostitute standing in a narrow lane with another man took him for a pimp and said, "Look he is asking me to marry him." Sukhdev wittingly remarked, "Don't do that, Bibiji, else how would we earn our livelihood?" Back in the room, Jaidev objected to this type of behavior. At this, Sukhdev said, "I can call myself successful if people in this unknown city take us (revolutionaries) for pimps."

During the English period, there rose a new class of clients—the young people for whom carnal pleasure held greater importance than entertainment. They were the troops, both Europeans and Indians, stationed in the cantonments and garrisons that the Company created, covering most of the important towns in the occupied territories. Living away from their families for long periods, they looked to kothas to fulfil their carnal needs.

It is also imperative to mention that in one respect, the British were clearly distinct from the Muslim victors—the latter, after a

victory, set the troops free to plunder and do what they liked to the women, while the British earmarked the areas for brothels or kothas in or near cantonments, where both courtesans and prostitutes set up their facilities. This factor mainly accounts for the fact that there are not many accusations of rape against the British troops.

If, around 1857, you visited any cantonment, you would invariably find at least one area dedicated solely to kothas. For example, Meerut, a prominent cantonment, had three such areas—one in the Sadar Bazar area of the cantonment and two in the city. Often, 'Out of Bounds' billboards were erected at their entry points, as the troops were prohibited from visiting these places. Nonetheless, the troops visited these areas somehow, and a large number of troops even contacted venereal diseases.

The tawaifs in the cantonment had preserved their dignity to some extent, and this is the reason that they were often referred to as *Nagarvadhus* (town wives), though the British preferred to call them nautch girls.

7

The Intriguing World of Nautch Girls

Any discussions on the nautch girls would be incomplete without unravelling the intricate web of their operations and the distinctiveness of their setup.

Until the Mughal period, they were looked at with respect due to their association with royalty and nobility. They were considered the epitome of fine culture, language, and literature, even though not all got a chance to perform at the royal court on a daily basis. Such women operated their own business houses, called kothas (as mentioned earlier), which served the upper middle class. They were recognized as the preservers and performers of high-class art and contributed to the evolving music and dance forms, especially Kathak, Dadra, Thumri, and the like.

These women learned these skills with perseverance. They hired well-known musicians and classical dancers and chose appropriate dance movements for themselves. This was how several of them

evolved their unique styles too. In fact, this is how Hindustani music found its origin in them. The singing of the United Provinces (now Uttar Pradesh) was known as *Purab Ang*, and it was quite popular in large cities even outside the province; the UP style of Dadra was especially popular in the Punjab. The singing of Banaras was also a part of this class but was sometimes referred to as *Banaras Ang*. *Tappa* was particularly popular in the Punjab, and some courtesans in the United Provinces too had picked it up.

In addition to the concerts, mehfils, and muzras, other contests were also held, namely, *Gazra*, *Jhoomar,* and *Dangal.* In Gazra, two of them sang in competition with each other, while in Jhoomar, the number rose to four or five. In *Dangal* (called *Prashnik* in earlier times), a large number of tawaifs from across a wide spectrum took part. It was like an open contest, but only a select few singer-courtesans could take part. Mostly, several of them would be lined up, and a musician would give them a line/couplet/stanza. Thereafter, each of them would display their talent in singing, dancing, or both, as might be the arrangement. The one who was acclaimed by all the patrons would be judged the winner and would win the rewards.

As this was not considered shameful, the nobles and the elite sent their wards to these kothas for training in the art of etiquette and appreciation of literature and poetry in Urdu, a language that was quickly gaining momentum in everyday conversations as a mixture of Persian and Hindi. The courtesans were also seen as the patrons of poor singers, dancers, and artists. Their trade brought them lucrative income and made them prosperous. They owned property and paid taxes, and as the record states, many of them were in the highest tax bracket in Lucknow and Bhopal. When the British confiscated the property of a large number of people following the 1857 Uprising, the names of several courtesans figured prominently in the lists.

This glory, however, did not prevail for long. With the decline of the Mughals and then the Nawabs, the kothas witnessed a fall; they declined from the exalted places looked at with awe and admiration to the places that people avoided mentioning in their daily discourse, and the visitors to these places were labelled as immoral.

At the start of the colonial period, the kothas came to be operated by a *Chaudharayan*, an older courtesan who normally owned and managed the premises. She kept strict control over the household, and her commands were binding on all members, men or women. She ensured that the task of training girls and musicians was accomplished well.

The income of the establishment was normally divided into three parts: one part each for the performing courtesan, the owner, and the remainder for training and maintenance of other staff, like musicians, chefs, guards, palanquin-bearers, and others. Some of them also employed tailors full time, and new fashion often originated at these kothas. They also employed some musclemen who kept a check on those who could attempt to enter the premises for purposes not served by the place.

With the entry of the lower-middle class and government officers, including troops, the quality of the kothas declined, and many nautch girls started to indulge in sex trade too, which had legal implications. So, running them became a more complicated affair and needed good management.

Despite this, if courtesans could come out to confront the British masters, it was due to the fact that they were subservient to no one and maintained their freedom of choice.

The British officers looked at these kothas as brothels, and such an attitude only distanced the high class from these places. A tawaif ruefully recalled the days when the visitors had to prove their status before entry into the kothas, but with time, the licensing, shorter

working hours, stricter police control, and raids led the profession towards a decline in quality.

The participation of courtesans in the 1857 Uprising brought harsh suppression at the hands of the British, as had happened with all other rebels. Many of them were given capital punishments, their property was confiscated, or heavy fines were levied on them. Also, several legislations were passed that further curtailed their business, like the Contagious Diseases Act, 1864, under which it was made mandatory for the courtesans to undergo tests and treatment for venereal diseases at regular intervals. The law was brought into existence in view of the fact that a large number of Company's troops had fallen victim to venereal diseases. Disease and morality were seen through a common lens to the extent that the steps undertaken to abolish prostitution were called 'moral hygiene'.

In the next few decades, several legislations were passed including the United Provinces Naik Girls Protection Act, 1929; United Provinces Minor Girls Protection Act, 1929; and United Provinces Suppression of Immoral Traffic Act, 1933, in addition to other steps. Such laws were also passed in other provinces with a view to curb human trafficking and prostitution. All these steps led to a gradual debasement of the profession into ordinary prostitution, especially when the patrons had already vanished.

The British had already brought these kothas into disrepute and termed all those who went there as immoral and dissolute. Now, they also employed policemen to check entries to such places. However, interestingly, as the troops needed these courtesans for sex services, several of the kothas were relocated to the cantonments, and for these, the young and healthy nautch girls were chosen. Consequently, this development did away with the remaining attraction to the kothas located outside the cantonments.

The courtesans were unhappy at the harm that the British had done to the profession, reducing them to the status of mere nautch

girls and prostitutes. It was a dramatic fall from being a celebrity to a *persona non grata*. The tawaifs, who could afford it, turned to seeking work in radio and films, and several of them even earned a big name there and are remembered even today. Of course, to hide their true identity, they had to replace 'Bai' from their names with 'Devi' or 'Jaan/Begum'. In fact, they were quite in demand owing to their training, quality of voice, and skill in dancing. Evidently, this became one of the key reasons that these dancing girls sided with those who rose against the British during the great upheaval.

They contributed to the Uprising in many ways, from supplying information, providing funds, serving them with food, and even taking up arms in several cases. Courtesans did this right from the time the British started to bring Indian territories under their control in 1757. The harsh repression at the hands of the British did not prevent them from making their contribution to the freedom struggle, which ultimately brought freedom to the country in 1947.

8

Ignominy Coupled with Oblivion

When it comes to giving credit to women in whatever profession or movement, we can see a marked disinterest among historians. The exceptions were only a few women who could not be overlooked, such as Rani Lakshmi Bai or Sarojini Naidu. And when it comes to the role of the women of a particular section, described even by legendary leaders like Mahatma Gandhi as 'fallen women', they have been completely blanked out from historiography of India. The term tawaif has now come to connote a whore or a dishonored woman.

Despite this bias, during my visit to different towns in connection with research on this book, I found that the role played by the tawaifs in the freedom struggle continues to thrive in folklore. Many of these women have become legends, and their influence is so great that many people refuse to accept them as tawaifs, as is the case with Begum Hazrat Mahal.

A historian in Kanpur, on the condition of anonymity, suggested that their life as a concubine should be obliterated from

history and such women should be presented as glorious freedom fighters, even at the cost of altering true history.

People see the term 'tawaif' as offensive and impolite, which should not be used in common discourse and history. They find it hard to digest the fact that several of these women started their career as young courtesans who then went on to make a name in the political field. Maybe, without their past being such, they would not have stood up to confront the mighty British Empire.

Prof. Lata Singh of Jawaharlal Nehru University, in her paper "Courtesans and the 1857 Rebellion," opposed those who want to erase their past professional lives as courtesans. She says: "The shift from the career of a courtesan to the political domain was not as abrupt as it is often made out to be . . . this transition was difficult for the conventional middle-class morality to accept. Consequently, they were left with no choice but to bring these women's professional life to the forefront which they simultaneously wanted to invisibilise or erase."

The fact that the sort of training that these courtesans got in the kothas helped them come to the fore as true fighters cannot be denied. They were as much citizens of the country, and their hearts beat for its freedom. They were more aware than others of what was happening around them due to their wide contacts in the society and administrative circles. They rose against the British individually and collectively. Some of them participated in the struggle directly, donning the soldier's dress and arms, while others created conditions or motivated others to fight against the oppressors. In every way, they displayed their exalted state of mind and unparalleled valor.

Notes:

---

1. Munshi Premchand, in his popular novel *Courtesan Quarters* (original name *Bazar-e-Husn* in Urdu and *Sewa Sadan* in Hindi), has described the type of life and

emotions that a *tawaif* undergoes. Amritlal Nagar had undertaken a prolonged research over three years to discover history from the primary and/or secondary witnesses; he too has depicted these women in his book *Ye Kothewalian (These Courtesans*).

2. In the present times, several women are actively making efforts to revive the exalted tradition of the tawaifs or courtesans; some of them are bringing their songs and dance styles to the fore; including Manjari Chaturvedi who is doing this task through 'The Courtesan Project'; the other important names include Malini Awasthi and Shubha Mudgal. They associate them with the positive things that they were known for then. You can watch several videos concerning them online.

Part II

Azizan Bai

9

Travesty of Justice

General Havelock, the well-known General, who crushed the 1857 Uprising at many places, looked haughtily at the pretty young lady brought in chains before him, her hands tied in the front with irons. The 25-year-old lady in chains was Aziz-un-Nissa, better known as Azizan Bai. The most well-known nautch girl of the town was brought before the General for a summary trial as she was accused of a rebellion against the Company.

"So, you know what things are like now. However, if you confess your crimes against the Crown, I'm willing to let you off," said the General in Hindustani in his unique assuring tone.

Havelock had studied the Persian and Hindustani languages in 1822 when he was planning to come to India, and all these years in India had only improved his skills at communicating with the native populace. He was a war-hardened general who had several battle victories to his credit right from the time he came to India in 1823.

Ever since the Uprising had broken out in Meerut, he was leading his troops across Awadh, crushing the revolutionaries whom the British preferred to call 'rebels', and now he was in Cawnpore (now Kanpur). Of course, he was going to die of dysentery in Lucknow the same year when he would be besieged by the revolutionaries.

As of now, Havelock was in command of the situation and was in the process of punishing the 'rebels'. Two cannons were lined on the ground, while a set of gallows stood not far from him. Ironically, these gallows were erected by the same people who were now being hanged on them. Many of the rebels were summarily sentenced to a gory death and were waiting for their turn to be hanged or blasted from the cannon's mouth.

When a cannon is fired, it instantly and violently kills the man tied on its mouth. It also generates a massive recoil; that is, the cannon moves back with a great jerk. To diminish this, the British tied one rebel each to its two wheels to check this recoil. They suffered no less distress, as the recoil often fractured their legs, thighs, or even spine, rendering them invalid lifelong.

Azizan's beautiful eyes rolled without a twitch on her face as she inspected the entire ground. Her lips scowled as she saw a soldier, with a lighted torch, move toward the back of the cannon. A rebel was tied to the mouth of the cannon, and two were tied at the back. Before anyone could track her displeasure or anxiety, she composed herself. She gazed at the General directly and merely smiled without saying a word.

The General had heard of the nautch girl, and he was ready to condone her 'guilt' if she confessed to her crimes and revealed the information he was seeking. He, in fact, wanted her to continue to adorn the kotha, which was a favorite haunt of many European officers. In fact, he himself wanted to see her muzra.

10

Lucknow to Kanpur

It was in Lucknow that Azizan was born to a tawaif mother in 1832. She was brought up in the kotha, in an atmosphere replete with singing and dancing. As an adolescent, she picked up the skills required to become a proficient courtesan. She was so fond of dancing that her mother often chided her for prolonged practice. At such times, she would say that she found solace in the sound of musical instruments and janglers that adorned her delicate, supple ankles. She picked up the fine nuances of singing at an early age. When she talked or sang, the listener could not help but be tranced by her delicate facial expressions that enlivened the entire surroundings.

These were the happy times for her. Her mother took pride in her skills and hoped that she would one day become the most favorable courtesan of the Nawab of Lucknow, under whose patronage the trade blossomed.

Lucknow, at this time, was the center that attracted tawaifs from across the country. They came to reap the fruits from the

overly caring Nawab and nobles. With the changing times, even the high government officers started to seek their services. Yet another segment of new clients comprised British officers, both civil and military. This development assured a thriving business in the time to come.

This pleasant situation, however, did not last long for Azizan. Her mother died, leaving her behind, still precarious at others' mercy, though she had wealth in the form of cash and jewellery. She did not take long to overcome the grief and keenly gauged the situation, realizing that due to more intense interference by the British resident, the Nawab was growing powerless.

Initially, the resident was the Governor General's ambassador to the Nawab's court, but with the Company becoming more powerful, he virtually became the ruler, leaving little power in the Nawab's hands. It had a dynamo effect as the income of the nobles and landlords slid down.

Moreover, with the worsening quality of the patrons, who wanted the tawaifs to 'warm up their beds' rather than the spirits with their music and dance, the situation went from bad to worse, especially for the courtesans who resisted this attitude. This development drove several of them away from Lucknow, while there were others who submitted to the carnal desires.

The youthful Azizan found that Lucknow could no longer be her place. Her dignity was at risk at the hands of the mighty nobles and landlords. She finally decided to abandon the place after a noble tried to hold her hand and push himself over her. She could not compromise with her dignity; this felt like an insult to her. With a broken heart, she made preparations to leave. Her eyes often moistened as she saw the place once looked at with awe and admiration gradually decline into a brothel.

Azizan, with her jewellery and money, took leave of the *Chaudharayan*, who made a last-ditch effort to convince her of a

rosy future, but without success. She headed to Kanpur, where a large cantonment was located. Moreover, she had heard that the place was yet full of people who enjoyed music and dance in their exalted form. She found a suitable place in the cantonment, got it repaired and decorated, and established herself. She hired dancers, musicians, and other staff. She knew well how to connect with her clients; her mannerisms charmed people. In a few weeks, her place was as vibrant as it gets and was the talk of the town.

It was early 1856 when the country's political landscape was undergoing a massive change. The East India Company was trying to add more territories by means fair or foul. Just eight years ago, in 1848, Lord Dalhousie, the Governor General, formulated a 'Doctrine of Lapse', under which, if a native ruler died without a natural heir, his adopted heir would not be eligible to inherit the throne, and his state would be annexed to British India. Consequently, a number of native states had been annexed, including Satara, Jaitpur-Sambhalpur, Baghat, Udaipur, Jhansi, Nagpur, Karoli, and many others. Dissatisfaction was simmering across the land.

Not content with this policy, the Company also declared that it could bring under its direct rule any territory if the ruler appeared to be incompetent. It was under this pretext that the Awadh state was annexed in 1856, and Nawab Wajid Ali Shah was sent off to Calcutta on a pension. It was like rubbing salt into the injury. None of the annexed states were powerful enough to take on the mighty Company. This simply meant that they could emerge victorious only if a large number of native states came together and acted jointly. Nana Saheb thought it incumbent upon himself to undertake this task.

After its victory in the third Anglo-Maratha battle in 1817–18, the East India Company gained control over the Maratha territory, and Peshwa Bajirao II was expelled and dispatched to a small town

called Bithur (near Kanpur) with an annual pension of 80,000 pounds. It was a large amount, which helped him lead a royal life.

Now, Bajirao II had no son, so he adopted three sons of a Deccani Brahmin who was a courtier in the Maratha state. The elder of these sons was Dhondu Pant, who came to be called Nana Saheb or Nana Rao, when he was declared the heir apparent to the throne and pension. He grew up in the company of Tantya Tope and Manikarnika Tambe (later Rani Lakshmibai of Jhansi); they played and trained together; it is no wonder that all of them rose to be exceptional revolutionaries during the 1857 Uprising.

When Peshwa Bajirao II died in 1851, the Company refused to acknowledge Nana Saheb as the heir under the Doctrine of Lapse. Moreover, it was contended that the Maratha state was no longer in existence, so there was no question of his having any title whatsoever. Nana Saheb even approached the British government in England through his friend and secretary, Azimullah Khan, but to no avail. By the time the final denial came, it was 1855, and ever since, Nana Saheb had been approaching different people, including rulers, native sepoys, and religious heads from both Hindu and Muslim faiths to rise in revolt.

There is evidence of him and Azimullah Khan visiting the Kumbh Mela, the largest Hindu religious fair, which was held at Haridwar in 1855. He was there to seek support from the saints and sages who had set up their camps on this occasion. Here, he met with Swami Purnanand and a young hermit who later came to be known as Swami Dayanand Saraswati. This hermit was instrumental in raising the banner of revolt at Meerut.

It was from this time that two campaigns were started: *Kamal Abhiyan* (lotus campaign) and *Chapati Abhiyan* (flatbread campaign). The British could never solve the mystery enveloping them. Under these campaigns, lotuses, and flatbreads were distributed in towns and villages across a large part of northern India, motivating people

to be prepared to rise in revolt when the call was given. It is believed that under these two campaigns, the date for the Uprising was fixed as May 31, 1857. These two campaigns in particular helped to make the Uprising one in which common people participated in large numbers right from the first day, which prompted Savarkar to call the Uprising the First War of Independence. His claim is often disputed by historians, scholars, and even politicians, who argue whether the Uprising can be termed a mutiny, a peasants' revolt, or an urban revolution. As we dive deeper into the topic, we will see that Savarkar was justified in saying so.

At this time, the Company's forces mainly comprised three presidency armies—Bengal Army, Madras Army, and Bombay Army. The Bengal Army operated in northern India and recruited troops mainly from the Punjab, Awadh, and Bihar regions. Awadh comprised most of the territories now forming eastern Uttar Pradesh, with considerable influence over Bihar. The sepoys from Awadh felt anguished when the state was usurped by the British and Nawab Wajib Ali Shah was exiled to Calcutta.

11

Making of a Revolutionary

Azizan proved to be an able manager. She regulated the timing of her performances so that the British and Indian troops were not together. She found that the British visitors, under the influence of liquor, often discussed what was going on in the army and administration. This opened up an avenue for her to know what was going on in the power corridors. She came into contact with some 'rebels' and passed on this information. She seemed to have found the purpose of her existence. Her patriotic sentiments were breaking on the barren sands of her life and were nurturing new ideas in her.

A frequent visitor to Azizan's place was an Indian sepoy named Shamsuddin, who belonged to the 2nd Cavalry. This tall and stout soldier was admired by other troops for his daredevilry. Azizan was attracted to him. As the two came closer, infinite love blossomed between the two souls, and they vowed to live together.

Shamsuddin, however, wished to accomplish a noble goal before tying the knot with her. He was dissatisfied with serving the

British, the very people who were plundering his country. The fact that he was one of the native soldiers who were aiding the British expand their territory and suppressing their own countrymen agonized him further. He was only waiting for an opportunity and Azizan was important to this cause. He primarily came to her for the information that she gathered. He was also in active contact with several revolutionaries, including Nana Saheb, who is believed to have visited Azizan's place at least once.

Impressed by each other's abilities and intentions, Azizan and Shamsuddin wished to live and die together, but destiny had different plans for them. Moreover, Azizan was not apologetic about her affairs becoming public; rather, she blushed when the co-courtesans talked about this.

Shamsuddin sometimes took Azizan out for horseback riding, an art she soon learned. She also learned sword-wielding and practiced it behind closed doors in her place. On two occasions, he taught her how to use firearms and took her to the banks of the Ganga, where she fired from the musket.

The signs for an uprising were emanating from different places in the country. The news of Mangal Pandey's rise in revolt and his supreme sacrifice at Barrackpore filtered into the town and circulated all over the country, spreading disaffection among the Indian sepoys as well as the common folk. The saints and faqirs had played a vital role in spreading this news, adding rumors to incite people. The sepoys from the disbanded units too were travelling to other units in the country, and the units at Kanpur were no exception.

Azizan is said to have taught her dancers and other workers how to keep an eye on the British visitors so as to get vital information. Any such information gathered from them was passed to the rebels promptly. Some of the rebels even found shelter in her place in the garb of her staff. The intention and probability of an open revolt against the British were expressed openly in several places.

Shamsuddin had clearly told her that he could marry only when the British were thrown out of the country. However, he made it a point to visit her daily. As the situation grew ripe for an uprising, he became too busy to visit her as his place was also used to shelter the rebels. If Azizan had any vital information to pass, she herself would visit his place in hiding. With time, Azizan continued her work of gathering intelligence through tracking the European visitors' conversations and facial expressions. Any signs of anxiety were also considered worthy of reporting.

The rebels used to meet at two places—one was Shamsuddin's place and the other was the residence of Subedar Tika Singh (later made general by Nana Saheb). These places were under the protection of Nana Saheb's people, guided by his two reliable servants, named Jwala Prasad and Mehmood Ali.

In addition, Azizan helped the revolutionaries in the form of pecuniary assistance and shelter too. V.D. Savarkar, in his book *The First War of Independence*, has described her as sepoys' favorite courtesan, who gave up the practice of selling her love in the market and instead showered it in the market of freedom struggle as a reward.

Once, Azizan lured a British officer in her trap when he showed signs of having doubts about Shamsuddin, and the rest was done by the revolutionaries. When Shamsuddin learned of this, he confronted Azizan saying, "Aren't you scared of doing these things? You could land in trouble; you don't know these white people."

Azizan only laughed, "What use is this beauty if it can't be put to use for the motherland!"

In the first week of May 1857, Shamsuddin did not turn up for several days together. Azizan was a patriot, but that did not mean she would deprive herself of the opportunity to have a glimpse of her lover. When the mehfil was over and the visitors had all gone off, she stealthily made her way to his place.

"Don't you realize how dangerous these times are?" Shamsuddin was seemingly unhappy with her visit.

"I'm simply restive if I don't see you daily," she replied, her moist eyes shining brilliantly in the dim light of the kerosene lamp.

Shamsuddin held her hand and said, "Just a few days more. Things are moving in the right direction. The day for the revolution has been fixed; it's the 31st of this month. We're getting ready. Nana Saheb will be heading with his force to Kanpur soon."

According to Travelyan, a highly reliable source from that era, Shamsuddin made a promise to Azizan on this occasion, vowing to fill her house with gleaming gold *mohurs* (coins), ensuring her future wealth and prosperity.

As Azizan shook her head lightly, her eyes expressed unease, "Take good care of yourself."

"God willing, everything will fall into place, it's just a matter of a few days before we can be together for all times to come," he said in an attempt to comfort her, and then added solemnly, "Azizan, you don't need to risk your life."

Azizan said in a soft but resolute voice, "This country is as much my *Aziz* (lover) as I am his *Azizan* (beloved)!" She took his leave with her heart resolute to do her work of intelligence-gathering more keenly in the hope that her beloved's words would come true soon.

12

The Spark of Revolution

Kanpur was buzzing with the information that the Uprising would take place on May 31, 1857, a Sunday. Those aware of it were bracing themselves to meet the changing currents. They were, however, bewildered, when in the middle of the month, they came across rumors about the breakout of the Uprising at Meerut on May 10 itself, three weeks before the decided date.

For General Hugh Wheeler, the military commander of Kanpur, this piece of confirmed information was received on May 18. Under him was deployed a division comprising three native infantry regiments (1st, 53rd and 56th) and one cavalry regiment (2nd), totaling around 3,000 troops.

Wheeler had adopted Indian traditions and had even married an Indian lady. He was popular among the native sepoys and enjoyed their confidence. When he received this news, he was still confident that his sepoys would not go against him, though he felt somewhat uneasy when he heard of some sepoys dropping off their families to their native places.

Wheeler conjectured that even if the sepoys under him rose in mutiny, they would march off to Delhi, as it had happened at Meerut and other places. He felt assured that he only needed to make some security arrangements to deal with the turbulence in the initial stages. He seemed to have forgotten that for the people of this region, the sepoys were local boys who were unhappy at Awadh's annexation by the British.

To meet any eventuality, Wheeler erected his defenses in a large complex of buildings to the south of the town. It was surrounded by a muddy boundary wall. He made adequate provisions for food, arms, and artillery. He also ordered all Europeans and families to take refuge there in case a rebellion broke out.

It was a surprising decision on his part because he had a more secure place to the north of the town where the magazine (artillery) was located. However, he felt assured that the sepoys would not rise against him, to the extent that he dispatched two of his companies for the defense of Lucknow.

As the revolutionaries' movement intensified, Wheeler thought that the revolt would take place on the festival of Eid, to be celebrated on May 24, 1857. This day was also the birthday of Queen Victoria. Each year, as a custom, all British cantonments fired a gun salute on this day. However, he decided to forgo the ceremony that year, as it could irk and alarm the rebels.

Wheeler's lapses in judgement extended even further. He was also misled by Nana Saheb's demeanor as he felt him to be in the imperialists' favor. He himself invited Nana Saheb to take over the defenses of the town. With this, the latter entered Kanpur with his three hundred warriors and two cannons.

On May 30, the sepoys at Kanpur knew that Meerut had already revolted, and they excitedly shouted slogans. Some of them even fired a few shots, but the situation remained under control.

The next day, in a unit posted along the Ganga bank at

Fatehgarh, near Kanpur, a group of native sepoys rose in revolt and attacked the British garrison. To bring them under control, Wheeler dispatched a company. In the ensuing confrontation, three English officers were killed, while one managed to flee to safety. The revolution, however, did not spread, and native regiments remained peaceful.

This development alarmed Wheeler, and he ordered all Europeans and their families to take shelter in the building earmarked for the purpose. To notch up the safety arrangements, he deployed two cannons pointing towards the native regiments. This deployment did not go well with the native sepoys, as this presented a major danger to them. Surprisingly, peace still prevailed.

On June 2, a drunk British troop fired at a native sepoy; the incident was reported to the officers, but no action was taken as the miscreant was a British. This created explosive discontent among the sepoys. In no time, rumors went around that there were plans to disarm the native sepoys, and that they would all be lined up in the parade ground and shot dead. Several other rumors were having a field day too.

The first major rebellion in Kanpur occurred on June 5, 1857, when the sepoys of the 2nd Cavalry attacked and killed Risaldar Major Bhavani Singh, an Indian loyal to the British, trying to impose discipline. This created unease among the sepoys belonging to other regiments. The British thought that a major rebellion was taking place, when on the contrary, it was not. Amid panic, they started bombarding the native lines.

As of now, about 150 native sepoys deployed in the magazine had not revolted. Deciding to bring it under his control, Nana Saheb headed to it. Surprisingly, he was welcomed, as he was believed to be loyal to the British. Once inside, he posted his men at crucial places and took over the artillery, and then he announced that he too was part of the Uprising.

Seeing the situation change in an instant, all native sepoys submitted to his authority. His strength swelled further as more and more native sepoys joined him. He gathered the cannons and treasury and moved towards the Grand Trunk Road. The joyful sepoys and other rebels shouted slogans, hailing 'the enemy-destroying Emperor of Hindustan'.

Azimullah Khan asked Nana Saheb, "What do you intend to do now?"

"What else? We ought to move to Delhi. The battle is raging there. If Delhi is conquered, the entire country will come under our control," said Nana Saheb with unprecedented hope shining in his eyes.

"There, Bahadur Shah Zafar has been declared the leader of the Uprising but you can't trust that old man with this huge task. For all we know, he'll only try to establish a Mughal rule," said Azimullah Khan thoughtfully.

"But you see, it's under him that the whole country can unite in this fight." Nana Saheb replied with respect for his secretary's wisdom. After a brief pause, he turned to his trusted advisor and inquired, "What do you suggest?"

"We should rather fight for a Maratha empire. We can start from occupying Kanpur, and Bithur is already under our control."

"Will that satisfy the revolutionaries?" said Nana Saheb looking at the slogan-shouting fighters.

"Clearly, what they want is the removal of the *firangi*s (Europeans)," said Azimullah Khan in a confident tone.

Nana Saheb's brow furrowed in contemplation for a moment; then, he made up his mind quickly and said, "Well, Azimullah, you're right."

Whatever the merit of this decision, one thing was now sure: the Uprising was bound to fail as the revolutionaries across different places were no longer fighting for a common goal. The

aim of having a unified front against the British was a long-lost idea now, despite many efforts.

Seeing Nana Saheb back in Kanpur, all native sepoys joined his forces, as did many common people. His strength soared to about 10,000–15,000 troops. In the evening, he sent a letter to the British commander stating that he intended to attack his garrison. Surprisingly, Wheeler did not take it seriously!

13

The New Avatar of Azizan

On the following day, Nana Saheb laid siege to the complex in which the British and their families were housed. Those in the garrison included the European troops, officers, traders, assistants, wives, and children, numbering approximately 1,000. Their condition inside the garrison was precarious—water was deficient, dysentery and cholera had broken out, while Nana Saheb's cannons were bringing misery.

But the British derived solace from the fact that they still did not launch a land attack. The cannons deployed at the mouth had kept the rebels away. The besieging force lost several sepoys to the shelling from the garrison; Shamsuddin was one of them. He had suffered grievous injuries from splinters. When this news was brought to Azizan, she visited the site. Everybody expected that she would bemoan the death, but no tears could be seen in her eyes; instead a resolute determination shone. She said that she wanted to take the place of her fallen lover.

Azizan went to her place and returned, this time in a man's

dress, adorned with the shining medals that she had removed from Shamsuddin's uniform. It was in this dress that she was seen by several people. She was seen in the company of Nana Saheb and Tantya Tope on more than one occasion. Azizan was not the only nautch girl to do this; several other nautch girls from her kotha too joined her. They played their part in the war by preparing meals and tending to the wounded. Occasionally, they aided in the distribution of ammunition. Moreover, they engaged troops in conversation, providing both entertainment and morale-boosting singing and dancing sessions. Azizan's group, the Mastani Toli, played a vital role in maintaining the warriors' spirits, offering a much-needed breath of fresh air on the battlefield.

During this time, Nanakchand, a lawyer loyal to the British, maintained his journal, which gives us a unique peek into the scenario. He wrote: "The armed Azizan shone like a flash of lightning; she would stand distributing sweets to the fatigued and wounded warriors." In his testimony to the enquiry committee formed one year after the Uprising under the chairmanship of Lt Col Williams, he described Azizan as he had seen her on the horseback "in male attire decorated with medals, armed with a brace of pistols" as she took part in the crusade. Another witness, Janakee Prasad, a trader, delineated her in the same manner and claimed that he had seen her as had thousands of others.

Azizan made one of the gun batteries her place of operation. It was located to the north of Wheeler's entrenchment between the 'racket court' and the 'chapel of ease'. Her battery shelled the entrenchment right from the first day of the siege. Nanakchand had written that she used to distribute arms and ammunition among the fighters, cared for the wounded, cooked food, sang for them, and was also seen distributing milk on the road. She remained in the battery all through the siege, despite heavy bombardment from the entrenchment.

While this confrontation continued, Nana Saheb declared Kanpur an open city. He was now planning for its administration. For instance, he had appointed one Hola Singh as the Chief Magistrate; he also formed his ministry, comprising Jwala Prasad, Azimullah Khan, and others under his direct command.

By June 21, almost one-third of the inhabitants in the entrenchment perished, and many were wounded too. Seeing their distressful situation, Wheeler requested Lucknow to send reinforcements, but to no avail, as Lucknow too was struggling at its own end.

June 23, 1857 was the centennial anniversary of the Battle of Plassey. It was prophesied that India would become a free nation on this day. To realize this prediction, Nana Saheb launched a land attack on the garrison, but its cannons did not allow his forces to come anywhere near it. The attack was repulsed, yet the siege continued. On the 24th, Wheeler wrote to Sir Henry Lawrence, Chief Commissioner of Awadh, a long letter seeking help. He added, "British spirit alone remains, but it cannot last forever." And then he concluded, "We have lost everything belonging to us, and have not even a change of linen. Surely we are not to die like rats in a cage." In response, Lawrence promised that 'Brigadier Havelock, with 400 Europeans and 300 Sikhs, guns, and cavalry, were to march from Allahabad immediately'. But destiny could not be averted.

The condition inside the entrenchment gradually turned from bad to worse, caused by incessant bombing and diseases. The inmates needed to be evacuated but was not possible without Nana Saheb's consent. Coincidentally, Nana Saheb sent a European prisoner as his messenger to Wheeler with a proposal to let him and his people sneak to Allahabad safely. Left with no other option, Wheeler accepted it.

This was seen as a sign of victory. Nana Saheb even took out a victory march on June 26, of which Azizan Bai and her

Mastani Toli, who toiled hard for these 21 days, were a part too. Azizan rode a horse in her male attire. Otto Travelyan, a civil servant, who served in India in 1860s, has in his book, *Cawnpore*, described Azizan as "the Demoiselle Theroigne of the Rebellion." Describing the scene further, he writes that ". . . she appeared on horseback amidst a group of her admirers, dressed in the uniform of her favored regiment, armed with pistols, decorated with medals." Her favored regiment, of course, was the 2nd Cavalry, in which Shamsuddin served.

This, however, was not the end of the conflict. Darker and more terrible things loomed on the horizon.

14

The Massacre

Following his offer, on June 27, 1857, Nana Saheb arranged for 40 boats at the Sati Chaura Ghat (now called Nana Rao Ghat) on the Ganga River. Showing his compassion, in addition to food, he also arranged for palanquins, elephants, and bullock-carts to carry the families, the wounded, and the sick. He even allowed them to carry small arms with them.

The British reached the bank at eight in the morning. To watch them go, a large number of people thronged the Ghat. The water level in the river was low. When the boats in the shallow water were occupied, they could not be rowed into the running stream. Confusion reigned as people pondered their next steps, but then came the unexpected! A piercing bugle call split the air. It served as a signal, prompting the rowers to abandon their boats and swim towards the riverbank. Explosions rocked the vicinity, setting a few boats ablaze. Finding themselves under attack, the confused British started to fire their weapons indiscriminately. In response,

some native cavalrymen rode their horses into the water and started attacking them with their swords.

Nana Saheb was accused of the attack, but he did not seem to have done it, as it was him who was helping the British and had even allowed them to carry small arms. If he had any evil designs, he would not have done so.

When informed of the sudden turn of events, Nana Saheb rushed to the Ghat immediately. He ordered that no harm must come to women and children; they should only be taken prisoner. Only four British troops could sneak out to save their lives. Some of them tried to flee on a boat, but a few of them were killed, while 12 of them were taken prisoners. These troops were taken to Savada Kothi, Nana Saheb's residence during the battle, where they were killed.

All the other prisoners, including women and children, were brought to Bibighar. The total number of women and children brought to Bibighar was approximately 200, with some of them succumbing to cholera and dysentery.

This event has been discussed in the book, *The Story of Cawnpore* by one Captain Thomson, who somehow saved himself on the Ghat.

15

Suppression of the Uprising

On July 1, 1857, Nana Saheb was proclaimed the Peshwa at Bithur, and the coronation ceremony was held in which he was seated on the throne.

To rescue Kanpur, General Henry Havelock was leading a large contingent to Kanpur. Nana Saheb thought that he would be able to stop this army at Allahabad itself in return for the release of these prisoners. However, when this proposal failed, he sent his army to confront Havelock. The two armies fought at Fatehgarh on July 12, and Nana Saheb was beaten in it. Another battle took place near a village called Awang on July 15, but he tasted defeat again.

It was this day that witnessed the heinous massacre, wherein all the prisoners at Bibighar were killed and thrown in the adjacent well. Nana Saheb was not in favor of any such atrocity, but with the overwhelming chaos, he could not do anything. It is also alleged that women were dishonored and mutilated.

However, Sir John Kaye, KCSI, FRS, has narrated a detailed account of these incidents and battles in his book, *Indian Mutiny of*

1857–58 (Vol. II). He has carried a clear note of denial below this narration and has noted: "Mr. Sherer and Mr. Thornhill, in their official reports, speak most distinctly in denial of the assertion that our women had been mutilated and dishonored."

Nana Saheb continued to struggle, fought several battles, and even declared himself the ruler of the Maratha state; however, he could not face the increasing sway of the besieging British forces. When things turned awry, it is believed that he made his way over to Nepal, where he died in 1859.

Tantya Tope, on the other hand, struggled too, and when he found himself weaker, he led his forces to Bundelkhand and joined Rani Lakshmibai of Jhansi. Not much is known about what became of him after the death of the legendary Lakshmibai. It is believed that he headed to the Narmada region and made efforts for a revolution in central India.

Col. GB Malleson, CSI, writes in his book, *History of the Indian Mutiny, 1857–59*, that Tantya Tope was betrayed by a trusted person, and it was on the basis of his information that he was arrested from the Paron jungles on April 7, 1859. He was court-martialed the next day and hanged on the 18th of the same month at Shivpuri. Malleson argues that Tantya Tope was never a British soldier or official, so he could not have been court-martialed, but such were the high-handed ways adopted by the British to crush the Uprising. Praising him, he further writes that Tantya Tope was "a wary, capable, astute man, he alone of all the natives brought by the mutiny to the front—Kunwar Singh and the Oudh Moulvi alone excepted—showed any great qualities of generalship. Tantia (Tantya) was a man to be feared. Fortunate was it for the British that the Gwalior soldiers had not earlier placed themselves under his orders, for his first act on taking up his office was to march them southwards to occupy a position which could threaten Kanhpur [Kanpur]."

The British were ruthless in retaliation, but owing to the incidents at Sati Chaura Ghat and Bibighar, they turned brutal. All those arrested were put to death by atrocious and violent means, including hanging, firing, and blasting from the cannon's mouth. Before they were put to death, they were brought to Bibighar and were forced to lick the blood-stained floor, irrespective of whether they were involved in the massacre here or not.

16

To the Gallows

And now, arrested along with other tawaifs and workers from her place, Azizan Bai was standing in chains before General Havelock, who was summarily disposing of the rebels. He was giving a death sentence to them all, though the manner of putting them to death varied.

On seeing not much reaction from Azizan, General Havelock grew a bit impatient and said again, "You're a rebel. There's no doubt about that, but if you confess to your crime, you will be forgiven. You can then run your place in peace. What do you say?" His final words could not be heard by anyone as the cannon blasted and pieces of a rebel's body stained the grassy area. The only voice was the groans of the two rebels, who had been tied to the wheels of the gun carriage to check the recoil as they had suffered multiple fractures.

Azizan seemed to be in a phantom world. Her entire life passed before her eyes like a fleeting panorama. With her lover, Shamsuddin, gone, she had no more desire to live. She said nothing and kept on staring at the General. She knew that her weakness

would only demoralize the revolutionaries who were still fighting elsewhere.

She said in a calm voice, "You, not we, are the rebels. You've betrayed the country that gave you rights to trade, and you've only taken advantage of our weakness. Until recently, you swore allegiance to the Emperor of Hindustan and worked as tax collectors but look at you now. Not to forget, you've tried to defile our religion."

"She must die," said the exasperated General in a dry voice to the Jemadar standing next to him.

She was taken and made to stand behind the queue of the rebels awaiting their death, either by shooting, hanging, or blasting.

When her turn came, Azizan was taken to the gallows. As the noose was wrapped around her delicate, long neck and pulled up, a shot of fire was heard, which pierced her chest. She is said to have managed to shout, "Bharat Mata Ki Jai!" (Hail Mother India!) and "Nana Rao Ki Jai!" (Hail Nana Rao).

Azizan was gone, but she did not know that her sacrifice would remain hidden from the annals of history. The only solace is that she remains etched in the local folklore.

An Awadhi folksong celebrates her zeal, and its last stanza goes thus:

"Bhed bataub Angrezan kai,
Jetna apni jaan ma.
Bhed khula tau kati Azizan
Gai dharti se asmaan ma."

(She revealed the English's secrets,
Putting at risk her life,
When her role was found out then Azizan
Flew from land to heaven.)

Part
III

Husna Bai

17

The Stigma

Husna Bai, or Husna Jaan, had just finished her first rendering in thumri. Before her on the low diwan rested the zamindar. He had been her regular client and patron for the past three years. Enthralled by the singing, he raised his head from the palm resting on the richly embroidered bolster. With admiration in his eyes, he extended his hand to gather a few notes from the plate before him, but suddenly his facial expression changed to that of bewilderment when he saw her stand up.

"Baiji, it's been only one song and you're leaving," said the zamindar in his commanding voice.

"I think I'm not well, maybe I'll sing later. In the meantime, my assistant will come and sing," said Husna Bai.

"You don't seem like your normal self," said the zamindar. "Is there something bothering you?"

"The times are changing rapidly, and my heart is restless," said Husna Bai as she strode away without giving a further explanation. Her voice missed the spontaneous liveliness she was known for.

With a thoughtful expression, the zamindar saw the renowned singer go behind the netted curtain and sit down on the low chair with a silver back, while her assistant walked in.

A well-respected singer, Husna Bai was the nominated *Chaudharayan* of Banaras. She had earned this reputed post because of her profound knowledge of Sanskrit, Persian, and Hindustani, along with her excellence in singing and other crafts, which cast a spell on the audience. Even Bhartendu Harish Chandra, the renowned litterateur, visited her to learn about arts and discuss literature. Her handwriting was described as 'manly', as she lived in a time when far more men were educated than women. She had her salon at Raja Darwaza near Dahal Mandi, popularly called Dal Mandi.

"Are you all right, Sarkar?" said the assistant sitting next to Husna Bai behind the curtain, from where they had a clear view of the open hall. This assistant had been training well and usually started the performance first before Husna Bai would take over. Astonishingly, her mistress had returned all of a sudden, though she often sang for one hour at the least. The assistant had been a witness to the picketing that had taken place at the staircase of the kotha that afternoon.

"How long can this go on like this?" Husna Bai mumbled to herself while the assistant looked at her blankly.

The country was passing through a crucial stage. Gandhi had returned from South Africa a few years ago and had gone around the land. Now, he was at the forefront of his first major campaign—the Non-cooperation Movement. It was based on a new idea which he had experimented with in South Africa, though without much success. Its basic ethos was based on *Ahimsa* (non-violence) and *Satyagraha* (insistence on truth). He dissuaded the Indians from taking part in any activity that 'sustained the British government and also economy in India', including the British industries and educational institutions. The movement had to manifest itself

through refusal to buy British goods, adoption of local handicrafts, and picket liquor shops.

Gandhi had adopted this mode of rising against the alien rulers because it kept up with the prevailing conditions of the common Indians, who were mostly powerless, poor, and helpless. He also wove social reform in this movement by giving the call to end untouchability. With an intent to make it widespread and acceptable to all communities, especially the Muslims, he linked it to the restoration of the Khilafat (rule of the Khalifa or Caliph) in Turkey.

Gandhi's main thrust was in response to the Rowlatt Act of March 1919, which had suspended the rights of political prisoners in sedition trials, and the heinous massacre at Jallianwala Bagh in Amritsar on April 13, 1919, on the day of the Baisakhi festival. He had been working for the movement to grow popular, which happened towards the end of 1920. The other reasons he ascribed for starting the movement included the economic exploitation of Indians at the hands of the British, hardships faced by the artisans, factory-made goods replacing handmade native goods, and large-scale conscription in the army in view of the First World War. He promised *Swaraj,* or self-rule, within one year if the movement was fully implemented. In October 1920, he wrote in the *Young India*: "Much laughter has been indulged in at my expense for having told the Congress audience at Calcutta that, if there was sufficient response to my program of Non-cooperation, Swaraj would be attained in one year. Some have ignored my condition and laughed because of the impossibility of getting Swaraj anyhow within one year."

The movement had caught the fancy of the youth as well. The revolutionaries supported Gandhi, abandoned their mission of throwing out the foreign masters by the use of force, and joined the fray. The movement had a huge impact. Strikes and hartals, boycott of government offices and educational institutions, resignations by

government employees and teachers, and boycott and bonfire of British goods left the British government in shock. In this wake, national colleges and institutions were set up all across the country. As the movement picked momentum with passing weeks, the government could do little but stare helplessly as Gandhi sought to include more and more classes of people, and now next on his agenda was to seek the active support of women while cleansing the society of all immoral elements.

Masses found it so easy to participate in the movement—what they needed to do in most cases was just gather a few people, raise a banner, go round the streets singing patriotic songs, and raise slogans. The more courageous ones would picket shops selling British goods and liquor. The idea of picketing too was simple; the protestors would stand outside the shop and apprise the customers about the British atrocities and why it was more important to buy native goods.

Gandhi wrote for *Young India* on August 11, 1921, "The fine fabric that we have imported from the West or the Far East has literally killed millions of our brothers and sisters, and delivered thousands of our dear sisters to a life of shame." And then he went on to ask people, including the women in the trade, to spin cotton of the finest quality possible. He wrote that the spinning wheel "should be as it was the widows' loving companion".

This perspective of morality and women's participation in the Non-cooperation Movement was accepted widely by the demonstrators, and they now started to picket the premises of the courtesans too, as they viewed their profession as immoral. Picketing against them had earlier occurred in Amritsar, and now the trend was spreading to other cities.

They were not in the wrong either, as Mahatma Gandhi had placed courtesans and prostitutes in one category of 'fallen women'. This adversely affected the trade in places where the courtesan

tradition was still surviving and had not yet fallen into the clutches of the British officers, who viewed them as mere nautch girls. Banaras was one such place.

And today, Husna Bai's place had been picketed, led by one Prem Kumar Khanna, and it perturbed her greatly. In financial terms, it had no impact as she served only a few patrons, and any other interested person could ascend the steps of her place situated on the first floor as soon as his antecedents and intentions were confirmed.

What pained her most was that her noble profession of singing and dancing had been equated with that of prostitutes. This was a great fall for her. She was so distracted and agitated by this development that she found it hard to sing. She was not satisfied with her performance of the one song that she had sung; she felt she could not bring out the spirited joy that was the essence of her singing and for which she was known.

As an individual and a citizen of the country, Husna Bai was in support of the nationwide campaign, and had been contributing to it. Whenever the volunteers visited Dahal Mandi to collect donations, she would send money to them.

"Baiji," the patron called from the hall, "if you're unwell or unable to sing, let me know. I'll leave, I can't wait any more."

Husna Bai unwillingly rose and came out. She started to sing how Radha awaited Krishna on the river bank, and when she sang another version of the same song on a different note, even the patron knew that she was not her own self. Rising to his feet, he said, "I think you need to rest. Will visit you soon."

Husna Bai too stood up, bowing to him in salutation.

18

Husna Bai: The Epitome of Grace

Of the four greatest singers of classical Hindustani music, Husna Bai alone belongs to the tawaif, or courtesan tradition. Despite a decline in reputation, she stuck to the roots of the structure and the elevations of this genre. Speaking of Husna Bai (together with 'Surshree' Kesarbai Kerkar, Girija Devi, and Kishori Amonkar), Kumud Dewan Jha, in her paper "The Alpha Songbirds: Independent and Vibrant", writes, "As women performers, they are the path-breakers. In terms of innovation, they have spawned their own *gharanas* [school/tradition] within the framework of the traditional and historical gharana in which they were trained. Their performances are imbued with a genius interpretation of raga and the literary underpinnings of the compositions they sing."

Hindustani classical music has largely been a male bastion, but these women have raised the bar. As far as Husna Bai was

concerned, it was all the more amazing because she overcame social hurdles that came her way, as her work was often seen through a narrow lens because she came from the tawaif tradition. Despite being termed 'baiji' she rose above the class of mere performers and created a niche for herself. She made the profession for women 'highly sought after and revered artists'.

For women, it was a taboo to sing in public, and when it came to a woman belonging to the courtesan tradition, like Husna Bai, it was a stigma. However, it did not deter her from singing, as she accorded the first and foremost place to music, and this helped her create a name for herself in all times to come.

Thumri was essentially a courtesan art, and it had entered the semi-classical field through new experiments at the hands of performers like Husna Bai. Just to note that Wajid Ali Shah, the Nawab of Lucknow, was the greatest patron of this genre, and he himself composed several thumris under the pen name Akhtar Piya. With the 1857 Uprising, the scope for most courtesans had shrunk terribly, bringing about their fall, while a few continued to survive through sheer hard work and skill, remaining oblivious to the realities of the times they lived in when their profession was no longer looked at with respect, and to this class belonged our protagonist of this story, Husna Bai.

Husna Bai performed in a limited sphere, as she performed publicly only in Banaras and before her patrons in her place. This is the reason that she is not as popular as other latter-day singers from the city, such as Siddheshwari and Rasoolan Bai, who performed across several cities. This restricted Husna Bai only within the United Provinces but she was well-known for her expertise in *khayal*, thumri, and *tappa* singing. A.N. Sharma compiled Husna Bai's thumri and its sub-genres under the title *Madhu Tarang* in his book *Bajanaama: A Study of Early Gramophone Records* (published by Kathachitra Prakashan). Though much less-known, the level of her

skill is placed in the same league with the performers par excellence such as Vidyadhari Bai, Badi Moti Bai, Siddheshwari Devi, Gauhar Jaan, and Rasoolan Bai.

Husna Bai was born and brought up in the kotha and, over the years, was trained by Thakur Prasad Mishra and the well-known sarangi player Pt. Shambhunath Mishra. She grasped a deeper understanding of tappa singing from affluent patrons of Banaras, including Chote Ramdas Ji. She received her initial training in singing and dancing from the musicians employed in the kotha, but her natural interest in the field led her to be under the tutelage of the masters of the city, and the outcome was scintillating. Her absolute command over singing led to her being established as the master, and earning the esteemed title of 'Sarkar', a term reserved for the most skilled artists.

A contemporary of the legendary litterateur of Banaras was Bhartendu Harish Chandra. Husna Bai often corresponded with him and sought his advice on poetic expression. It was at his insistence that she composed the *Geet Govind* (composed by the twelfth century Hindi poet Jaidev), and made several of the songs popular. For instance, we have:

Amal-Kamal-Dal-Lochan Bhav Mochan E
Tribhuvan-Bhuvan-Nidhan Jai Jai Dev Hare.

Unfortunately, there are no records that mention her name.

She was well-known in local circles, including the landed gentry and royalty. Consequently, she was initiated into a new role. Husna Bai continued to adorn the high traditions of the tawaifs, who were known for their Adab, Tehzeeb, and Nafasat. There is a legend about her high tawaif etiquette.

Once, when she was performing in the hall, a wealthy landlord started to ascend the staircase with a thumping sound. As he

appeared at the entrance upstairs, she stopped singing, looked at him sternly, and said, "Please go away. I can't sing for you."

"Why . . . why hesitate? Look at the notes I've brought for you," the landlord tried to impress her with his wealth.

With a sarcastic smile, Husna Bai said, "It's the nursery of music. If you don't know the basic etiquette of climbing up the stairs, I'm sorry, but I think you would know little about singing and how to appreciate it. Please leave."

19

Kashi Tawaif Sabha: A New Path

Husna Bai, respected and admired for her singing, was aware of the threat being faced by her noble profession ever since the British had come to India. Despite all the negative terms being ascribed to it, she had maintained her dignity. The brief picketing by the protestors before her place was an incidence that had perturbed her greatly, as it could bring her somewhat stigmatized profession into complete disrepute.

There is an interesting episode about Prem Kumar Khanna, who led the picketing at her place. He was a small-time trader who, under the influence of the Arya Samaj, took to picketing courtesans' places. If he could not gather any people on a day, he would go all alone to do his bidding. These actions stemmed from all types of negative things that he had heard about the courtesans. He was not wrong either.

While Husna Bai had maintained the purity of her profession, there were other tawaifs in the city who had not been able to do so and had mixed prostitution with the trade. It was at their hands that the profession suffered a blot, leading to its decline in the past few decades, as they had adopted sensual movements in their dance and illicit senses in their singing. Husna Bai could never imagine sinking to such depths. She would have to find a way out of this mess.

This was one such day when Khanna was all alone, yet he had decided to do his work. Perspiring profusely in the hot afternoon, he had hardly taken a step or two in the alley when he fell down unconscious. Coincidentally, Husna Bai was returning home, and finding him lying senseless in the pathway, she took him in the palanquin while she herself walked the remaining distance.

At her place, Khanna was looked after well. Regaining consciousness, he was shocked to find himself in the hospitality of the very ladies whom he had opposed all these days. In the conversations that followed, he was fully convinced that there was nothing immoral about the tawaifs, so he now turned to be a Gandhian who believed in their rehabilitation rather than their ouster from the place.

The patron had long departed, and the musicians and other performers had gone to their respective chambers, when Husnawale Das walked in and sat beside Husna Bai. He was her lover and was a Hindu. and they both wanted to get married one day. His name was in fact not Husnawale, but he had come to be known as such owing to his association with the renowned courtesan.

Normally, he avoided entering this part of the premises, but learning of her agitated mental state, he had come to console her. He held her hand and massaged it lightly without saying a word. When he found Husna Bai had regained her composure to some extent, he asked very softly, "What pains you?"

"Are we *Veshyas*? No, we aren't. Nor, shall I ever be," said Husna Bai. "We belong to a glorious tradition, which is the hallmark of etiquette. Until recently, the gentry sent their sons to us for training. And now, these stupid people…they equate us with *randis*. This is simply unbearable!"

"They are led by Gandhiji," said Husnawale Das.

"No, they *claim* that they are led by him. Ambitiously, they have extended the scope of their social reform but are unable to sift chaff from grain. A Veshya's trade can be immoral, but so is not the case with mine," said Husna Bai in anguish. "We're sure to earn a stigma from it."

"What do you intend to do now?"

"We need to implement the Gandhian spirit in its positive sense," emphasized Husna Bai, and then continued, "Look, Gandhiji has called upon the prostitutes to jettison the life of prostitution and take on other careers. Now, the question is—Can they enter other professions so easily? People wouldn't accept them. They can go to them when the city is engulfed in the dark, but they can't interact with them when it's daylight. I don't think they can adopt other careers. We'll have to think more broadly."

With these words, Husna Bai sank deeper in thoughts and left for her chamber in a trance, leaving Husnawale Das where he was.

The year 1920 was drawing to a close. Gandhi was on his visit to Banaras; it was his second visit to the city this year. In fact, he was on a specific mission to uplift the women under the aegis of the Non-cooperation Movement and had planned to travel right up to Nainital over the next few days. He was also scheduled to march through the streets near Dahal Mandi, just near which, in Raja Darwaza, Husna Bai had her kotha.

As she received this information, she took an unusual decision! She wanted to avail this opportunity to see Gandhiji and even wanted to take a few of her courtesans with her. The street was

barricaded with ropes held by the volunteers on either side of it. She stood behind the rope just midway between two volunteers, while the other ladies of her place were on her left and right, forming a single line. Seeing so many women line up drew the attention of the volunteers, but as soon as they identified them, even the volunteers with white caps tried to keep a distance from them. Prem Kumar Khanna was the only exception; he ensured that they stood at a place where they could have a broad view.

For common people, it was even more baffling. How could they be seen with the tawaifs on the street in broad daylight? Of course, it would be another thing by night. They stood away from them, though they would steal a glance to look at them every now and then and pass comments among themselves.

"People are keeping away from us," remarked one of the courtesans.

"Yes, it's daytime," said another in an obvious tone.

"It's good for us; at least we won't be crushed in the crowd," said another as she smiled. The others followed suit.

Little caring for what people might be thinking, Husna Bai waited for the great leader, who was running a little behind schedule. The sun was shining overhead providing warmth on that winter afternoon, as people waited patiently. Some slogans were raised intermittently.

The word spread that Gandhi had turned into the street; people were now more alert as they bent over the ropes held by the volunteers as their eager eyes looked far to catch a glimpse. They could see a group of people clad in white marching down the street. He was not among them. They were the enthusiastic volunteers who walked ahead of him, raising slogans and asking people to be patient.

Not far behind emerged Gandhi, with several people at his heels. He walked slowly, looking at both sides and raising his hand

to acknowledge their greetings. Some of the people would say a word or two, and he would shake his head at them.

"Mahatma ji! Mahatma ji!" almost cried Husna Bai as Gandhiji approached her. "Please listen to me."

He looked at her and stopped, with the characteristic smile on his face, which made his face look still rounder. At the very first sight, he understood who these ladies were. He only shook his head up and down, as if asking to speak up.

"Mahatma ji, you've put all of us in the same category and that's not right," said Husna Bai.

"Perception is very important in life, so there's need for you to embrace other walks of life! You have to break free from the shackles of the *Dhani* [rich man or owner]."

"What else can we do?"

"Take up the charkha for a livelihood. Why don't you take the lead? It's also a part of the Non-cooperation Movement. Rise and emancipate the fallen women as only you can know how to best do it," said Gandhiji as he stepped ahead.

The volunteers and people had fallen silent when the dialogue was being conducted, and now they burst into shouting slogans once again.

Husna Bai turned and walked away, followed by her ladies. Her eyes were shining with confidence. The leader's words had done wonders for her. Back in her place, she shut herself in her chamber. She was in deep thought and was writing something rigorously in a notebook. She remained in this state for hours.

Two days later, Husna Bai's place was vibrant with a lot of movement. In response to her invitation to all the courtesans in the entire area to lunch, as many as 60 had turned up. As they sat down on the matted floor, she took her seat on her low silver chair. Near the wall on the left sat Prem Kumar Khanna, silently studying who was doing what.

Husna Bai welcomed them and then said, “I’ve invited you all for a purpose. You already know the kind of problems our profession is facing. We are here to discuss them and take decisions that will maintain the exalted dignity of women. But these should be in consonance with the fact that our sisters are not starving and are able to lead a respectable life. I asked Gandhiji what we could do in our case. His advice was to take up the charkha. And now, I seek your suggestions in this regard.”

“Charkha alone cannot sustain us,” came a voice.

“If we take up the charkha, our skill in singing and dancing will go to waste,” said another.

“These are, of course, reasonable objections,” said Husna Bai. “I’ve got an idea, if you’ll like. You know picketing by the over-enthusiastic volunteers has forced several courtesans to flee from Amritsar, and by the look of things here, some of us might have to do that as well. Gandhiji says that we should lead a dignified life, that simply means that we are in need of rehabilitation.”

She could see many of them shake their heads in agreement. She resumed, “What he meant by taking up the charkha is simply that we become part of the Non-cooperation Movement. Our country is facing many problems, and we cannot hope these to be solved effectively under the foreign masters. So, we need to take the plunge for national service while helping ourselves gain dignity. How about singing religious and patriotic songs?” said Husna Bai.

Several eyebrows went up at these words. Finally, a remark came by, “But who will come and listen to religious songs from us?”

“And forget if anyone will ever come with a wad of notes to listen to such songs,” said another.

“Even those who loudly advocate for women’s reform hesitate to come near us. You know what happened with Gauhar Jaan!” a third one remarked.

Now let us recount the riveting tale of the renowned courtesan, Gauhar Jaan that is talked about in Vikram Sampath's book *My Name Is Gauhar Jaan.*

Earlier that year, Gandhi had contacted her to take advantage of her popularity to raise money for the Swaraj Fund. On this, she said that she would conduct a fund-raising concert and donate the entire amount that she would collect. However, with this, she attached a condition that Gandhi himself would have to attend the concert, to which he consented. On the day of the concert, Gandhiji did not come but instead sent Maulana Shaukat Ali as his representative. In response to this, she gave Shaukat Ali only half of the amount of ₹ 24,000 that was collected. After the concert, she said, "The legendary Mahatma who speaks of honesty and sincerity doesn't seem to keep his word given to a tawaif as she is a fallen woman. He has sent you instead, keeping only half of his promise. So, Maulana Saheb, I too keep half of my word and give you 12,000 and not 24,000 which I have collected."

"I've nothing to say about the other leaders but let us not forget that Gandhiji is different from other leaders and so-called social reformers who want us finished and gone. But that is not the case with Gandhiji; he wants us to rehabilitate and adopt other professions so that we don't have to live a life of ignominy. Let us follow what he wants us to do. For us, our welfare is linked with the national movement, so we must do our bit in it. Most of us have been singing sensual songs; now we'll replace them with religious and patriotic songs. What do you say?"

"The question remains the same. Do you think people will shower notes and guineas when we sing religious and patriotic songs?" a courtesan said.

Husna Bai was ready for this situation. She calmly said, stressing every word, "Yes, true. No one is going to shower money on you. But then you see, the religious musical assemblies earn quite a bit. Some of us are quite resourceful, I'm one of them. We can present ourselves as a joint front. We may not be able to earn large sums, but rest assured, we all will be able to lead a dignified, respectable life." She paused for a while to see the impact of her words, and then resumed, "Don't you agree with me that we all will be able to lead a dignified, respectable life?" she repeated herself with hope in her voice. As expected, an affirmative reply came about, but in a doubtful tone.

She now divulged her plan, "We'll change the track of our lives under the aegis of a new organization. I assure you, we'll be able to meet our objective."

"What organization?"

"An organization of which all would be members. Now suggest what we should name it," she said.

"Gayika va Nartika Sangh."

"Dharmik va Rashtravadi Sabha."

"Kashi Mahila Uddharak Sabha."

Several suggestions came by. Husna Bai considered all of them keenly, and then spoke, "Let's not forget the high traditions that we belong to. Not very long ago, the kings, and nawabs, and zamindars sent their wards to us for training in etiquette. We're tawaifs, and we're not ashamed of being so. All we want is to save the profession from indignity. I propose its name as Kashi Tawaif Sabha. Do you all approve of it?"

The hall reverberated with a loud "yes". Husna Bai concluded that it would be a registered body.

Prem Kumar Khanna also spoke on this occasion. He called upon the ladies in the simplest language. He said that they needed to shun immoral life, obscenity, immoral songs, and sensual dances,

and embrace social reform, which they could do by marrying their sisters and daughters. He stressed that it was more honorable to wear simple clothes to lead a chaste life than to wear expensive clothes and glittering ornaments. He also spoke against drinking and meat-eating.

In the next few minutes, the executive committee was constituted. While it discussed to finalize the charter of the Sabha, the others shifted to the adjoining hall, where lunch was served. A few minutes later, Husna Bai was serving the guests herself. She seemed to know how to run the organization and was making a bid to redefine the contours of leadership. Consequently, Husna Bai held a series of meetings with more tawaifs, musicians, and leaders in order to manifest the Sabha into reality.

20

The Inaugural Session

The Kashi Tawaif Sabha was established, and hectic preparations were made for its inaugural session because Husna Bai wanted to launch it in such a way that common people would have a positive perception of the tawaifs. This extraordinary meeting was held in August 1921. She sent invitations to a large number of political, social, and religious leaders, though only a few of them were courageous enough to give assent. The responsibility for its arrangement was taken by Vidyadhari Bai, a well-known singer of the time. Not many details are available about this inaugural meeting, but the complete text of her presidential speech was published in *Varvadhu Vivechan* several years later, in 1929 (by Sahitya Sadan, Amritsar).

In her speech, she first talked about the negative attitude of people towards the tawaifs and recounted how exalted the profession was in tradition. She was very well aware of the prevailing social and political situation in the country and said that there was a need to rehabilitate women and protect them from entering the

profession as a result of the barbarous massacre of people at the hands of the foreign masters.

She described how Gandhi had inspired her to undertake that step. She also quoted what he had said in Nainital a few days ago, where he harshly criticized the humiliating customs of devadasi and *nayak* in the Kumaon region, appealing to people to give them up. (In order to understand this, it is crucial to describe this evil custom. The people of the Nayak clan of the Kumaon-Garhwal region forced their daughters, born of the women they bought from Khas-Rajputs, into prostitution. The social reform movement from 1857 to 1929 and several laws during this period helped to eradicate this custom to a great extent. However, there were still some who continued to sell their daughters out of the region for money).

Husna Bai called upon people to embrace the charkha, both as a mark of their contribution to the freedom struggle and as a means of livelihood. In order to ensure their rehabilitation, she advised them to spin cotton when they had free time, while they continued their forays into the public display of their exalted art.

As per A.N. Sharma, in the chapter "To be like a Joan of Arc", Husna Bai called upon the courtesans to learn from the life of Joan of Arc and the women of Chittorgarh. She was aware of the problem that some of them had brought the trade disrepute by their actions, so she exhorted them to wear iron shackles instead of gold ornaments, to keep away from undignified life. She also motivated them to embrace *khadi* and swadeshi (cotton and indigenous) goods.

Referring to the courtesans' performing career, she asked them to take to nationalistic compositions and advised them to adopt the patriotic songs of Vidyadhari Bai, a contemporary of her. Towards the close of her speech, Husna Bai asked the tawaifs to go through self-reform and take part in the freedom struggle. Moreover, she gave the credit for establishing the Kashi Tawaif Sabha to

Vidyadhari Bai. Thus, Husna Bai ensured that the courtesans were able to veer away from the life of indignity and to sustain their lives by spinning cotton and singing songs.

Before the singing commenced towards the close of the meeting, Vidyadhari Bai addressed a note of thanks to all those who had dared to take part in the meeting.

In the same inaugural session, several courtesans displayed their skill at singing patriotic songs. She herself sang:

Mandir mein chand chamakta, masjid mein hai murli ki taan,
Makka ho chahe Vrindavan, hote aapas mein qurbaan.

(The moon shines in the temple while Krishna's tune is played in the mosque,
Whether it is Mecca or Vrindavan, they are inclined to sacrifice for each other.)

The most famous song in most concerts after this awakening was the one composed by Vidyadhari Bai. They continued to sing this song despite objections from the police and other government officials:

Here are its opening lines:

Chun chun ke phool le lo armaan rah na jaye,
Ye Hind ka bageecha gulzar rah na jaye.
Ye woh chaman nahin hai lene se ho ujaad,
Ulfat ka jismein kuchh ehsaan rah na jaye.

(Gather flowers leaving no ambition unfulfilled,
The garden of India should not remain flourishing.
This is not the garden which can be destroyed by exploitation,
No gratitude of love should remain anymore.)

The recording of this song has not survived, but it has been sung by several singers, including Malini Awasthi and Shubha Mudgal, among others, and some of these videos can be viewed on YouTube.

Paradoxically, the Sabha was constituted following the call of Gandhi, yet on numerous occasions he refused to accept the courtesans as members of the Congress. The meeting was reported by the local daily *Aaj* on August 10, 1921.

In the coming years, the *Kashi Tawaif Sangh*, which also came to be called *Gayika Sangh*, worked to secure the tawaifs from the scourge of criminal cases being lodged against them under the new laws in different provinces. It issued a code of conduct for the members and made it compulsory for all tawaifs to follow it. It also issued licenses to the registered tawaifs. These licenses had no legal validity, but the law enforcement agencies took favorable notice of them, as the association had become quite popular owing to the well-known tawaifs being its members and their patrons being in powerful positions, including in the government. Later, the male musicians of the kothas were also enrolled as its members. Widening its scope, the association also dealt with the disputes that arose between the members.

With time, Husna Bai stood apart from all singers in the singing of patriotic and nationalistic songs. Not only this, she inspired her contemporary singers, both courtesans and others, to embrace this genre in the national interest.

However, her romantic journey was plagued with sadness. Her Hindu lover, Husnawale Das, died when she was planning to marry him. He might have departed physically, yet he left a lasting impression on her psyche. In his memory, she built a temple and an inn called the Sri Radha-Krishna Temple and the Sri Krishna Dharmashala, respectively. These two survive to this date. On enquiry, the officials at the temple did not know who built it. So far

as the inn is concerned, its ownership lies with an old man living in Kolkata whose grandson was reluctant to show the ownership records. The pilgrims come and stay at the inn, located just near Kashi Vishwanath Temple, but they show little curiosity about uncovering the hidden and profound tale of struggle and love that lies behind these walls.

In 1959, Amritlal Nagar conducted a series of interviews with tawaifs and wrote the book *Ye Kothewalian*. The legendary Vidyadhari Bai affirmed that Husna (Bai) had earned a great name for herself. She recalled that Gandhiji asked her and other singers to sing nationalistic songs in the concerts that they held in the *Riyasats* (princely states) and cities. Similarly, the well-known Motibai too said that she had gone to see Gauhar Jaan with Husna Bai, who herself was a renowned singer then. A music lover, Raikrishnadas, recalled Husna Bai in these words: "The senior *tawaifs* of our childhood were Saraswati and Husna Bai. Husna wrote to and received letters from Bharatendu Harish Chandra. When I came of age, Husna was aged about fifty. Once he happened to get five or six pictures of Bhartendu from Husna. Her handwriting was beautiful, and she wrote in a fine masculine style. She also had a daughter who was married off, but did not survive long. Husna too lost her mental equilibrium later."

Recalling her, another music lover, Srikrishnaprasad Gaur, said that Husna looked after her lover, Husnawale Das, very well. Yet another person, Vinodshankar Vyas, said that Husna had sung in her *Janeu Sanskar* (Hindu sacred thread ceremony for child) celebration. A writer Vachaspati Pathak recalled in the interview that Husna (Bai) was well-known and said, "Once the former ruler of a Bengal estate was present in Husna's place and in some context, she started to sing. The ruler himself was an accomplished musician; he drew the tabla and started. They went on singing the whole night." He further confirms the story that

she was very generous and got a Dharmashala constructed in the memory of her Hindu lover. He also says that she went insane in old age and looked monkey-like then.

Interestingly, a poem was also written by one Sher Bahadur Singh Verma, better known as Babu Bachchu Singh 'Bhakta' Vaishnav, compiling the names of one hundred well-known tawaifs contemporary to Bhartendu Harish Chandra in a poem titled *Veshya Stotra*, and the name of Husna Bai appears in its seventh couplet, as under:

Hyder, Mishsrijaan, Nawaban
Gilli, Gunchadahan, Gulavan.
Vilayati, Husna o Hooran
Najjo, Rangbahar, Zahuran.

Part IV

Begum Samru

21

Suicide or Treachery

It was midnight. Pitch dark enveloped the area in a sheet of gloom, though faint glimmers of hope seeped through the dense mango tree canopies, illuminated by the crescent moon. This feeble light barely guided the party along their dusty path to the east. This could be the reason that it was led by a *mashalchi*, a torchbearer with a torch whose flame flickered as he moved with hurried steps. Of course, he was only showing a little part of the path ahead, though he served like a beacon for those who trod after him. At his heels, he was followed by eight soldiers, two of whom held muskets while others had unsheathed swords, ready to pounce on the likely opponents. Just behind them, riding a horse, was a young, energetic Frenchman, closely followed by a palanquin. The party also had a rearguard with about sixteen armed soldiers. All of them were scampering through the wooded area. The destination was the Ganga River in Meerut, from where they had planned to take a boat to Anupshahr for the journey to a haven in Bihar or Bengal.

In the palanquin was Begum Samru, the ruler of the principality of Sardhana. Usually confident and composed, she did not seem her normal self today, nor did she seem the one who had commanded her troops against the mighty armies on more occasions than one. In fact, she had reached the crossroads of her life when she had to choose between power and love, and she went for the latter. It was in this bid that she was fleeing secretly. The decision to flee for the powerful ruler was not easy and was going to have repercussions.

Anxiety enveloped her dark, round eyes as she saw her lover riding just ahead of the palanquin. He looked behind every now and then, and when he saw the curtain move aside and the Begum's hand wave up and down, he slowed down the horse and came along with. The horseman was Le Vaisseau, her lover and second husband; she had married him just recently but had kept it a secret.*

After her first husband, Walter Reinhardt Sombre's death in 1778, she had been administering her principality of Sardhana quite well, but she was not happy with her personal life. There were several Europeans employed in her court and army, and many of them eyed her as, even at 40, she was young and pretty. George Thomas, her principal lieutenant, was possibly one of them. Even the Begum seemed to have a soft corner for him, but ever since Le Vaisseau had joined her troops in 1790, she was all for this tall and handsome young man. He was educated and accomplished, came from an elite family, and was quite distinct from the savage, uneducated people surrounding her. She herself had never been to school but had received training as a tawaif, and as a tawaif's daughter, etiquette flowed in her veins.

---

* The Begam's marriage with Le Vaisseau was solemnized by a missionary, Rev. Fr. Gregory O.C.D. in 1793. He was the same priest who had baptized her into Christianity (Roman Catholic) in 1781.

As the ruler, she often had to face court intrigues and rivalries and resolving them did not give her a high purpose. She was an efficient ruler, but she had to face occasional cases of insubordination from her officers and troops. She felt that if she dared to reveal her second marriage, there could be a revolt among her troops. This fear impeded the Frenchman's free access to her chamber. He was to approach her in secrecy every time, and this was the supposed situation she was fleeing from, because his movements could not be hidden from the attendants, and this could potentially give rise to rumors.

The Begum realized that her marriage was unconventional and all kinds of rumors were afloat. She had been in the midst of politics for several years. When in the company of her first husband, she had observed from close quarters different shades of life. She had learnt much from the way different clans conducted themselves and how people of these clans behaved—she admired the *Jats* for their cunningness as well as patience; she commended the Sikhs for their reckless daring and giving death no value; she praised the foreign mercenaries for their dashing intrepidity and foresight; she learnt a lesson or two from the Rajputs' dynastic quarrels; she was a great admirer of the Marathas' perennial readiness for action and endurance for suffering; but she learnt most from the Mughals how they sought pleasure and adopted treacherous ways—all these together had led to the East India Company's rising stars. The Begum had learnt much from the prevailing political situation in the land. Sombre died when she was at the peak of her youth, and maybe now that same youthful energy guided her to live an ordinary life full of love, rather than a luxurious life devoid of love.

The unrest was being fomented by those who could hope to make the most of it. She had her own sources to know that mutiny was in the air. She was also convinced that George Thomas was intriguing with her army units, which were then stationed with the

Emperor in Delhi under the command of Sombre's son, Zafaryab Khan, born from his first wife, Bari Bibi. While George Thomas himself was in service with Appa Khande Rao, the Maratha chief of northern India.

Consequently, this led to her fleeing from the very same mutiny, intrigue, and conspiracy to lead a life with love and peace in the company of Le Vaisseau. The plan to do the same had been an elaborate one. This is true that she had left secretly, but it was not entirely unplanned. She had been in correspondence with the Marathas and Company's government for safe passage. She had also sent Father Gregory to Calcutta to see the Governor General, but he denied permission. The Begum wrote a letter again, which was approved by the Calcutta Council, allowing her to settle down at Patna with her family and attendants but without troops or military. This approval, however, did not seem to have reached her.

These efforts proved fruitless as the troops sensed the plan for flight before any reply could be received. It was at the behest of George Thomas that Legois, a commander in Begum's army, led the revolt and invited Zafaryab Khan to come over and take over the principality.

Seeing the unfavorable situation rapidly developing around her, the Begum decided to flee by night. However, little did she know that she would not be able to go far.

They had barely gone three miles from the palace, near a village called Khirwa, heading towards the Ganges, located to the east, with plans to cross the sacred river into the British territory, when the terrible incident took place. La Vaisseau slowed down his horse to come along the palanquin.

"Anything you wish to say?"

"I don't know…my left eye is twitching, it's a bad omen!"

It was the first time that La Vaisseau felt fright in her voice, although he was not able to clearly see her face in the dark. He

did not know if twitching of the eye meant anything negative or positive. To reassure her, he said, "In my part of the world, it's rather a good sign. Something good is certainly coming. I'm right here with you and will always be."

He bucked up the horse to go back to his position, when a commotion rose in the air accompanied with the sound of trotting horses and gunfire from behind. He at once pulled the reins and turned around to confront the situation. Seeing him, the Begum screamed, "What are you doing? Let's get going."

"We gotta face them!" said La Vaisseau with resolve in his voice and the revolver ready in his hand.

"It's all hopeless!"

Before he could move, a gunshot was heard, and a shot scratched his cheek, which knocked off his hat. He had hardly composed himself when he heard a pitiful voice emanating from the palanquin. He turned again, ordered the bearers to stop, and peeped into the palanquin.

"NO!" His heart sank as he witnessed his biggest nightmare. The Begum was slumped in the palanquin, lying in a pool of blood. A dagger was lying near her hand. Evidently, she had stabbed herself on the side of the chest. He did not know whether she was dead or alive. "Oh, why did I ever enter into that suicide pact with you? But now that you've done your part heroically, and now I ought to do mine," he cried remorsefully.

Despite being on horseback and having the option to escape, his commitment to honor his word kept him rooted, steadfast in his resolve. He pointed his pistol at his temple and pulled the trigger, and with it, fell from his horse lifeless. He had executed his part of the pact, but little did he know that the Begum was still alive.

Was it an attempt to commit suicide? Or was it treachery, a ruse to get La Vaisseau to commit suicide? Doubts prevail as to what actually happened.

Listening to the commotion and sounds of gunfire, she knew that the revolting troops were in the vicinity and her escape was no more possible. She had entered a suicide pact with La Vaisseau and time to execute it had just come. She moved the curtain aside and looked at him. He was heading backward; if he clashed with the enemy, he was sure to die. Hopelessly she drew her dagger and hit herself. It glanced on her rib but without making a deep wound; it had caused bleeding; she slumped on the floor unconscious. The wound, extending over several inches, was superficial, though it caused much bleeding, reddening the white cloth that covered her waist. It was due to its shallowness that some people accused her of treachery.

22

Between Life and Death

Pain in the wound brought Begum Samru back to consciousness. She realized that she was in a very uncomfortable position, standing on her feet, unable to move her hands. Alarmed, she opened her eyes. She found herself tied to the gun carriage just outside the palace; both her upper arms were tied to the bars under the barrel. The sun shone brightly overhead, heating the iron gun. Her uncomfortable position, together with the heat, made it quite unbearable, but she was not the one to be easily subdued. "I suppose I need to wait before I come back to myself," she murmured to herself. Uttering the word 'I' several times filled her with a resolve to face the consequences and turn the table on the adversary if an opportunity arose.

She was more thirsty than hungry, and hoped that her adversary would be compassionate enough to give her water, if not food, in that scorching heat. She also felt that no medication or dressing had been applied to her wound, though she was no longer bleeding. The blood must have coagulated there, restricting

the bleeding. She wondered if her enemy wanted her to die in that position. She did not know if it was Zafaryab Khan or any other person who had ordered her to be put in this uncomfortable position. As per her information prior to her flight, it was he who had conspired to take over the principality. She expected this the least from someone whom she loved and who was the son of her first husband and his first wife.

The sun had completed its day-long journey and was gradually sinking in the west. Begum looked at the red sphere which was gradually dimming in splendor while its glory touched higher realms. "Like you I might be sinking at the moment, but you will rise in the morning, and so will I," she murmured to herself. Even the second day passed without any trace of food or water. Out of hunger, she felt weak, she knew she could not survive long without water. She found it hard to keep her eyes open. For a bystander, with closed eyes and famished body, it was difficult to determine whether she was asleep, awake, or senseless, she seemed to be lifeless. Lack of food and water was evident in her eyes and her complexion grew lusterless and pale. She had no sense of time and was unaware of how long it had been since the sun dipped below the horizon and rose on the other side of the earth.

She kept hanging down her head with eyes closed until she was mildly touched. She made an effort to open her eyes even and in the dim moonlight, saw a woman beforc her. She looked keenly at her, in an effort to recognize her but was unable to do so.

"Begum Sahiba, have this water, you must be very thirsty," said the woman as she placed a wide pot to her lips. It felt like nectar. She drank a few sips slowly, and then thought that this opportunity could be snatched away from her any moment, so she started to gulp faster. To her dismay, the woman took the pot away.

"Give me more," whispered the Begum.

"You should eat first," said the woman as she now fed her boiled rice mixed with pulse. The food was cold. It was kept hidden since evening meal served to the attendants. The Begum had tasted this food earlier when she went to their cookhouse to check if they got food of satisfactory quality. She swallowed more than she chewed.

"Don't eat much, it might make you throw up," said the woman, "I'd try to come again before the sunrise."

Before going, she also applied some paste on her wound giving her a soothing feeling. Then she stole away without waiting for a 'thank you' from the noble lady.

The Begum tried to recall for long who she was. She came like a ray of hope amidst the darkness. She had given her hope when she needed it most. The little food that she had got gave her much needed energy. She was able to think more sensibly now. Lastly, she remembered she was one of her maids working in the kitchen. She could be her savior; maybe one of her supporters had sent her. She decided that she could send across a message to her benefactor through this woman. This very thought alerted her. She thought who could come to her rescue in that dire situation and what message she needed to send. She now waited for the maid anxiously, while she recollected the recent events that landed her up in this situation.

After the death of her first husband Walter Reinhardt, better known as Sombre or Samru Sahib, in 1778, Begum Samru carried his name forward. She took over the reins of his principality in her hands and proved to be an efficient administrator and commander. She preserved his dignity through military campaigns against the enemies and welfare measures for the subjects. She embraced Catholicism in 1781, though she continued to follow her Islamic traditions to a great extent. It was soothing to see European and Islamic cultures and traditions blending in her palace and parties.

Evidently, her loving husband had not insisted on her conversion, she did it of her own free will long after his death.

A decade of separation from her husband vibrated the pangs of soft emotions in her. She was in her early forties—still youthful, energetic, and pretty. She has been described to be 'a small dainty woman of delicate features, with a fair complexion and large eyes'. She was polite and graceful to those around her, and guests enjoyed her company. There were several in her service who had an eye on her. George Thomas thought that she loved her, but that was not true. Instead, she had softer sentiments for much younger La Vaisseau, the French commander, which revolved round the most sublime feeling of love. He had entered his service about 1790, long after George Thomas did.

George Thomas had earlier served as the commander of the Begum's army, and as a reward for his commendable services in the administration and battlefield, he was appointed as the Collector of the subdivision of Tappal and was her chief advisor too. When La Vaisseau, a Frenchman, entered her service and drew her personal attention, George Thomas seemed to envy her, as the Begum's attention towards him had deviated.

A sort of competition began between the two. The animosity between George Thomas and La Vaisseau touched new heights. As the latter was at Sardhana, he took every opportunity to spread rumors about the former, creating suspicion in the Begum's mind. He said that George Thomas was dismissing the tried and tested French officers and was hand in glove with the enemies. A lie, told several times, turns into truth, that is what the Mughal ruler Akbar said. The Begum, too, began to believe that George Thomas's loyalty was questionable. Not only this, she also illtreated his wife, who was still at Sardhana.

George Thomas now knew that things were no longer in his favor; he first rushed at the head of a small army to rescue his

family from Sardhana and then returned to Tappal, where he raised the banner of revolt.

The Begum herself headed to Tappal to crush the Uprising. Seeing the precarious situation that could boil down to a bloody conflict, George Thomas took refuge in the fort, but knew that he would not be able to withstand the onslaught. Therefore, he sought Mahadji Scindia's intervention, and thus Shah Nizamuddin, the Maratha ruler's resident at the Imperial Court, intervened. The Begum too felt somewhat grateful for the fine service George Thomas had rendered to her, so she allowed him to leave her *jagir* unharmed. This occurred towards the end of 1792, and in early 1793, he was commissioned into service with Appa Khande Rao, a general under Mahadji, then campaigning in northern India.

The Begum also heard the rumors that were afloat about her relationship with George Thomas. Some people said that he left her service to follow a more independent path, while others said that since the Begum was ageing he was no longer infatuated by her and was falling for maidens of hers. When the Begum came to know of such things, she only murmured, "Baseless! Rubbish!" She was right, as it was *she* who had rewarded him with the jagir (subdivision) of Tappal and later married him to one of her chief maids of European descent whom she considered her adopted daughter—this meant that the relation between them was like that of a mother and son.

The Begum, on the other hand, was all love for La Vaisseau. Her love was so deep that she was even ready to risk her position. However, she wanted this relationship to remain a secret, so she asked him to keep away when others could be watching. Despite her repeated instructions to him to keep it a secret and not reveal it under any circumstances, he paid little attention. He kept telling people about his romantic affairs with her to bolster his position

among them. After all, having an amorous relationship with the ruler simply meant that he was all powerful.

The Begum had specifically asked him not to visit her when people were around, but he would still enter her chamber on one or the other pretext. The more he disobeyed, the more infatuated the Begum became; his charm had completely engulfed her. She was somehow trying to strike a balance between her state duties and her love duties, but the more she tried, the more she failed.

She needed advice on this vital issue—*love.* The issue, however, was such that she could not confide in anyone as she had sensed an unfavorable atmosphere arising around her. She had to find a solution herself, but the solution she arrived at proved to be a disaster. She did not realize that the love relationship was like a bad omen for her, and so it was for La Vaisseau.

Finally, she married La Vaisseau in 1793, after his specific promise that he would do everything that was needed to keep it a secret, come what may. This was the reason that it was solemnized in private. Other than the priest, two other reliable military officers were the only witnesses, one of them being M. Saleur, as he was the one who would never revolt against the Begum.

However, her attraction seemed more potent than his promise. La Vaisseau carried on with his ways. He thought that he had now gotten a free-pass to visit her any time of day or night; maybe he also thought that revealing the secret marriage could empower him.

His persistent conduct put the Begum in a quandary. She was deeply in love with him, but found his conduct unbearable and harmful to her interests as the ruler. She believed if her marriage was revealed, her troops would rise in rebellion, and her fears were not unfounded. Ironically, she found in him a loving person in whose arms she found solace.

The Begum had asked La Vaisseau to conduct himself as an army officer, and not as her husband, but in vain. He was not ready

to receive other army officers as his equivalents, while the others were peeved at his superior conduct. Some of the commanders declared that no man could command them if he did not treat them equally. The situation was coming to a head.

The Begum sank in deep contemplation; a solution was the need of the hour. She needed to overcome this perplexing situation. This mental state was also the reason why people thought that she had created a drama to get rid of La Vaisseau; but this could not be true keeping in mind the things that were going to take place in the time to come.

The situation worsened when La Vaisseau demoted an army commander named Legois, replacing him with one of his own junior officers. Legois was a close friend of George Thomas, and the two had participated in several campaigns together. When Legois sensed that the Begum could attack Jhajjar, where George Thomas was then stationed on a mission to bring the Rajputs, Sikhs, and Haryana under Maratha control, he advised the Begum to desist from the mission, as it could harm his friend's well-being. His demotion came as a rude shock for other army officers too, who felt uncomfortable because of the ways of La Vaisseau. The signs of a mutiny were in the air.

The Begum was, however, convinced that she must punish George Thomas, as he had harmed her own as well as the Mughal territories. She marched to Jhajjar, leading four of her battalions in addition to twenty guns and three squadrons of cavaliers, and camped about 17 *kos* or 30 kilometers, southeast of Jhajjar.

The troops under her command were not comfortable with the way they were being treated, and now they were convinced that this mission was meant to punish only George Thomas. They could tolerate no more of it and broke out in an open revolt.

The Begum had no other way left but to retreat to Sardhana as quickly as she could, but not without losing two of her battalions

that abandoned her and marched to Delhi to put themselves under the command of Zafaryab Khan, Sombre's son from his first wife.

The Begum was back in Sardhana but was unsure about her and her paramour's safety. They could be thrown behind bars any time, or worse, assassinated. Now, she wanted to abandon Sardhana to embrace her love life fully. It was with this in mind that they sought help from the British as well as the Marathas for safe exit from Sardhana and safe passage through their territories, seeking a place to settle down in Bengal or Bihar, but to no avail. She wrote these letters on April 2, 1795, and one month later, on May 6. The situation was, in the meantime, growing restless, and they needed to do something urgently.

Taking notice of the letters, Governor General Sir John Shore wrote to Major Palmer, the British agent with the Marathas at Delhi, to act in favor of the Begum. The Begum had good relations with Mahadji Scindia, but he had died the previous year, and the Maratha command of northern India was now with Lakwa Dada and Jagu Bapu, the representatives of Scindia. They demanded 12 lakhs as the price of taking over the territory of Sardhana. In contrast, Begum demanded 4 lakhs as the cost of arms and other paraphernalia that Sardhana had acquired under her and her late husband.

It was also settled that one of the Maratha commanders would take over her territory, while Zafaryab Khan would be pensioned off on 2,000 rupees a month for life, and La Vaisseau would be allowed in their territories as a prisoner on parole who could live with his wife at Chandranagore, which was until recently a French settlement and was under the control of the East India Company presently. It was probably done because La Vaisseau was a Frenchman.

When all this was happening, Zafaryab Khan thought that he had legal and moral rights over the principality as he was the son

of the late Sombre and perceived himself as stronger after two of Begum's battalions defected to him. He declared himself the Chief of Sardhana and marched to seize the Begum and La Vaisseau. Little did he realize that he would need approval for his aggression from the powers that be.

The rapidly developing situation demanded urgent action on the part of Begum and they made a plan to elope by night with gold and property that they could collect, resolving to live and die together. They decided that if one was killed or captured, the other would follow suit. It was in this bid that La Vaisseau shot himself, while the Begum found herself tied to the gun carriage.

Hanging her head down in extreme pain, she could hear the jeering sound of the '*raits*' (people) and troops who had gathered at some distance. She did not know what lay in store for her, but the little food in her stomach gave her some hope.

23

The Deliverance

Having usurped the principality of Sardhana, Zafaryab Khan was now its *Jagirdar,* or ruler, though he still needed the approval of the sovereign. He was an incapable person and lacked experience as a ruler. This elevation had certainly elated him, which manifested in the form of unwise decisions and miscalculations. Rather than taking care of the administration and bringing the army in order, he indulged in entertainment, while leaving Begum in the scorching heat without considering that there could be some of her supporters too. Maybe he thought that he could enjoy it for a few days only, as his newfound status was subject to the approval and recognition of the Mughal emperor, who himself was under the overlordship of the Marathas.

Instead of taking a glorious stance, he forged a letter in the Begum's name to the Governor General. He thought that he could easily trick the East India Company. He wrote that the Begum was surrendering her right to rule in his favor as he was the legitimate

heir to Sombre. He dispatched this letter through Colonel Ware, the British Commanding Officer at Anupshahr.

The colonel, however, was unsure whether he had the propriety to forward the letter to the Governor General, nor did he know the contents of the letter. So, he sent it to Palmer, the British resident with Scindia in Delhi, who eventually sent the letter to the Governor General with a covering letter in which he expressed his apprehension that the letter could be "fictitious and framed by Zafaryab Khan in the Begum's name." He was of the firm opinion that it could have been extorted from her under duress in order 'to obtain from this government an acknowledgement of his usurped authority'. He also wrote that the Begum either had no knowledge of it, was compelled to affix her seal, or the seals were not in her possession at all. He also noted that it was a difficult task to convey a message to the Begum without Zafaryab Khan knowing it, and any intervention could also offend the Maratha sentiments. The content of the covering letter ensured that the Governor General took no cognizance of the matter.

Meanwhile, Zafaryab Khan was enjoying himself. Instead of consolidating his position, he engaged himself in such fake letters. Not only this, his willful entertainments now bordered debauchery. Time favors those who make the most of the opportunity, but Zafaryab did not seem to know this tenet.

It was dark in the wee hours when the maid appeared again. With a soft whisper and touch on the hand, she awoke the Begum. She gave her some water, food, and milk.

By this time, the Begum had made up her mind that she would seek assistance from none other than George Thomas, the very commander whom she had expelled from her jagir and against whom she had marched just recently, leading to the defection of two of her battalions. She whispered, "Can you do me a favor?"

"I am ordered to be at your command, Begum Sahiba."

"Ordered to be at my command!" the Begum repeated the words and understood that help was at hand and she had to make use of it. "Who is he?"

"Saleur Sahib," the maid murmured.

The Begum realized that she was thinking along the right lines, as she knew that Saleur and George Thomas were close friends.

"Tell him to send a message to his friend at Jhajjar. He would do the needful."

As the maid was about to bow before going, the Begum added, "And La Vaisseau? What happened to him?"

"He's no more. I've heard he shot himself."

"What!" exclaimed the Begum before controlling her emotions. She did not want to look weak before an ordinary maid. "Ah! He was a true man who kept his word," said the Begum. "Where is he buried?"

"His body was brought here and kicked about before it was thrown in a ditch." The maid did not have the courage to look up. She softly jerked her head before moving away.

The Begum silently wept over her lover's demise. Each of her limbs was fully tired. In some corner of her heart, she wished to die too. The maid had given her some hope, but her condition was growing from bad to worse, and she felt she would break down from this torture. 'How long will I be able to resist death? This position is beyond the limits of toleration. Maybe death would bring my deliverance too!' She relapsed into silence; only heaven knew if it was sleep or unconsciousness.

On his part, Colonel M. Saleur was making an effort to get the Begum relieved of the torment she was suffering on the gun carriage. He had protested when she was taken to the gun carriage, but there was no one to pay heed to him. He had tried to talk to other officers, but in vain. However, he continued to convince

them that this treatment was inhumane for the Begum who had been their favorite once, and that her paramour was already dead. He also warned them, "Should she come back to power, they would have tough times to face."

In a week, the initial euphoria subsided, and some opinions were raised in her favor. Finally, she was released and put in confinement. It was after a long time that she had a long, sound sleep, despite the bed not being so comfortable. Good and bad dreams had kept her mind busy, sometimes shaking her awake.

The state of confusion continued in Sardhana. The commanders and troops had thought that they would be delivered of the strict Begum, but to their dismay, they found that they had fallen out of the frying pan into the fire. A feeling of revulsion against the new ruler was increasingly occupying their minds. All this while, the state of indecision continued.

The Begum was in confinement from about the middle of October 1795, and now it was the month of June in 1796. The area witnessed abundant rainfall over four months, which was the secret behind the rich crops here. It, however, made it very difficult, if not impossible, to undertake a military mission during this rainy season, so this season marked relative peace.

The Begum had been sending distress messages to George Thomas, who finally made up his mind. In secret deliberations with M. Saleur, he marched his troops towards Sardhana and camped at Khatauli, about 8 kos (or 15 km) northeast of his final destination. It could not have been easy for M. Saleur to make his friend agree, as he was unhappy with the Begum for the ugly treatment of his family, crushing his revolt at Tappal, and then marching to subdue him in Jhajjar.

Once George Thomas agreed to rescue the Begum, he confided in the Maratha chief on a promise of payment of one lakh and twenty thousand rupees from her. He also promised the

chief that the Marathas could keep the territory of Sardhana only if they helped restore it to the Begum.

Before entering Sardhana, George Thomas got announced in the town to the beat of drums, "There is no chance of amnesty to those who would obstruct restoration of the Begum to the masnad [throne]." He also got it announced that he was acting on behalf of the Maratha chiefs, and all those who resisted should expect no leniency.

And before his final movement, he sent a message to the revolting troops saying, "Should the Begum die under your torture being inflicted on her mind and body, the [Maratha] minister will immediately resume the lands from which your payment is made, and will also disband you all as you are worthless to him or the [Mughal] Emperor."

With these announcements, George Thomas felt that there could be a plot to bring some harm to the Begum, so without waiting for his entire force to be ready, he immediately marched at the head of fifty mounted troops, and four hundred of his infantrymen were to follow them soon.

As he entered the fort area, the mutineers saw that it was only a small force, and they could easily vanquish it. However, before they could take any action, the rising dust in the distance intimated them about a larger army approaching. They were apprehensive that the entire Maratha army was there. Their demeanor changed in a flash. They not only became submissive, but also agreed to follow the orders.

The Begum was immediately released from confinement and restored to power. She was seated on her masnad on July 9, 1796. She was in prison for close to nine months, during which she faced massive hardships. She had grown weak, but the determination and confidence on her face reflected that she was in command.

24

The Aftermath

Immediately, a war council was summoned. A covenant was drafted by about 30 European officers, only one of whom could sign his name. They acknowledged that they would abide by all the commands of the Begum and would recognize none other than her as their commander. Then they affixed their seals to it. A few of them, who did not want to display their illiteracy, just put their initials. They also took a solemn oath of allegiance to her.

The Begum was a transformed persona now. Despite her restoration, she suffered massive ill-repute owing to her love affair. She wanted to reform all this and was determined to reinvent herself in a new avatar. She kept her personal happiness and weak sentiments on the fringes, and worked as an able ruler was supposed to do. Now, all her attention was focused on the management of her vast territories and the welfare of her subjects. From now on, never ever did she allow her weak impulses to command her. She was entering a new phase of life, and she would be remembered for this. She was already known for her astute administration, able

military leadership, and insightful interaction with other rulers. Before she could look into the administration of her principality, there were certain things that needed her immediate attention.

In the reinstallation ceremony, a Maratha commander was also present. He and his troops needed to be seen off. He, on behalf of the Maratha chief Bapu Scindia, happily received the sum of one lakh and fifty thousand rupees, in the form of cash and promissory note, from the Begum, thirty thousand more than the promised amount. With the restoration of normalcy, the Maratha army quit the territory and returned to its garrisons.

The Begum put her army under the command of M. Saleur, a Frenchman; he was the only one to have signed the covenant. He had displayed his loyalty when the Begum needed it most. Not only this, it was he who had managed to feed the Begum through maids, bring his co-officers to their senses about what they were doing, and bring in assistance from George Thomas.

Zafaryab Khan was arrested and packed off to Delhi, where he died in 1802. He was buried in Agra beside his father in the Roman Catholic Cemetery. Despite all the evil things that he had done to her, the Begum loved him immensely; she went to Delhi to meet his mother and Sombre's first wife, called Bari Bibi, to share her sorrow.

The Begum was grateful to all those who had served her during her trying times. She was especially thankful to her savior, George Thomas, who led an interesting and adventurous life. She requested that he stay on and take over the command of her troops, but he had his own plans. He aspired to become an independent ruler one day, with his own currency, which made it imperative for him to continue with what he was doing under the Maratha chieftains. She bid him and his wife goodbye; his wife of European descent was earlier the Begum's maid of honor, whom she had adopted as her daughter. It would be interesting to know more about his exploits.

Born in 1756 at Tipperary, Ireland, George Thomas docked in a British naval ship at Madras as a day-wager. Sensing the great demand for foreign mercenaries, he deserted and formed a band of Pindaris. He fought different commanders and came to limelight. He took service under Begum Samru, winning several battles for her, and thus rose through the ranks in her army.

George was transferred to Tappal as the commander. When, under the influence of La Vaisseau, the Begum happened to disrespect his wife, he led an army and brought his family back to safety. Back at Tappal, he broke out in an open revolt but retreated from her territory and joined Appa Khande Rao Holkar, the Maratha governor of the Mewat territory. Under him, he launched several successful campaigns in Rajasthan, Haryana, and Shekhawati. Promoted as the jagirdar of Jhajjar, he harassed the Mughal territories, compelling the blind Mughal emperor Shah Alam II to seek Begum Samru's help, who came but had to withdraw as her troops were still loyal to George; two of her battalions deserted her as well. This led to her unsuccessful elopement with La Vaisseau. As we know it now, it was George who saved her despite her ill-treatment.

George emerged as an able ruler, strengthened his territory, and looked after his people. He also built the fort named Georgegarh, which over time corrupted to Jahazgarh.

When Appa Khande Rao died in 1797, George declared independence, established his capital at Hansi, and attacked and occupied Rohtak and Hissar. He loved being called Raja from Tipperary, after his homeland. He established a mint, realizing his dream.

George made several bids to expand his territory against the powerful Marathas and Sikhs, although without success. He rebuilt the Asigarh Fort at Hansi. At its prime, his territory extended from the Ghaggar in the north to the Rewari and Pataudi parganas in the

south, divided into four parganas for efficient administration. He had a powerful army comprising 6,000 footmen divided into eight battalions, supported by fifty field guns and 1,000 cavaliers. He paid attention to industrial development and encouraged workmen and artificers of all kinds to settle in his kingdom. Moreover, he established factories to manufacture artillery, muskets, matchlocks, and gunpowder. He also built Jahaj Kothi and Jahaj Pul at Hissar.

George Thomas ruled until 1801, when he was routed and driven out by the Sikhs. He was fleeing on a ship to Calcutta when he died near Murshidabad. It was during this journey that he narrated his life story to his biographer, William Francklin, who published it as *Military Memoirs of George Thomas*. His grave is located in Berhampur.

25

The First Step at Dance

It doesn't matter that she lived and ruled two centuries ago over a small principality, Sardhana; there was something in her magical personality that people continue to remember her, not only in the area but also beyond it. She was a Muslim-turned-Christian, yet this did not deter people of all faiths from visiting Sardhana church to praise the architecture and, above all, to pray for their wellbeing. Her entire life is rooted in mystery, romance, adventures, and campaigns.

Her early life is shrouded in obscurity. Different scholars and historians have described her origin differently, but all of them agree that she was born in Kotana, about 60 kilometres northwest of Meerut or about 30 kilometres north of Baghpat. There are diverse opinions about the year of her birth too; it has been put between 1751 and 1753. The Sardhana Church, in its booklet written by Fr. Patrick, puts the year of her birth as 1753, while there are several historians who do not agree with this. Dyce Sombre, the adopted son and Sombre's heir, in a letter to Pope Gregory XVI,

has put her age at 85 (solar) years on her death, which places her birth in 1750–51. William Francklin, George Thomas's biographer, who also worked with Begum Samru for some time, put her age at 45 when he talked about the events in 1796, which again puts her birth in 1751.

As the historians do not agree on the year of her birth, they do not agree on her ancestry either. Most of them agree that she was born of the second wife of a man named Lutf Ali Khan who had settled down at Kotana. Atkinson has said that she was born of a concubine of Asad Khan, but there is probability that it was Lutf Ali Khan's another name. While Sleeman has described her as a Sayyidani, or lineal descendant of Muhammad, Francklin has said that she was the daughter of a Mughal nobleman. However, Bussy, the French commander, was informed by his agents in northern India that she came from a Kashmiri family. There are chances that her father was a Sayyidani, who worked as a Mughal noble but had fallen in disfavor and settled down at Kotana.

The Begum was named Farzana at birth. She was very small, not yet ten years of age, when her father died. Her mother was subjected to ill-treatment by her stepson, and when it became unbearable, she made up her mind to leave. Wandering from place to place, she and her small daughter finally arrived in Shahjahanabad, Delhi. It was a glorious Mughal town with wide streets and means of entertainment, with the imposing Red Fort overlooking Chandni Chowk. Everybody seemed happy and wealthy, but the famished, starved, and fatigued duo found none who could feed them and give them refuge. Walking here and there and finding no help anywhere, with no more energy left in them, they just lay down on the naked floor outside a large, prettily-carved old door. Perhaps they were more tired than hungry and were engulfed by deep slumber in no time. They cared little that the door was obstructed by them. It was probably the year 1760.

With the first rays of the sun, they were awakened from sleep. When the lady of the house opened the door to broom, she was moved by their pitiable condition, as she was facing bad days too and lived alone in that large house. The mother soon realized that it was a kotha and not an ordinary house. Before her marriage, she too was a nautch girl and had worked in the same locality. She had come to this locality but could not locate the kotha where she worked about ten years ago. She decided to stay on, as it was no ordinary brothel but a center of dance and music; her dignity would be preserved here. She also noticed that the place had fallen on bad days. Soon, she came to know that the *Chaudharayan*, or owner, had no young dancer, and she was eyeing the young, pretty girl, Farzana. Nowhere else to go, she consented, and it was how Farzana's training started in dance, music, and etiquette.

It did not take more than three years for Farzana to learn and master every trick that the *Chaudharayan* taught her. The growing girl, too, appeared to have been made for music and dance.

Soon, the kotha was opened to music and dance lovers. The *Chaudharayan* had also managed to have a couple of other dancers and singers, but Farzana became the focal point. She enthralled them with her new styles of singing and dancing. Passing through her adolescence, she had become a star of sorts. People thronged to the kotha to watch her performance, and many of them were ready to empty out their pockets and become her patron. But the *Chaudharayan* knew that she had come to possess a mine of gems, so she curiously waited for the higher bidder. Earlier, she had lost out on all her singers and dancers to competition and patrons without having minted money, and she did not want that to recur this time. She took all her care, right from nutrition to dressing to training. She was sure that her renown would bring the bidder she was looking for.

Farzana, at the threshold of youth, had physical features that could entangle anyone in her charm. Her remarkable beauty, small stature with supple limbs, and dark expressive eyes, coupled with extraordinary intelligence and tactful conversation, formed the dream combination for a bright career ahead.

26

The Nautch Girl's Spell

It was the year 1765. The previous night had been drenched in relentless rain, persisting until noon the next day. The lingering coolness in the air created a favorable atmosphere, drawing more visitors to the bustling market. With Farzana's presence, the number of visitors to the kotha had shot up, so had its income. Despite insistence of several wealthy people on becoming her patron, the Chaudharayan had raised the bar as she wanted someone powerful and wealthy, not just wealthy.

As the evening set in, Farzana was in her chamber getting ready for the performance when she felt that there was something out of the ordinary happening around . This brought her out of her chamber. She found the hall being decorated with flowers as if being prepared for a special guest. The masnads were covered with new satin sheets, and two servants were busy shining the spittoon, hookah, and other metalware to further elevate the festive mood. To her amazement, all this was being supervised by the Chaudharayan herself.

Farzana looked to the Chaudharayan with a question in her eyes and found that she was looking at her very intently. She examined her from head to toe and then said, "Today I am expecting someone special. I want you to wear your best dress."

With her resplendent eyes signaling affirmation, Farzana walked back to her chamber, and then, out of curiosity, looked down the window into the market. She found that the florist was decorating the entrance while a person was sprinkling perfume all around. "He must be someone very special," she murmured as she stood before the life-size mirror. The maid came soon after and helped her get ready. She aspired to fulfill the heartfelt desires of her beloved Chaudharayan.

Ironically, no special guest was scheduled. There was hearsay afloat in the market that Samru was in town and was likely to visit the market. The Chaudharayan was preparing herself to attract him to her place. She was confident that he could be a suitable patron for Farzana, as he fit into her scheme of things.

The turbulent political situation in the country had brought Walter Reinhardt, better known as Sombre or Samru, a freelance mercenary, to Delhi. He was probably still in the service of Shuja-ud-Daula, the Nawab of Awadh and Grand Vizier of the Mughal Empire, or maybe he was here looking for a new master. Some historians have stated that he was in the service of Jawahar Singh, the Raja of Bharatpur at this time and was on the mission to occupy Delhi. However, as far as the facts are concerned, Jawahar Singh had ordered this mission in 1764, which had ended in failure by February 16, 1765, when the Jat ruler of Bharatpur returned from Delhi. Therefore, there are few chances that Sombre was in his service at this point in time. It is very likely that he joined his service in about August 1765, because he transferred the charge of his brigade to the Nawab of Awadh the same month, as he had received a favorable bargain from Bharatpur. This fact can also be

supported by the letter of John Carnac, Commanding Officer of the Company forces, who was also involved in negotiations with Shuja-ud-Daula and Mughal ruler Shah Alam II. He wrote to Clive on July 28, 1765, saying that Sombre had retired into the Jat chief's district of Agra and he wanted him to be delivered to the Company forces to be punished for his brutality against the British.

As the *mashals* lit up the walking corridor along the main road, nightlife came to life in the market. Regular buyers and sellers gradually receded, while the people now seen on the streets had only one purpose in mind—entertainment. And this was very easily identified from their demeanor and dress, and this market was well-known for fine performances in music and dance as well as satisfaction of carnal desires.

Many of them were on *machans* (the single seat carried on the shoulder by two pallbearers) or horseback. The night was growing dark, but the area had become quite colorful as the sound of musical instruments and singing started to filter into the street. Many of them wanted to climb up the steps of Farzana's kotha, but the staircase was blocked by a guard who told them that there was no performance that day. The disappointed visitors turned away, wondering in disbelief why the entrance was so lavishly decorated.

About this time, at the entrance of the market, stopped a tall and healthy European, surrounded by armed horsemen. He got down, passed the reins to one of his troops, and started to walk. Four of his troops followed him on foot, while others waited. He was Sombre. It was he for whom the Chaudharayan had made special arrangements, though no prior appointment was fixed for the rendezvous.

Listening to the pimps, he kept walking with his usual thumping steps. He had not gone far when he found a woman standing in the pathway. She bowed and saluted him saying, "*Huzoor*, I have the gem that you're looking for. Spare a little time to have a glance."

Convinced, Sombre shook his head. The decorated gate seemed to invite him too. Without thinking more, he climbed up the stairs. He was respectfully seated on the masnad. Resting against the plush bolster, he instinctively grasped the hookah pipe, savoring its fragrant smoke. Absent-mindedly, he exhaled, his thoughts slipping away. Wide-eyed, he found himself in a momentary haze, forgetting the purpose of his action, his surprise echoing in his widened eyes.

There stood before him a youthful damsel, small in height, adored with a light smile and resplendent eyes, adding glory to her bright, fair complexion. He first felt it was a statue, but with the tabla and harmonium starting, the girl came to life. She had started with a slow melody. The glamorous beauty displayed subtle dancing steps. He was hooked to her in fascination that would last a lifetime.

The performance was on with the third song depicting Krishna's love for Radha in the forest, when Sombre beckoned the Chaudharayan to come near.

"*Ji* huzoor, how do you like my gem?" she asked and her hopes were not belied.

"I'd like to have her in my harem. What do you say?"

"She deserves to be in your harem, no doubt, but she is the only source of my livelihood."

And then a round of bargaining started. When she rose, a wide smile adorned her broad cheeks. Farzana's mother seemed to have no say in all this.

When there are no records, several legends evolve. How Farzana entered Sombre's life has another story too, but it is not very trustworthy. As per it, Jawahar Singh, while returning from Delhi, took Farzana along with him, but the mother queen Hansia, alias Rani Kishori (Maharaja Suraj Mal's wife), objected to her presence there as she did not like her son to be tied to the 'apron strings of a dancer'. It was at her behest that Jawahar Singh gave

her away in *dola* (bride in palanquin) to Sombre, who gratefully received this damsel.

Howsoever, Farzana might have come into Sombre's life, he married her. He was already married though. His first wife was Bari Bibi, and he had a son from her who would later be given the title of Zafaryab Khan by the Emperor.

With Farzana by his side, Sombre felt as happy as he could be. From a proficient, sensuous dancer, she gradually evolved into a skilled warrior and commander. From now on, she was to accompany him in all campaigns until sometime before his death. She came to be known as Begum Samru. The time had come when more of her qualities would be revealed.

27

Samru Sahib

India's modern history, especially unfolding in the latter half of the 18th century, is so full of paradoxes that many of the facts are simply unbelievable. What makes this period fascinating for historians and readers is the emergence of European and Indian mercenaries and the freelancers who shaped these turbulent and uncertain times.

At this time, the central power was the Mughal empire, but with Aurangzeb's death early that century, its power started to erode. Nadir Shah gave it a rude shock in 1739. Then started a saga of exploitation, usurpation, wars of succession, and dismemberment. The once glorious Mughal dynasty lost its shine at the hands of even petty chiefs.

In central India, the Marathas flourished under Shivaji and Chhatrapati Shahu, but with the latter's death in 1749 and their defeat at the Battle of Panipat in 1761, their power declined. But Mahadji Scindia restored the Maratha influence over northern

India, this time more as a regional power than as a central power, which again subsided with his death in 1794.

Down south, Hyder Ali and his son Tipu Sultan were struggling to hold their own against the expanding British with the aid of the Marathas and the Nizam of Hyderabad. Madras (Tamil Nadu) was already under the British control by now.

In the east, the British gained firm control over Bengal following the Battle of Plassey in 1757 and then the Battle of Buxar in 1764, though they needed sovereign approval from the Mughal ruler.

The political situation was so uncertain that one never knew who would be an ally or enemy in the next battle. It was during such times that the Europeans started to play a major role. They first entered India as humble merchants, but with time, emerged as warriors and arbiters of India's political power. They entered India not only as part of their trading companies but in individual capacities too. In the past, they served under the Mughal rulers, Nawabs, and Hindu rulers, as the Indians were considered more competent administrators and commanders. However, things began to change with time, and rightly so.

The Indian princes and commanders observed that the European military talent was astonishing; however, the truth was the other way round. The Indians had not done much to upgrade their military strategies and weapons. During the rule of the early Mughals and even under Hyder Ali (of Mysore), Indian technology and wargames could be compared with the best of European armies. But they lost the edge as they became more focused on maintaining their status quo rather than investing in advancement. The Europeans, on the other hand, adopted and improved anything they came across. A case in point was the use of rockets by Mysore. Indians lost that technology, but the Europeans took it back to their native place and improved it greatly. While Indians lost the initiative

even in simpler military wares like swords, Europeans destroyed the foundries. Moreover, Indians had lost the alloy technology by which sturdier swords were cast earlier.

The foreign talent might be in great demand, but this never meant that the native military talent had exhausted itself. We had fine military leaders in the likes of Mahadji Scindia, Tukoji Holkar, and Hyder Ali, and able statesmen in the likes of Nana Fadnavis and Mirza Najaf Khan. In contrast, the military adventurers were not of remarkable military genius, but they were certainly enterprising, energetic, determined, and resourceful, though they could not have been described as anything more than mediocre warriors in their homelands, nor had they received any military training back home.

A perception prevailed in India that every European possessed spontaneous talent in warfare. Such thinking was not altogether unfounded. The victories scored by Dupleix with a small body of French troops and sepoys to defeat the stronger Indian side were only one of the proofs. Even when the Europeans lost battles, they were admired for their sheer maneuvers on the battlefield. The beginning was marked by the recruitment of these mercenaries by Mahadji Scindia to high posts to train his men in the art of warfare. With this, even the smaller native kingdoms did not lag, and now Europeans could be seen leading their military affairs across kingdoms, states, and principalities—big and small.

The Europeans working in trading companies carried back the stories about India's prosperity, which attracted more young men from there. Not all, however, could be employed in trading companies, so they donned the attire of mercenaries. To their surprise, they were warmly welcomed by native princes. A few decades ago, they were given subordinate posts, but now they were made the commanders. Some of the enterprising youths formed their own bands of mercenaries and joined the forces of any prince

who would pay for their services—there was no place for morality or loyalty. They often switched sides more often than they changed clothes. Some of them even established their own kingdoms, as did George Thomas. So, this was a period of adventure, romance and daring, and opportunities to showcase the fighting spirit were numerous. Among them, one who has made a mark for himself was Walter Reinhardt, whose memory was immortalized by the work his widow Begum Samru did.

Born circa 1725 in Germany, Reinhardt ran away from home to join the French troops and arrived in India at Pondicherry (Puducherry) circa 1750. He headed to Chandranagore (West Bengal). In 1757, the British seized the factory here, and the French defeat was imminent, so he abandoned his employers and wandered about before joining the forces of Gurgin Khan, the Armenian General of Mir Qasim, the Nawab of Bengal. Two battalions were put under his command. Now, he was called Sombre, which later corrupted to Samru, as he adopted a Mughal life complete with a *zenana* (harem). He also sufficiently mastered Persian and local tongues.

Treason, however, was in his blood. It was at this time that Mir Qasim wanted to enforce his authority against the British and emancipate his subjects from the undue trade favors and tax concessions granted to the East India Company through an armed conflict.

In 1763, Mir Qasim ordered an invasion of the Company offices at Patna. A number of Europeans, including Resident Mr. Ellis, were captured and ordered to be executed. It was Samru who carried out the execution of these 51 prisoners on October 5, 1763, and with this, he invited the wrath of the English, who wanted him dead or alive. It was like a massive slur on his character. This act later forced him to flee from the areas influenced by the English.

Samru showed exceptional battle skills, impressing Gurgin Khan and Najaf Khan, who later became the supreme commanders of the Mughal forces.

The unenviable relationship between Mir Qasim and the Company led to a final showdown in the Battle of Buxar on October 22–23, 1764. To aid Mir Qasim, Nawab of Awadh Shuja-ud-Daula and Mughal ruler Shah Alam II were also present. In this battle, Samru's three battalions were the only disciplined force; however, his maneuvers were not to the liking of Mir Qasim and Shuja-ud-Daula. Samru could foresee defeat, therefore, he retreated from the battle, leaving Mir Qasim to his fate. Now, he was headed to northern India. He first visited Delhi, where Begum Samru joined his zenana, before he joined the services of Jawahar Singh, the Jat chief of Bharatpur.

Bharatpur was an influential state, with its territory extending from Meerut and Rohtak in the north to Dholpur and Agra (covering the present-day states of Uttar Pradesh, Rajasthan, Madhya Pradesh, and Haryana). After Maharaja Suraj Mal's death on December 25, 1763, Jawahar Singh ascended the throne. He was an obdurate fighter and thought little before starting a campaign. This was the reason that he lost more battles despite having competent commanders like Samru and Madec. He created several enemies through his campaigns, which did not benefit him much. Samru and Madec helped him gain many territories, but Jawahar could not retain them.

The English were expanding their influence and were interested in forming an alliance with Bharatpur on the condition that Samru should be dismissed from the service. Jawahar Singh refused this offer. Later, in 1767, he formed an alliance with the English against the Marathas, but without compromising on Samru. This shows his clout. He continued to show his competence in battle after battle.

Jawahar Singh was murdered in 1768, after which instability enveloped Bharatpur. He was succeeded by Ratan Singh, but he could rule for only ten and a half months before he too was murdered. The next to become the ruler was infant Kheri Singh, and the crown soon went to Nawal Singh, but he was an inefficient and cowardly ruler. He started a battle with the Marathas, but his inefficiency resulted in his defeat with 2,000 dead and 5,000 other casualties. His fleeing army left behind all the artillery pieces, with the exception of two field guns, which were carried back by Samru. He ably covered the retreat, protecting his fleeing men from the chasing Marathas.

Nawal Singh, out of his mindless tactics, lost another battle, suffering a huge loss. At this point, Samru decided to change his master. He had impressed Najaf Khan, the Mughal commander, and Amir-ul-Umra previously and again in the last battle, so he invited him to join his camp, which Samru did gratefully. The Mughal emperor too disregarded the prospect of the English ire.

Najaf Khan allotted Samru with the fief of Panipat and Sonipat and deployed him against Nawal Singh, his ex-employer, who did not live much long after. Samru played an important part in the battles at several locations. Unfortunately, Bharatpur fell in the last battle despite the unmatched valor displayed by the Jat warriors. Even the Jat women shone with raw courage. They stood behind their men, holding spears and swords. When the men fired their muskets, the women snatched away the muskets, replacing them with new weapons while they reloaded the muskets. And when defeat was imminent, they induced them to cut their heads first before falling to the enemy swords.

Madec writes that the three wives of Nawal Singh asked the royal eunuch to cut off their heads while they lay down on the floor. The eunuch did their bidding and then cut himself and fell over the corpses.

During his career as a mercenary, Samru had seen so much blood that he felt revulsion. He now wanted to lead a peaceful life, and Najaf Khan helped him achieve this objective. In 1777, he was given the jagir, a princely grant of lands, for his maintenance. Lying in the Doab, its territory extended from Aligarh to Muzaffarnagar, with an income of 6 lakh rupees per annum. Samru found Sardhana, a village 12 miles to the north-west of Meerut, suitable for his residence, after which the jagir came to be known as the principality of Sardhana. At this time, according to General Polier, his force comprised three battalions of footmen, 200 cavaliers, and 14 guns, well mounted and well served with everything necessary.

Samru's dream of living a peaceful life still eluded him. Soon after the grant, he was sent to Agra as its governor to establish order. He undertook some constructions here, one of which was the renovation of the old Jesuit church. This church had been existing right since the time of Akbar but had seen ups and downs as it was demolished by Shah Jahan and later by the Afghans under Ahmad Shah Abdali. The Latin inscription on the church bears testimony to his contribution. This church is also called the Cradle of Christianity in northern India. Samru also built his palace, surrounded by an octagonal wall with eight gates, though nothing of it can be seen now other than a few carved sand-stone pillars on the Agra-Fatehpur Sikri Road.

Samru did not live long at Agra. As per the letter of M. Visage, the French commandant at Gohad, he died 'of a neglected cold'. He was buried there in his garden, and his remains were later transferred to the Agra churchyard. His tombstone bears a Portuguese inscription and mentions his death to have occurred on May 4, 1778. Giving a sketch of his character, J. Baille Fraser, in his book *Military Memoir of Lt Col J. Skinner, CB*, concludes, "Sumroo appears to have been a man whose evil propensities far

outweigh the good; he was stern and bloody-minded, in no degree remarkable for fidelity or devotion to his employers, and though we cannot imagine him void of those qualities which attach the soldiery to their officer, we can see little in his career to indicate anything more than the hard, unscrupulous, and reckless, though bold, military adventurer."

28

Rise of the Begum

Not many weeks had passed since marriage when one day, Samru was about to go out to attend a meeting when, he saw a curious scene. Farzana was closely examining the swords, one after another. Surprised, he said, "What do you intend to do?"

"Just looking for a sword suitable for myself," said Farzana with a confident smile on her face.

"These delicate hands are not meant for swords, are they? said he, "And I've already taught you how to use a dagger, haven't I?"

"Yes, you're very much there for me, but sometimes we can reverse our roles," said Farzana as her tinkling laughter filled the chamber. "You'll be even more surprised when I ask you to train me in horse-riding."

"Really? I'd love that. None of these swords would suit your petite figure. I'll get you a sword by this evening," said Samru before stepping out, and the very next moment he was back again, "And yes, your horse training begins today."

Ever since Samru came into possession of Farzana, the little pretty dance girl, he found her company inevitable wherever he might be. He wanted her to be by his side all the time, even on the battlefield. She proved to be a quick learner and observer. With her youthful energy and agility, she had time for everything, right from looking after the kitchen to taking part in the commanders' meetings, from earning sword-wielding to horse-riding and taking the field on the elephant. She established rapport with the ordinary troops through enquiring about their well-being. At times, she supervised the treatment of the wounded and sick soldiers. It took her a few months to attain this position.

She often had suggestions on diverse aspects of their life including officers' conduct and agenda points in meetings. Whenever she appeared before others, a thin netted veil adored her lively face. She was a sight to behold when she was on the battlefield. In the beginning, her elephant would remain behind her husband's, with added security of the cavaliers. Things, however, changed with time as Samru found many of her suggestions very effective and useful.

She pointed out several shortcomings in his operations; one of them was camouflage, an idea ahead of her time. That was the age when warriors often wore distinct, colorful dresses that could be made out from a distance; she observed that this made them easy targets for the enemy firing and bombardment. She often advised him which tactic to follow in which situation and how to form the charge.

In a few months, Farzana had grown to be a trusted lieutenant who would take independent charge of the force in certain skirmishes. Even her commanders trusted her leadership at a time when working under a woman was looked down upon. In the beginning, they looked at her as a liability, but soon they found an asset in her, so innovative were her ideas. Though she never

operated a cannon, she knew everything about it: kinds, loading, charging, aiming, carrying, supplies, and much more. She had a keen interest in learning about everything, right from administration to operation. In a few months, she was making more and more decisions on behalf of her husband, the stern military campaigner.

As her clout enhanced, Farzana very subtly motivated Samru to opt for a more peaceful and settled life. Even with the grant of principality, the aspired dream of a settled life did not come true. He was first assigned the fortress of Agra, where he died not long after. By this time, she was better known as the Begum.

Samru and Farzana had no child between them, while he had a son, Zafaryab Khan from his first wife, Bari Bibi. His son's name was, in fact, a title that Shah Alam had bestowed on him at the Begum's request. He ought to have inherited Samru's fortunes and forces, but he, being a man of weak intelligence, was thought unfit even as a nominal heir. On the other hand, Shah Alam, Najaf Khan, and officers of Samru's own force expressed confidence in the Begum's leadership.

Thus, she was now the ruling princess, under the overall fiefdom of the Mughal emperor, and had an army of her own. At this time, her army comprised 4,000 footmen, horsemen, and artillery men, officered by 82 Europeans, under the overall command of Pauli, a German. However, she found him involved in an intrigue, and as a result, got him murdered. This undoubtedly cautioned officers that she should not be taken lightly.

With the reins in her hands, Begum Samru now settled down at Sardhana, the seat of administration. She had seen how different rulers managed their territories. She adopted the best practices that suited her. She went among common people, inspired farmers and traders, provided security, and built basic infrastructure for irrigation and travel. As people grew prosperous, so did the revenue. Higher revenue meant she could make more investment

in the infrastructure. Several contemporary writers have remarked that her territory was greener than that of other adjoining states and much better than the British territory.

As she matured as a ruler, some changes seeped in. Three years after her husband's death, she, of her free accord, embraced Christianity with her stepson, Zafaryab Khan. She converted to Roman Catholicism on May 7, 1781. She was baptized by Fr. Gregario, a Roman Catholic priest, and she was given the new name of Joanna. Zafaryab Khan, too, was renamed Louis Balthazar Reinhardt.

29

Begum Samru: The Emperor's Sheild

The prevailing times were vicious. Love for gold, not loyalty, guided people. The Maratha power was on the rise under Mahadji Scindia, who was now the viceregent of the Emperor of Delhi; it was he who, in practice held the reins over northern India. Despite this fact, there were rulers and chiefs who wanted to break away from the empire to claim sovereignty, and the Rajputana was the most vigorous in expressing this sentiment. Raja Pratap Singh of Jaipur took the lead as he gathered several chiefs into a confederacy and withheld the customary tribute paid to the Mughal emperor. Mahadji Scindia marched in person to subdue the combined force, but his own house was not in order due to greed-induced treachery, leading to his rout in the battle that ensued at Ajmer towards the latter half of 1787. Defeated and humiliated, he retreated towards the Deccan and camped at Gwalior, awaiting reinforcements.

Taking cue from this defeat and likely Rajput invasion, his deputy and in-charge of Delhi, Shah Nizam-ud-din, fortified the garrison around the Red Fort and city of Delhi. He was neither capable of maintaining his hold over the empire during Mahadji's absence nor did he know from where the actual threat was more likely to emanate.

Ghulam Qadir, an Afghan Ruhella, is a controversial figure in history. His father, Zabita Khan, was the Mir Bakshi (head of the army) in the Mughal court but later went on to lead a Ruhella rebellion. At the emperor's bidding, Mahadji led a military campaign against him. While Zabita Khan fled to safety, Ghulam Qadir, then about eight years old, was captured with other family members and kept at Ghausgarh (Saharanpur). It is also rumored that he was castrated during this time, though this does not seem to be true. His father later regained the emperor's favor and was reinstated in the royal court.

Zabita Khan died in early 1785, and Ghulam Qadir wished to take his place in the court as the leader of the Afghan Ruhellas. He arrived with his army and camped on the eastern bank of the Yamuna, opposite the Red Fort. His cause was supported by Manzur Ali Khan, the *nazir* (head of the Mughal harem), who facilitated his audience with Shah Alam II, the Emperor, in August–September 1787. The treacherous nazir wanted to use Ghulam Qadir to eliminate the Hindu and Maratha influence on the royal court. Shah Alam, on the contrary, turned down his claim.

Shah Nizam-ud-din saw this threat; however, he underrated Abdul Qadir's strength. He crossed the river with a small force and attacked his camp, only to suffer a humiliating defeat. He also realized the threat that the nazir could pose to him, so he retreated to Ballamgarh (Ballabhgarh) fort, approx. 35 kilometers south of Delhi.

Abdul Qadir knew that the fort was defenseless and it offered him the most appropriate opportunity to get what he wanted. In

less than 10 days after the emperor turned down his claim, precisely on September 5, 1787, he entered the fort again, this time at the head of 2,000 armed troops. The feeble emperor succumbed to the pressure and appointed him the Mir Bakshi, Regent as well as *Amir-ul-umara* (head of the nobles). The emperor was virtually his prisoner, and his intention was to lay his hands on the Mughal treasure; little did he realize that the coffers were as good as empty. He found no gems, gold, or silver but still believed that the hapless emperor knew where the treasure lay.

Despite his elevation, Abdul Qadir was aware that his position was not a stable one, and he would have to make efforts to create more support in his favor as well as eliminate any threat that he might face. A potent force to challenge his authority could be Begum Samru, who had considerable influence on the royal court.

At this time, Begum Samru was in Panipat confronting the Sikhs. She immediately set out for Delhi and camped just outside the fort with her four battalions and artillery pieces, led by French officers. She knew the intruder was cunning and deceptive. She was disgusted over how he became the Amir-ul-umara and how shabbily he had treated the emperor, whom she respected from the deepest depths of her heart.

The wily Abdul Qadir knew that trick, not power, could bring the Begum in his favor. He approached her camp with only two attendants. He was kept waiting for about half an hour before he was brought to the Begum's camp. She was seated on a high chair, adorned in her martial dress which she wore when going on a military campaign. She had four alert bodyguards, two on each side, while a minister stood waiting for her command.

Looking at the splendor that the Begum displayed, Ghulam Qadir bowed to salute and said, "Begum, you're like my sister, in fact, you're my sister. I've an attractive proposal, that would bring mutual benefit to this pair of sister and brother." Every word of his

was wrapped in sweetness, but the Begum knew how sour it was. Still, she wanted to know what was in his mind, so she offered him a seat and said, "Go on."

"Well, if you concur, we could work together," paused Ghulam Qadir to see the effect of his words and then continued, "You are aware that the empire is in weak hands and the prevailing times present us an opportunity to rule the land; we can divide it between us."

The Begum was seething with anger, but she did not allow the same to reflect in her facial expression. She continued, "What do you think we can do?"

"You'll attack the fort while my troops inside the fort will present no opposition. Not only this, but one of my battalions will join you from across the river. In no time, we will be in the commanding position. In the ensuing negotiations, I'll represent the Emperor, and you know what all we can achieve," chuckled Ghulam Qadir, his eyes swirling with slyness, and his cheeks creasing deeply as he erupted into hearty laughter.

The Begum shook her head in affirmation. The elated Ghulam Qadir took her leave, while she kept sitting and thinking about how she could avert this threat and display her loyalty towards the emperor and Mahadji Scindia. She wished to come true to the trust that had been reposed in her.

On the morrow, as per the plan, Ghulam Qadir sent a well-equipped battalion across the Yamuna. As soon as its last soldier had landed, the entire force was taken captive.

Alarmed, Ghulam Qadir sent a messenger to the Emperor, asking him, on the threat of invasion, to evict the Begum and her army from the premises. With her around, the relaxed emperor had courage enough to ridicule the messenger. This only angered Ghulam Qadir. He ordered cannonading the fort, which was adequately responded to by the Begum's force.

Ghulam Qadir was about to order a physical assault when he came to know that Prince Jawan Bakht was leading a strong army to the capital. Seeing his bleak chances, he could think of only one thing—retreat. Before leaving, he pleaded before the emperor to forgive him for his rude behaviour and returned all the treasure and arms that he had grabbed. He quit Delhi to go back to his principality in Saharanpur, still nursing ill-will that personifies him as one of the most shameful personalities in Indian history. He utilized the intervening period by occupying more territories, expanding his army, and plundering the areas not under his direct control; even Begum Samru's territories suffered at his hands.

For her commendable conduct, the emperor felt immensely grateful and bestowed on Begum Samru the title of Zeb-un-Nisa, meaning 'Adornment of the Fair Sex'. He was more than pleased with her, not knowing that destiny would present more opportunities to feel more grateful to her.

30

The Daughterly Begum

Presently, the Mughal empire was facing the most precarious of times. Its revenues and territories were fast vanishing, while the challenges were growing stronger. The regional and petty chiefs like Ghulam Qadir had caused great harm to its prestige. To restore the glory that his forefathers once enjoyed, Shah Alam II finally decided to take to the field himself. He had also received an invitation from the Rajput king Pratap Singh of Jaipur to reconquer the lost possessions from the local usurpers.

Setting out on 4th of January, 1788, Shah Alam arrived at Bharwas, about 10 kilometers south of Rewari (now in Haryana), where he met Pratap Singh early next month. He insisted on the payment of overdue tribute, but Pratap Singh expressed his inability to do so in view of the Maratha onslaught. In the end, he happily went away, handing the emperor only a promissory note for 25,000 rupees. This was like a setback for cash-starved Shah Alam, as lack of money was already thinning his forces, as 50 to

100 troops deserted almost daily. The only satisfaction was that the Begum's three battalions stood strong by him.

The emperor then decided to check on Najaf Quli Khan, who was then expanding his influence and was presently garrisoned at Gokulgarh, about 4 kilometers away. First, a message was sent to him, but he treated the sovereign's message most willfully. On the contrary, he presented a counter claim to the post of Regent, as he was the only heir of Mirza Najaf Khan, being the adopted son.

Shah Alam decided to launch a campaign. He camped in the middle with the Mughal forces on his left and Begum Samru's three battalions on the right, while he commanded one division of Mughal forces under Badal Beg Khan to go ahead. It seemed as if this party was going for a picnic, as all personnel, with a few exceptions, drank themselves to senselessness all night. Najaf Quli Khan's spies reported this, so he decided to avail the opportunity. He himself was a drunkard, yet he did not touch it that night as he knew what reward it could bring.

In the wee hours of March 12, Najaf launched a nightly sally. The Mughal force was devastated and dispersed. The Sikhs in the rebel camp headed to the Emperor's camp to reap the rewards.

Begum Samru had a disciplined army at her disposal. When she saw the enemy's onslaught and the Emperor's precarious position, she immediately sent forth one of her battalions under George Thomas and ensured his safety. It was due to her that the Emperor was saved from certain ignominy.

Shah Alam was in a dilemma. With his available resources, he could neither crush the rebel nor was he in a position to sustain his army. Begum Samru came to his rescue again. She brought the two parties to mediation. To satisfy the imperial ego, Najaf Quli Khan was presented before the sovereign with his hands tied with a scarf. He was forgiven and restored to all his posts and territories. Not only this, but he was also given a *khil'at*, the robe of honour.

The embarrassed emperor returned to his capital in March 1788. There, he acknowledged Begum Samru's loyalty and pronounced her his most beloved daughter. He also presented her with a *khil'at* (robe of honour) as well as the charge of the jagir of Badshahpur-Jharsa, just near Delhi, which further elevated her influence. George Thomas was decorated with a *khil'at* as well.

31

The Return of the Prince

Prince Jawan Bakht, being the eldest son of Shah Alam II, was the heir apparent. When the emperor was away from Delhi for 12 years, it was the prince who ruled as the Regent. Shah Alam returned to Delhi in 1772 under the protection of the Maratha general Mahadji Scindia, who became the *Vakil-i-Mutlaq* (Viceregent). The evolving conspiracy at the court was beyond the taste of the prince, who now stood stripped of all his power. Dismayed, he abandoned Delhi in 1784 and reached Lucknow, where he was welcomed by Warren Hastings. His father wanted him back in Delhi, but he did not agree.

In 1787, when Shah Alam faced threats from petty chiefs, he wrote letters to Mahadji Scindia and his son to reinforce him. The Maratha chieftain had recently suffered a defeat at Ajmer, but still he sent Ambaji Rao with a small force. The *nazir*, Manzur Ali Khan was, however, engaged in intrigue again. Earlier, he had conspired with Ghulam Qadir. He staunchly opposed the Hindus, particularly Maratha influence over the court. He maligned the

Marathas and aroused suspicion in the sovereign's heart, to the extent of getting his approval for an assault on Ambaji Rao. Fortunately, Begum Samru was around; she intervened and escorted the Marathas to safety.

Then at Agra, Prince Jawan Bakht realized the Begum's significance in court affairs and sent a messenger, Khair-ud-din, to her when she was camping at Faridabad. He arrived by *dak*, taking only six hours, but he had to wait for some time before he was presented in the audience of the Begum.

When he entered the *shamiana* (tent), he found the Begum sitting on the throne behind a thin screen, with a formal durbar in which her French, Armenian, and Portuguese military officers were present in their ceremonial attire. After the introductory tedious formality, the Begum said, "Yes, what brings you here?"

"Who is there on earth who would not be fascinated by your glory? May your glory persist to infinity!" said Khair-ud-din, trying to flatter her obsequiously.

The Begum was little interested in these pretensions. She retorted in a soft but firm voice, "That cannot be an answer to my question, can it?"

The cautioned messenger then said, "Huzoor, the prince is much perturbed by the situation prevailing at the court. He wants to reinstate the Mughal glory as it existed during the reigns of the great Mughals."

"I too wish for this to be realized. Does your master possess any manly and heroic attributes to justify this?" the Begum enquired.

Khair-ud-din, however, misunderstood the question. He thought she was asking about his master's physical charm. He said, "The day is not far when he will be with you. He is as handsome as one can be."

The Begum maintained her calm with difficulty, and this time her voice was stern, "What kind of joke is this? I only asked if he had enough vigor to wield swords and win kingdoms, or he only possesses the passion to play the tabor and the drum!"

Khair-ud-din knew that he was caught on the wrong foot and immediately tried to amend things, "I mean, Huzoor, that he is brave and adventurous. He couldn't have asked for your company had he been a mere pleasure-seeker."

She forgave him for his folly, for the prince ought not suffer for want of wisdom in his messenger. She dismissed him saying, "My good wishes to the prince. When he is before the Emperor, one of my platoons will be right there in full strength to support his demand for regency." Despite his foolery, the messenger was lucky to have achieved what he had come for.

Shah Alam was happy that his son and heir-apparent was back after a long absence, especially in a time of such distress. He wanted to assign him the management of the state, the army, and the treasury. But that was not to be!

The nazir was a master at his game of intrigue, and the Emperor was a mere puppet in his hands. The rise of the prince simply meant his downfall. He used the same old trick, which was to create doubts in the Emperor's mind, who grew less confident of his own son. Even his trusted Begum Samru was not around at this time to resolve this matter.

On his part, the prince was not worthy of the confidence. He fell prey to the nazir's conspiracy and did his bidding by capturing his father and becoming the *de facto* emperor. He had ambitions that could not be realized without character, competence, and material resources, and he had none of them.

Shah Alam somehow got rid of his son just after 13 days as the subadar of Agra, which was not even under the Mughal control.

Disappointed, he sought refuge with Ghulam Qadir in Doab, only to become more disappointed. He then took refuge in the British territory in February 1788, lived as a heartbroken youth in Banaras, and died there three months later. He never knew that a great calamity was about to befall his father!

32

The Emperor Is Blinded

Tugging hard at the Emperor's beard with his left hand and tossing the blood-stained eyeball up and down, which had just been gouged out with his right, Ghulam Qadir howled like a devil with a vicious gaze at the bleeding, blinded victim on the throne, "Get me the painter! I want this painted!" He summoned the painter, thinking he was creating history, not realizing how shameful this act was.

The sorry tale of the imbecile, feeble ruler of the great Mughal dynasty was unfolding in a horrendous, deplorable manner. How things came to such a pass needs to be explored briefly, in which Begum Samru once again played a vital role.

The story now manifests a phenomenon that can be called divine justice for incompetence, cruelty, conspiracy, and treason.

In the absence of Prince Jawan Bakht, Begum Samru was looking after his affairs. Elsewhere, Delhi was vulnerable and up for grabs. Ghulam Qadir had failed in his earlier attempt and thought

that destiny had presented him with another opportunity so soon. Hence, he decided to make the most of it.

Above all, he had an attractive offer from Malika-i-Zamani, the wife of the deceased emperor Muhammad Shah. She lived in a grand haveli outside the fort and had amassed a great fortune. She had nursed Ahmad Shah, her stepson, who was deprived of his throne and eyesight by Shah Alam's father. Malika-i-Zamani offered Ghulam Qadir to replace Shah Alam with Bidar Bakht, the son of Ahmad Shah, and promised him twelve lakhs for this. Another widow of Muhammad Shah, Sahiba Mahal, would contribute to this amount. In some accounts, this amount is said to be ten lakhs. Either way, it was a very large sum those days.

Ghulam Qadir's mouth watered at this palatable offer, and he knew he could lay his hands on the Mughal treasure in addition to this great sum. He had utilized the intervening period by strengthening his army, adding artillery pieces, and recruiting fresh troops by gathering a handsome booty after plundering various territories, including Meerut, Ghaziabad, Patparganj, and Shahdara. Now, he was ready for the onslaught to quench his unfathomable thirst for treasure and retribution.

Shah Alam had come to a helpless state owing to his incompetence, and he was about to pay a heavy price for it. He had, in fact, perceived this threat and wanted to oppose Ghulam Qadir's access to Delhi. He immediately sent two of his emissaries to Mahadji Scindia with the robes of highest honor and an invitation to come to Delhi. Mahadji, however, had more important things to look after following his victory over Ismail Beg in Agra. He sent a contingent of only 2,000 horses under Ravloji and Bhagirath Rao from Mathura on July 8, 1788, and promised that he himself would be there soon.

The Lal Paltan, as the emperor's bodyguards were called, was present in the fort and could have averted Ghulam Qadir's entry.

The treacherous nazir Manzur Ali Khan was apprehensive that he and his associates would be punished for their past treachery by Mahadji Scindia, so he started conniving once again. He convinced the emperor about the good intentions of Ghulam Qadir and to send his loyal 2,000-strong personal guards out of the fort to join the invader's camp. The unsuspecting Emperor gave in and invited calamity upon himself. Consequently, on July 14, 1788, the invader entered the fort and palace without any opposition and posted his troops everywhere.

The helpless Emperor realized his folly and trembled at the evil omen. This forced the loyal generals Himmat Bahadur and Ravloji, who found themselves no match for Ghulam Qadir, to withdraw to Faridabad, about 25 kilometers to the south. Moreover, even Begum Samru could not come to the rescue as she was not in the vicinity. Thus, the capital lay at the mercy of the heartless invader.

Seeing everything under his control, the arrogant and egocentric Ghulam Qadir was about to do some eccentric things that even the most atrocious of invaders would not think of. On July 15, he was able to gain access to the palace again in complicity with the nazir. With this began a sorry tale of distress and disgrace for the royal family, which would last for the next two and a half months.

Entering the Emperor's chamber with heavy steps, he pushed Shah Alam aside on the masnad and sat down beside him, demanding the hidden treasures. The weak emperor pleaded that the imperial treasury was as good as empty, but Ghulam Qadir would not accept that as an answer. He looked here, there, and everywhere for gold and gems, but virtually got nothing worth mentioning.

Peeved at not getting any treasure, Ghulam Qadir imprisoned the princes and flogged them before others. He kept the women and children without food for days. He even punished the servants and killed a couple of them, lest they have the courage to supply food to the victims clandestinely.

Angered over his hectic but futile search for treasure over the next two weeks, Ghulam Qadir, on July 30, dethroned and imprisoned Shah Alam and placed Bidar Bakht, a son of the late emperor Ahmad Shah, on the throne in the Diwan-i-Khas, with the title Nasir-ud-din Muhammad Jahan Shah. He was amazed at this swift transition from a prison cell to the throne, out of sheer luck. Shah Alam, on the other hand, was kept in the prison-quarters known as *Salatin*.

This was what Ghulam Qadir had done for Malika-i-Zamani for a large sum, but he was not content with this; he wanted the Mughal treasure. His cruelty reached its lowest ebb on August 10. All these days, he had been torturing Shah Alam with threats. The *Ibratnama* in Elliot (as quoted by Brajendranath Banerji in *Begum Samru*) describes his helplessness in these words: "Qadir went to Shah Alam, and said, 'Find me some gold, or I will send you to join the dead.' Shah Alam reviled and reproached him, saying, 'I am in your power, cut off my head, for it is better to die than to live like this.'"

It was ultimately on this fateful day that Ghulam Qadir pounced on Shah Alam, pushing him down. As the victim tried to resist, Qandahari Khan and Purdil Khan held his hands while two others held one leg each. And then, on the command of his master, Qandhari Khan used his Afghani dagger to gouge out his eye.

Without caring for the wailings and fruitless efforts of the victim to get free, he dug out the other eyeball himself, and while tossing it in his hand, he sent for the court painter. He screamed at the top of his voice, "I want you to paint me like this! I . . . sitting on his chest, digging out his eye." Then Shah Alam was left in the cell with no one to care for his bleeding eyes. Savagery was at its extreme now.

However, Ghulam Qadir's abominable thirst for barbarity was not yet quenched. He was still devoid of the treasure, though the Ruhellas were leaving no place undug where they could hope to get something worthwhile.

His wrath now turned to the seraglio. Even the dreaded invaders like Nadir Shah and Ahmad Shah Durrani did not have the heart to disrespect the royal ladies. He plundered the personal belongings of the ladies, which they had accumulated over decades. He even took away their gold and silver embroidered apparels and deprived them of their silverware. His men beat the maids and eunuchs, several of them to death.

Ghulam Qadir was about to target their personal dignity next. Not long after, he ordered his men to bring the beautiful princesses before him as he sat drinking in the Moti Mahal with his compatriots. They were made to dance without a veil or screen. He and his companions did such indescribable indecent acts to the princesses. Unable to bear the torture anymore, three of the princesses committed suicide, jumping into the Yamuna from the ramparts. Terror was so rampant that one wife of the new Emperor died because of extreme fear and anxiety. Two of the former Empresses are said to have died of starvation. In all, 21 princes and princesses died, and the condition of others was no good.

Akbar Shah, Shah Alam's heir to the throne, was forced to drink and dance in public view.

Ghulam Qadir was ferocious not only in his deeds but also in his speech. He used a foul language without batting an eyelid, even before the ladies. When he forced Akbar Shah to dance, he cynically said, "Without you being singers and dancers, I could not have attained this position." Once he taunted the princesses saying, "One day I am going to allow my Ruhellas to drag you all to their rooms without wedlock, so that a manlier race is born to the Mughals." Some texts suggest that a few princesses were transferred from the Mughal harem to Ghulam Qadir's harem at Ghausgarh, others speak this about the most beautiful dancers. In the words of the historian Jadunath Sarkar, "It was a dance of demons for nine weeks."

33

The Nemesis

Ghulam Qadir next demanded from Malika-i-Zamani the amount she had promised. She was in league with him for the accession of her grandson. Not only this, she played an active role in the atrocities unleashed on the family of Shah Alam; they were thrown in the prison at Salimgarh Fort even without a change of clothing.

Malika-i-Zamani contended that he had already gathered wealth amounting to much more than the promised 12 lakh rupees, so he must leave the palace. In reply, he said, "All this was part of the spoils of treasure from my father's capital at Ghausgarh."

On August 22, Ghulam Qadir forced Malika-i-Zamani and Sahiba Mahal out of their mansions, with the clothes they were at that time wearing, placed them on the terrace of the octagonal tower in the city, and exposed them to the gaze of the common people on the river-bank for hours together, without water or food. In the meantime, their mansions were dug up, and everything was removed from there that could have value. The royal ladies were

suffering humiliation of the worst kind even though their grandson was on the throne. What an irony!

The threat of torture or the promise of reward to the maidservants bore the maximum fruit for the Ruhella. They revealed the most precious gems, jewellery, and clothing, collected over generations. Ironically, to the amazement of Ghulam Qadir, even the most renowned jeweler in the city could not value them and said that they were so precious that even he could not guess their actual price.

Ghulam Qadir did not spare even the nazir, Manzur Ali. When the traitor could produce no wealth from the palace, a fine of seven lakhs was imposed on him. To force him to pay out, he was beaten, dragged into a latrine, and threatened that excrement would be stuffed into his mouth. His house was plundered too, from which the find amounted to about 40,000 rupees and 5,000 gold coins, in addition to jewellery, silverware, and precious clothing. And when he ultimately fled from Delhi, he took the nazir with him.

The total spoils from Delhi fetched him about 25 crore worth of money, coins, gems, jewellery, and other valuable things. He had unleashed barbarity that could not be even dreamed of. And now, it was his turn to pay for his evil acts.

Mahadji Scindia and Begum Samru—either of whom could have saved Shah Alam from the undignified agony—are often blamed for taking their own sweet time before they came to the rescue. Let us find out how true this allegation was.

At this time, the latter was at Tappal, while a substantial part of her army was engaged in Agra under the former's campaign against Ismail Beg and Ghulam Qadir. Moreover, she had to look after the discontentment of the landed community, which took some time to resolve. However, looking at the gravity of the situation in Delhi and her loyalty towards Shah Alam, these issues were not as pressing as to warrant her inexplicable delay.

Mahadji Scindia, on the other hand, was at Agra when the news reached him. He had just secured a victory over Ghulam Qadir in Agra on June 17, but the retreating army had destroyed the ferry boats and captured the oarsmen. This forbade the Maratha army to cross over the Yamuna and go after him. Mahadji sent his general Rana Khan with the army to Mathura to arrange boats and cross over the flooding river into the Doab, while he busied himself in safeguarding his position. He himself reached Mathura on the 4th and waited for Ranjit Singh Jat to join him four days later. He sent 2,000 of his horse-mounted troops to Delhi, but that was not sufficient to meet Ghulam Qadir's threat. He was well aware of the hostile environment north of the Chambal and could not have gone there without having made some necessary preparations. Moreover, he was not confident of the Mughal troops, who were with him presently but had switched sides earlier. One could not help but wonder if they would not deceive him a third time. Even Shah Alam had warned him about their faithless character. Moreover, it would mean a very long supply and communication line to Delhi, which could be threatened by the adversaries. His reinforcement from the Deccan was unwilling to march to Delhi in view of the arrears in pay, and resources had to be managed for this as well. Adding to his problems were the conspiracies in the Maratha empire, and he had to ensure his security in this aspect. Thus, preparation took him some time before he could proceed to Delhi in strength. Unfortunately, Ghulam Qadir had wreaked havoc in Delhi much before that.

Anyway, the day of deliverance for Shah Alam seemed to have arrived at long last. Mahadji Scindia, as soon as he was reinforced with a large force from the Deccan, ordered his army to proceed to Delhi under the general Rana Khan. This force occupied old Delhi on September 28 and, proceeding further, occupied the city on October 2. Ghulam Qadir's troops were being forced back, and

they ultimately took refuge in the fort. The Marathas were assisted in this endeavor by Begum Samru and Ismail Beg. The latter of the two was cheated of his share by Ghulam Qadir, so he joined the forces against him. The time had finally arrived when justice was served to this reckless perpetrator.

The Marathas cut off the food supply to the fort and started bombing. Ghulam Qadir sensed that he could not maintain himself in the fort for long, so he started to send his baggage to Ghausgarh via Salimgarh, while he himself led his garrison in the fort. In the Doab, his convoy carrying treasure was looted by the Sikhs and Gujjars in liaison with the Marathas.

Meanwhile, Ghulam Qadir's atrocities continued unabated in the palace. He would often visit it and extort his parting gift from Bidar Bakht and Shah Alam, carrying away some of their sons as captives.

On October 10, in the evening, Ghulam Qadir was thinking where he could find more treasure when a powder magazine blew up, causing a volcanic explosion in the fort. It had happened due to the Ruhella troops' carelessness in drawing munitions. He took it as an evil omen and is reported to have said, 'Now the fort refuses to keep me.' He packed off his baggage and finally crossed over the Yamuna on boats with all his men.

The following day, when the Marathas resumed their cannonade, the princes imprisoned on the ramparts informed them that the palace had been vacated. A soldier was immediately sent by rope-ladder to open the fort gates.

Inside the fort and palace, Ravloji Scindia found a very terrible scene. All the princes, princesses, and servants were starving badly. Shah Alam and even Bidar Bakht were as good as half dead as food was nowhere to be found. They were immediately given food and water. Barbers and maidservants were fetched to groom the royal members.

After this, a hunt was launched to trace Ghulam Qadir and the spoils that he had carried away. On October 16, the blind Shah Alam II was restored to the throne, and *Khutba* was read in his name from the pulpit of the Jami Masjid. The Scindia flag was hoisted that would flutter there for the next 13 years, only to be replaced by the British one.

Ghulam Qadir was yet to be brought to justice. More Maratha troops poured in from the Deccan and went after him, fighting several pitched battles in the process. As he had proved a hard nut to crack, his food supplies were struck at. The fort at Aligarh was won over by the Marathas as well.

On November 3, Rana Khan's and Begum Samru's troops put tremendous pressure on Ghulam Qadir's troops, causing anxiety among them. Suffering the loss of men and material, he took refuge in Meerut Fort on November 4. At this, the Marathas encircled and blockaded it. Lack of food caused havoc with the besieged men and animals, many of whom perished. He tried to assassinate the princes still captive with him, but was prevented by his own commander.

A month and a half passed. At last, Ghulam Qadir decided to abandon the fort for Ghausgarh. On the night of December 17, he shot out from there with 500 of his horsemen. A Maratha patrol led by Jiva Dada pursued and attacked the party, causing much harm. Ghulam Qadir hid himself in the dark, so did his horsemen. When the attackers retreated, he did not find anyone from his party around. He mounted his horse and rode in a direction that he thought led to Ghausgarh, but his horse tripped over a crevice and broke its leg.

Meanwhile, when Ghulam Qadir's troops at Meerut Fort learned of his flight, the majority of them dispersed. The Marathas entered the fort and took charge of it. They released the princes, who were in a pitiable state, and collected the booty that had been

left behind. Some of his supporters, including a few commanders and the nazir, Manzur Ali, were taken prisoner. There were about 3,000 Ruhella troops in the fort who were stripped of their arms and clothing and were ordered to leave, while some of them had to be beaten away.

Ghulam Qadir, on the other hand, now limped without a clue about his destination. As the early rays of the sun hit, he sighted a village called Bamnauli, near Shamli. Here, he took refuge with a Brahmin, and offered him a handsome reward for providing a horse and a guide to Ghausgarh. Identifying the perpetrator, the host informed the nearest Maratha camp, and thus, he was captured on December 19. He and other prisoners were sent to Mahadji Scindia, who was then camping at Mathura.

The Maratha leader wanted to know about the treasure that the culprit had plundered from Delhi. Shah Alam was not happy about this and wanted him to be punished harshly. At last, on February 28, 1789, when Mahadji Scindia received a sharp letter from the Emperor, he finally decided to punish the prisoner for his misdeeds.

The heartless criminal deserved a harsh punishment. On March 3, his nose and ears were cut off, and his eyeballs were extracted; these were sent to the emperor. The next day, his hands and feet were cut off and sent to the emperor. He bled to death, and then his headless body was suspended from a tree. It is said that when the Emperor fumbled with the gory contents in the small chest, he felt greatly gratified. After all, the edict of eye-for-eye had been realized.

It was the Nazir's turn next. He was thrown to the mercy of an elephant, and it was not long before the beast crushed the life out of him.

Seeing everything under control, Begum Samru recalled her troops to Sardhana. Her commanders related to her the incidents that left a bitter taste in her mouth for days together.

34

The Sorceress Begum

Was Begum Samru a sorceress—a witch?

This is what the enemies believed, and they were quite confident about it. Her troops had earned great respect from their own and their opponents' commanders. She had groomed her army on the European model, and all her army officers were Europeans. She herself was adept at using tactics that the opponents found hard to respond to. Even when the armies she supported were routed on the battlefield, her own battalions escaped unscathed. This was one tactic that had helped her preserve her force on several occasions. Like her husband, she believed that it was better to retreat today in order to score a victory tomorrow. For her, reckless bravery was simply stupidity if it meant certain destruction and defeat. Her art of retreat had amazed even the well-known commanders of her time.

It was widely believed that she possessed magic powers. Right since her ascent as the ruler of Sardhana, her battalions had taken an active part in a number of campaigns and had emerged

victorious, causing losses to the enemy camp. She herself took to the battlefield on several occasions. J. Baille Fraser, in his book *Military Memoir of Lt Col J. Skinner, CB* (1851), writes, "By means of her uncommon ability and discretion, united to a masculine firmness and intrepidity, and aided by this force . . . she managed to preserve her country nearly unmolested, and her authority generally unimpaired, during a period of surrounding storm and tempest, which shook several great powers from their thrones."

Whenever she was seen leading her troops, the enemy troops were flabbergasted. They believed that she would spread her *chaddar* (shawl) to destroy her enemies. In his book, *Memoirs of George Thomas*, William Francklin writes, "The people in the Dekhan [Deccan], who knew the Begum by reputation, believed her to be a witch, who destroyed her enemies by throwing her *chadir* at them." In this context, the word *chadir* probably meant 'chain-shot' (several projectiles fired together from a cannon) rather than 'shawl'.

The difficult phase of her life was over, during which she eloped with La Vaisseau and suffered for a long time in captivity. Back in power, she now invested herself in looking after her principality.

Her first husband, Sombre's poor relations with the British did not deter her from making a solemn effort to mitigate the enmity into cooperation. She displayed in measure that, despite her loyalty to the Mughals, she had no desire to get into any unnecessary conflict with any other power. Her sole aim was to administer her estate well, and as history testifies, she had shown signs of this inclination right from the early period of her rule.

As early as 1791, Colonel Stuart, the British commanding officer at Anupshahr, was abducted by a Sikh band led by Banga Singh, who asked for a ransom of one lakh rupees, in addition to making other demands. The British offered twenty thousand rupees for his release, but the negotiations failed. They then contacted the Begum for assistance in the matter.

The Begum entered into a dialogue with the Sikhs and displayed her diplomatic qualities. At this time, her own army was deployed at Panipat against the very Sikhs, yet she succeeded in convincing them to release the captive for only ₹ 15,000. She secured custody and journeyed fifteen miles to receive him midway and to escort him back to Sardhana *en route* to Delhi. The Governor General himself expressed gratitude for this and reimbursed her. He noted on April 18, 1792: "Major Palmer be instructed to remit the sum disbursed on this occasion by Zeb-un-Nisa to that lady, and that Mr. Stuart be requested to send her, on the part of Government, such a present as he may think most proper, accompanied by a letter containing suitable acknowledgements of her laudable exertions in behalf of Lt Col. Stuart." Again in 1794, Sir John Shore requested her help in capturing the deserters from his army at Cawnpore and Fatehgarh.

Until 1803, Begum Samru remained attached to the Mughals, directly under the Maratha influence, with the blind Shah Alam being Emperor only in name. Three of her battalions were deployed under Scindia's command, yet she avoided any conflict with the British and kept in constant touch with them. When she eloped with La Vaisseau, she had plans to retire into the British territory and had entered into correspondence with Sir John Shore and other British officers for this purpose. She even used to invite the important British officers at Meerut and other adjacent towns for a lavish stay and party on the eve of Christmas every year.

The British, after the occupation of Bengal and Bihar, were exploiting people in every way possible, which led to an exponential rise in their revenue collection as well as trade. This helped them aspire for expansion of their control over newer territories, and this was to bring in its wake more battles in the Deccan and elsewhere.

In the battle of Assaye, fought on September 23, 1803, the Marathas tasted a decisive defeat at the hands of the British. With

this, the British sway spread over the Mughals and northern India. In it, five of Begum Samru's six battalions took part, in addition to her fifteen guns of artillery. While the Marathas suffered a massive number of casualties, her troops under M. Legois were able to come out of the battle almost unharmed after giving the British stiff resistance. Hard fighting in this battle by her troops was sure to have a negative impact. J. Baille Fraser quotes Skinner in these words: "It is a remarkable thing, and much to the credit of the Begam's [Begum's] troops, that some four or five of her battalions were the only part of Sindhia's army that went off unbroken from the field of Assaye: they were charged by our [British] cavalry towards the close of the day, but without effect; Col. Maxwell who commanded, being killed in the charge by a grape-shot."

Interestingly, Begum Samru did not wish for her troops to take part in the battle against the British, and she wrote letters to her commander, M. Legois, expressing the same. Yet he was not in a position to withdraw considering the prevailing conditions, and he was perforce compelled to take part in the fighting. This factor later negatively affected Wellesley's decision on whether to trust the Begum's loyalty towards his government or not.

35

Switching Side

With the decline of the Marathas and the Mughals coming under the British influence as a consequence, the time for introspection had arrived for Begum Samru. She realized that she could no longer rely on them as overlords, as the threat could come from the British, who had set their eyes on expanding their influence over the territories not under their control. This meant that her principality could be next in line, as it was very near Meerut.

She had, in fact, sensed this even earlier, which is apparent in her letter in January 1802 to the British officer. In another letter to the Governor General on August 4, 1802, she expressed her willingness to put her territory and army under the British charge. On February 1, 1803, she pleaded in her letter written in Persian: ". . . I being aligned with the British Government from the core of my heart, I cannot resist my desire that your Lordship should preserve me . . . I have a force stationed in the Deccan which your Lordship must consider as awaiting your orders."

So, the best option for her was to take shelter under the British to keep her principality safe. However, a number of factors went against her, and she pondered on how to overcome them. The foremost of these was that her first husband, Sombre, was like a devil for the imperialist British, who could not apprehend him despite their best efforts. Secondly, despite the overall defeat of the Marathas at Assaye, the fighting of her own troops left the British flabbergasted. Her troops had achieved this in several skirmishes. Above all, it was Wellesley, the Governor General, who himself had started the Second Anglo-Maratha War, of which the Battle of Assaye was a part.

Keeping these factors in mind, Begum Samru was aware that it would not be easy for her to seek any British favor. As expected, when she approached Wellesley—smarting under her army's stiff resistance—suspected her loyalty and asked her to surrender all her possessions on the promise of being given a small territory west of the Yamuna River. In her meeting with Lord Lake, she hoped that this arrangement would give her a higher British rank and that she would be able to derive greater benefits from the British as their ally. However, doubts eclipsed her mind soon after. She was asked to meet the British Resident in Delhi for the final agreement.

The evolving situation called for her to put her best foot forward as a diplomat. She knew she could not withstand the British onslaught, so what could save her, and her principality was her wit and presence of mind. In any case, fighting a battle was not an option. What she could do in this situation was somehow delay the execution of the Governor General's decision until the situation was in her favor. This could be done if his attention was diverted to more pressing issues, and she decided to manufacture these.

The Marathas were defeated but not completely crushed. The very next year, under Holkar, they defeated the British in the Rajputana and besieged Delhi. Seeing a ray of hope, the

Begum sent him a confidential message that she was with him. Interestingly, the British Resident in Delhi at this time was Sir David Ochterlony, the godfather of David Ochterlony Dyce Sombre, her adopted son and heir.

She met him on November 12, 1803. She was anxious that the territory to be assigned to her might not be equal to the one that she was relinquishing, so within a week of this, she wrote a letter to Lord Wellesley saying that she had expended a large sum in creating facilities at Sardhana and the territory being assigned should match it. She also demanded that such territory 'may be compact and undivided, with a view to its successful management.'

In reply to this, Lord Wellesley wrote, reaffirming his decision to transfer her a suitable territory and demanding that she cede her principality immediately while it would take some time before assigning her the offered territory, and he promised 'ample compensation from the British Government for any loss of revenue which may be occasioned by the delay in selecting and transferring to your authority the districts to be assigned to you on the western side of the Jamuna'.

She knew this was not enough; it was a mere promise while she was asked to cede her territory immediately. It could be a trick to rob her of her jagir. She sensed a deception in the deal. Adopting more dilatory tactics, she instigated the Sikhs to raid the British territory. While these raids kept the British busy, she was presented with another opportunity when she was approached for rescuing yet another British official from them.

The Begum kept doing these small favors while keeping the British in good humor with lavish parties and expensive gifts to satiate their vanity. All this while, she kept in correspondence with the British authorities. On February 3, 1804, she wrote to Lt Col Ochterlony, making her case for an immediate transfer of territory to her. She wrote: ". . . it is proper you should consider that when I

go away from here, I require a place to stay in, where I may reside with my family and dependents. There are near a thousand destitute persons and lame and blind people in this district for whom a place of abode is necessary." She expressed her displeasure and even gave a hidden warning, saying, ". . . and I am not lame."

Ochterlony was quick to respond that the British government intended to do no deception. However, she was also accused of entering into a secret bond with Jaswant Rao Holkar. Coming under pressure due to this accusation, she agreed to give up all her parganas other than that of Sardhana, which she was to vacate as soon as she was assigned a new territory. She also defended that she was not 'in hand in glove' with the Maratha chieftain, assuring that 'no person yet can charge me of treachery in the past 40 years.' In this letter, she also denied that she had anything to do with the king of Kabul. She asserted that as an influential ruler, it was natural for her to send her envoys to various rulers and *jagirdars*, but that could not be considered substantial proof of her scheming against the British.

What his officers could see clearly, Lord Wellesley did not want to see. He seemed inclined to punish the Begum for no fault of hers. This is evident from his Agent, Archibald Seton, who on December 10, 1804, wrote in his report: "As the situation of the Begum both from the geographical position of her country, and from the nature of her military strength, is or appears to me to be, such as to render her either a most useful ally or a very troublesome enemy . . ." At this time, both Holkar and Ranjit Singh were trying to woo the Begum in their favor, and when Saharanpur fell to the Sikhs, Seton was alarmed and wrote that she could, in retaliation, attack the British army at Saharanpur, so there was a need to conciliate her immediately.

Begum Samru, in fact, was playing for both parties to remain secure. When Ochterlony asked her of some favors in material

for the operations in Saharanpur, she quickly obliged. This brought him on her side, and now he was of the opinion that 'keeping her jagir in her possession during her life was all needed to win her over.'

Yet Wellesley remained adamant. Due to a little change in his mindset, he concurred for the Begum to be allowed to retain the possession of her jagir, but with reduced troops and replacement of the French officers with the British ones. The emergency likely to arise, as mentioned here, was that of the British defeat in the Bharatpur campaign, but this did not happen. Thus, the Begum continued to remain in command of Sardhana.

It was her sheer good luck that Lord Wellesley did not continue as the Governor General much longer; otherwise she could have been forced to evict her possessions. Fortune favors the brave, and brave she was.

Time ticked by. She kept herself safe until July 1805, when Lord Cornwallis was appointed Governor General for the second time. Interestingly, he occupied this office only for about nine weeks, as if destiny wanted to do its bit for the Begum. He reinstated her to the *jaedad* (assets) in the Doab 'on the same terms she now holds it.' He wrote to her expressing his gratitude for the service she had rendered to the British and how she secured the release of another British official. He wrote, "I have resolved to leave you in the unmolested possession of your *jagir*, with all the rights and privileges which you have hitherto enjoyed." Not only this, he sent Guthrie, the rescued officer, to Sardhana to finalize the terms of the treaty between her and the British. The final treaty was signed in August 1805. It expressly said that she would remain in possession of her assets as long as she lived, while her troops would always be ready for any service to the East India Company. This treaty also bound her not to have any relations with any other state or power.

Thus, Begum Samru was reduced to having only administrative powers within her estate, and this marked the end of her political career. She deputed half of her troops in the service of the British at her own expense, while she retained the other half for her own protection and other administrative needs.

36

The Begum as a Ruler

Begum Samru had several shades to her personality, which together made her a successful ruler. Let us begin this chapter with an interesting incident.

Once, she went to pay an informal visit to Lord Lake, the English General of northern India. Even though she was 54 at the time, she looked very pretty. When Lake was informed of her arrival, he himself came to receive her at the gate. As he found her climbing down the coach, guarded by armed soldiers on either side, he was spellbound by her beauty, or maybe the wine he had gulped had started to show its impact. Without a care for decorum, he took the graceful lady in his arms and put the marks of his lips on hers.

This was simply scandalous, insulting, and shocking. As she patiently but firmly removed his hands from around her, she could perceive the changing demeanor of her loyal guards, who had their hands on their hilts and eyes red in anger.

The tactful Begum knew that it could snowball into a controversy. She smiled to her guards and other onlookers as

if nothing alarming had occurred and said, "So you can see, gentlemen, how a padre receives his penitent daughter."

To the relief of all those present, she had dealt with the situation very tactfully. She had displayed this quality on more occasions than one. Without this wit, she could not have survived and preserved her jagir for as long as 58 years. All these years, she put her judgement, foresight, and intrepidity to their best use while she was surrounded by powerful and greedy powers. It was remarkable for her to prove her caliber as an administrator and commander in the midst of the challenging political spectrum in the country, which demanded the best of men and even more of the fairer sex.

The Begum overcame all the challenges with flying colors while several thrones trembled across the land. She left her mark not only on the territories under her control, but across the national scene. The big powers like the British, the Marathas, and the Mughals respected her, while her adversaries like the Ruhellas, the Sikhs, and the Afghans looked at her in awe.

Until 1805, she had taken part in a number of campaigns herself while her battalions remained deployed under one or the other powers all through. After entering into the treaty with the British, she was called to take part in a campaign only once, and that was against Bharatpur. In 1826, her troops were part of the siege under the Commander-in-Chief, Lord Combermere. The Begum, now at the ripe age of about 73 years, led her battalions herself. However, Combermere forbade all native chiefs, including her, from leading their troops and from taking part in storming the fort, until then considered impregnable. She was advised to stay put at Mathura. At this, she remonstrated, calling the order nonsense. Major Archer, Aide-de-camp to Combermere, quotes her words: ". . . if I don't go to Bharatpur, all Hindustan will say I am grown a coward in my old age." In another instance, he has

compared her with 'the honor of a similarity of character with our Elizabeth.'

Her army had earned battle honors in several campaigns and was the cause of envy for many rulers across the land. Mrs. Deane, a British officer's wife, visited Sardhana in 1809; she has described her army vividly: "She has a regular cantonment here for her troops, and a strong fort containing some good houses, which are inhabited by the officers and their families. Her soldiers are tall, stout men, with light complexions, hooked noses, and strongly marked features, being principally Rajputs, who are the best soldiers, but much addicted to chewing opium, generally proud, and often insolent. Their uniform is a dress of dark blue broad cloth, reaching to the feet, with scarlet turbans and waistbands. Her park of artillery seemed also in excellent order: most of the large guns stood in a line in front of the palace gates." Bacon, on the other hand, has described her officers as dressing themselves variedly while the troops wore vests of dark yellow cloth, with some attention to conformity. He writes, "They are not very military in appearance, but are said to be good soldiers, both in courage and hardihood."

As per various writers and records, the strength of her army varied from time to time. The number of her battalions varied from four in 1787 to five in 1802 to six in 1836. One battalion consisted of about 500 troops and her cavalry varied from 200 to 400, and her artillery pieces, from 85 to 20 to 25. In 1836, her army was recorded to comprise a total of 4,464 men, including her bodyguards, cavalry, and artillery. In 1805, the total amount paid to a battalion as salary was ₹ 6,595, which was increased during campaigns and tenure in the Deccan by ₹ 4,246. After her death, three of her battalions were assimilated into the British army, and the remaining sought service in the Punjab under Ranjit Singh.

Begum Samru was very particular about how she conducted herself in public. When she was to interact with the native subjects,

she would always wear a netted veil, and also conduct her royal duties in court from behind a screen. However, she would not use a screen or veil when she interacted with the British. Whenever she was the host of a party, she would make sure to give one or the other present to all the ladies present and would continue to sit in the hall, smoking her hookah, until all the guests had departed.

The 1805 agreement with Lord Cornwalis limited her power absolutely to her jagir alone. As she did not have any external matter to deviate her attention, she devoted all her time to her people. She encouraged trade and agriculture and took numerous steps to encourage the farmers to cultivate every inch of the land. During floods and droughts, she assisted farmers with farm loans, called *taqavi*. This had resulted in increased revenue, which brought prosperity to her as well as her subjects. In addition to this, she built bridges and roads. The road from Sardhana to Meerut is said to have been built by her, on which she charged tolls from traders and pilgrims.

She ensured law and order to allow traders to travel through her territory without fear. She built *serais* (inns) or *piaos* (water stations) for travelers' comfort. This brought her abundant returns. When her husband was granted the estate, the revenue was estimated to be 6 lakh rupees, which shot up to ten lakhs in about three decades. People from even nearby territories came and settled there, leading to a denser population when compared to Meerut.

The administration of both civil and criminal justice was vested in her, though she was obliged to inform the British if she wanted to punish a culprit with a death sentence.

The booklet *Sardhana*, edited by Fr. Patrick of Sardhana Church, quotes from Capt. W. Franklin's book *Shah Aulum* as follows: "An unremitting attention to the cultivation of the land, a mild and upright administration, and care for the welfare of the inhabitants, has enabled this small tract to view with the most cultivated parts

of Hindustan, and to yield a revenue of ten lakhs of rupees per annum." This book further quotes from Major Archer's book *Tours in Upper India*: "Here fields look greener and more flourishing and the population of her villages appear happier and more prosperous than those of the [East India] Company's province. Her care is unremitting and her protection sure."

It is true that she charged a high rate of revenue, which was a cause of hardship for the cultivators, but she ensured that it was not a cause of penury for them. To ensure that they worked hard, armed guards are said to have been posted in villages, resulting in greenery and apparent prosperity. The situation turned for the worse as she aged, and her heir, Dyce Sombre, meddled in the administration and increased the rate of revenue. It was during this stage that things worsened. Criticizing this state, Atkinson writes, "As long as the Begam retained possession of her energy and strength, this system flourished. But when her heir attempted to meddle in the administration, during the last few years of her life, the fictitious nature of the prosperity of her estates became apparent."

Yet, this criticism appears unfounded. The evidence lies in the spontaneous outpouring of grief exhibited by ordinary people upon her passing, a testament to her impact and connection with the masses. She continues to be remembered even today for her just policies. It is also rumored that she meted out harsh barbaric punishments at times, including burying the culprits alive, but this accusation has not yet been proved.

The unconfirmed incident of her awarding capital punishment to two slave girls tells us that once, these girls were accused of putting the Begum's house in Mathura on fire so that they could elope with their paramours who were the guards at this house. The crime got investigated, and when found guilty, the two girls were severely flogged and then buried alive in a pit just in front of her tent. Even if this incident is true, it was not uncommon

in the prevailing circumstances wherein criminals were given even harsher and crueler punishments.

Begum Samru was a great builder too, and her personality comes alive through several structures she built during her lifetime, the most important of these being the Sardhana Church and her palace at Sardhana. The church is known as 'Basilica Shrine of Our Lady of Graces' and is visited by people of all faiths, its fine architecture being the prime attraction. It is believed that its main dome was covered in gold, which the well-known robber Sultana Daku carried away. However, this is not verified. It is currently a protected monument under the care of the Archeological Survey of India.

For her own residence, she built a two-storey palace in Anglo-Indo style, completed in 1835, so she got only about one year to live in this palatial building. It currently functions as St. Charles Inter College. Prior to shifting to this palace, she lived in two places—one at Sardhana, currently working as St. John's Seminary, and another at Meerut, called Begum Bagh, named after her, a palace surrounded by a lavish garden. Now, no trace of her garden or palace is found, only a multi-storey residential complex exists there.

She also had a large residential building at Khirwa, near Sardhana, where she sometimes went for a change of air. She also had a palace at Chandni Chowk with a spiraling garden, gifted to her by Emperor Akbar Shah for her services to the empire, and presently, the Central Bank of India operates from here, though we can find no trace of the garden now. She had private property in several places, including land, gardens, and markets in different towns. In addition to these, she built two churches at Meerut, one for the European Catholics and the other for the Indian Christians.

As the Begum advanced in years, she realized that death was an inevitable reality. She had seen violent deaths from close quarters on more than one occasion but she was destined to pass away

peacefully. What perturbed her most was what would become of her dependents, who might be left without any support after her.

She decided to make some provision for their sustenance. To ensure this, she wrote to the Governor General with a request to make a monthly allowance of 7,500 sikka rupees in favor of her dependents from her assets. A sikka Rupee was a silver coin weighing 192 gm (Calcutta sikka) or 180 gm (Farrukhabad sikka), made from pure silver mixed with about 10 percent alloy, and from this fact, the amount of her benefaction can be guessed. In support of her demand, on July 9, 1807, the Delhi Resident wrote to the Secretary to the Government that this provision was meant for 'the relatives of those who have fallen in her service, and the loss of whom deprives them of all support.' When Lord Minto became the next Governor General, he was happy to accede to her petition as 'just and reasonable' and further noted that 'the general tenor of her conduct to merit every practicable degree of favor and indulgence on the part of the British Government was graciously pleased to comply with her request'. He also conveyed his decision to her saying, how her spirit of concern for the dependents was 'consistent with that spirit of liberality and justice which distinguishes your character'.

After her death, the British Government in India sanctioned life-pensions for 668 people who were left in a state of destitution. The list did not include some of those recommended by her heir, Dyce Sombre, who then made for them a provision of 2,000 pounds per annum out of his private income.

The Begum executed her first will in English on December 16, 1831, by which she appointed David Ochterlony Dyce and Clemence Brown, a colonel, her executors. She ratified the content of this will three years later, this time in Persian, in which she was well conversant. By these wills, she divested herself of her personal property in favor of her adopted son, David Ochterlony Dyce. He

was now required to identify himself as one of the Sombre family therefore, he suffixed Sombre to his name.

The Begum's generosity has been admired by several contemporary writers. Bacon went to the extent of calling her 'notoriously generous' who would 'loosen her purse-strings, distributing freely to the indigent.' She donated large sums to churches in India and abroad, including the Pope of Rome and the Church of England. She also created funds for instruction in Christianity and for the poor. Moreover, in Calcutta, she established the Poor Fund with 50,000 sonat (47,800 sikka) in government bonds, the interest of which was to be used for the liberation of prisoners suffering in jails for their inability to pay small debts. She also made provisions for several other churches, including those located in Agra, Calcutta, Bombay, and Madras. In addition, she created endowments for the maintenance of the religious and charitable institutions she established.

Bacon has also pointed out that while she was no miser in donating to any public institution, she was not so 'open-handed' in smaller matters as well. She would permit no expenditure in her household without her explicit consent, and she inspected the financial records herself.

The Begum is said to be tolerant of all faiths, and people of different faiths resided in her principality. As per the North-Western Province Gazette, she harbored a liberal attitude towards Hindu and Musalman institutions, though there are no instances of the same.

The Begum ruled the principality of Sardhana for about 58 years. She breathed her last on the morning of January 27, 1836. With her death, a proclamation was read in the presence of RNC Hamilton, Magistrate of Meerut, in her palace, by which her jagir was being annexed by the British Government. Of course, her personal property was not touched.

The letter, written by Governor General Lord Bentinck in 1835 on the occasion of leaving India for England, is proof enough of the exalted state of mind that the Begum possessed. He writes, "I cannot leave India without expressing the sincere esteem I entertain for your Highness's character. The benevolence of disposition and extensive charity which have endeared you to thousands, have excited in my mind sentiments of the warmest admiration; and I trust that you may yet be preserved for many years the solace of the orphan and widow, and the sure resource of your numerous dependents. Tomorrow morning I embark for England, and my prayers and best wishes attend you, and all others who like you exert themselves for the benefit of the people of India."

No modern history book is deemed comprehensive without acknowledging her, such is the significance of her contributions and influence on contemporary politics. Over time, she has become a mystical and spiritual figure who is revered even today. A proof of this revered belief is the story that tells us that the mirrors in her palace at Sardhana were smashed and taken away by people as they believed that looking into them could cure goiter. There is no doubt that her valor and persona have etched her name in the pages of history.

Part V

Begum Hazrat Mahal

37

Mahak Pari

Mirza Wajid Ali, the Prince of Awadh, sat on his *masnad* cross-legged, contemplating his new play that he would enact with the *paris* (fairies/beauties) of his *harem*. He had established a Parikhana in his palace, so fond he was of youthful damsels. He did not know how many *paris* he had; they numbered more than a hundred for sure, and when he would become the Nawab, their number would rise to over three hundred.

To make his time pleasant with them, he wrote, sang, acted, and danced. He was in fact a skilled dancer, a pupil of Maharaj Thakur Prasad, a renowned *ustad* (teacher). For the past few days, he was mentally stagnated, finding himself unable to shape his thoughts into songs and plays. This had happened to him earlier as well, and he could overcome this impediment through new inspiration, which was always in the form of new damsels.

His lusterless eyes were a sign that he urgently needed inspiration, and his wish was immediately fulfilled. An attendant

briskly walked in and saluted, bowing low with shining eyes, "*Huzoor*, Amman and Imaman are here."

The prince knew what it meant. His eyes lit up with sheer happiness, and he waved his hand in assent with his gaze fixed on the entrance.

The attendant soon returned with two courtesans. It was not the first time that Amman and Imaman were before him. On several occasions, they had supplied him with girls, many of whom now adorned his *harem*.

"Of late, you have been asking for a high price," said the prince.

"This time we have a pure pearl, *huzoor*! More glorious than you have seen ever before," said Amman.

"How much?" asked the prince eagerly.

"Let us present her in your attendance, *huzoor*, and then we'll leave to you how much we deserve for your service," said Imaman with a sharp smile on her face. She clapped, and with this, an adolescent girl stepped into the chamber.

She had a pretty oval face, adorned with a sharp nose, sleek lips, and dense hair parted in the middle; her big, bright black eyes casting a magical spell. He could hold himself no longer. He almost pounced to his feet, as if he had been waiting for this moment for a long time. Rushing, he took her in his embrace, fearing she would vanish into thin air if he were late, even by fraction of a second.

He did not realize for how long he was in this spell. When he came back to his senses, a broad smile emerged on his face. Without releasing her from the embrace, he moved to the masnad, sat down with the girl beside him, and said, "*Takhliya*! (Leave!)"

"*Huzoor* . . ." Amman wanted to say something, but the prince interrupted her, "I said go. Come tomorrow after having thought through what you want for her. That will be granted."

As the two bowed low to salute, Imaman said, "*Huzoor*, her name is . . ."

"She's sprinkled her fragrance all around here, so I name her Mahak Pari, right?"

With this, a new girl entered the harem, but she was not destined to be an ordinary Pari; she would carve out a golden page in history for herself.

This incident took place when a large section of the populace was facing extreme penury because of careless Nawabs, atrocious British officials, and a volatile political situation. In these precarious times, there was no dearth of poor parents who would sell out their little daughters to courtesans or brothels, wishing that they could one day find a wealthy patron and lead a luxurious life. All such girls were not as fortunate as Mahak Pari. Having the prince as her patron and husband was like hitting the gold mine, for most of such girls landed in cheap brothels and lived a terrible life as their beauty eluded them.

It is not known whether Mahak Pari was sold or kidnapped from a poor household. She came into the possession of these two courtesans, who invested their time and energy to mold her into a courtesan. Charm and training, coupled with innate traits, bloomed her in such a way that the prince was lost in her beauty for a long time. Soon, she became the mother of his son, which only elevated her status. She was now married to the prince, and rose from Pari to Begum. Her father-in-law and Nawab of Awadh, Amjad Ali Shah, was so happy with this that he named her Iftkhar-ul-Nissa Begum. In 1846, Wajid Ali Shah, an accomplished poet, wrote a song for this occasion. It goes as follows:

Bahut is Pari ka rutba badha
Ki paya khitab Iftkhar-ul-Nissa.

(The status of this Pari was greatly enhanced
That she was granted the title of Iftkhar-ul-Nissa.)

The son was named Ramzan Ali as he was born in the month of Ramzan, but his grandfather called him Mirza Birjis Qadr Bahadur. It was this latter name that he came to be known by. Birjis Qadr was not the only son of Wajid Ali Shah; he had three more sons from other Begums, but it was Ramzan who brought him good luck, or so it seemed.

The heir apparent to the throne was Prince Mirza Mustafa Ali Khan, who was in the bad books of the East India Company, and so Amjad Ali Shah was forced to declare Wajid Ali Shah as the heir apparent. The discarded prince Mustafa never wore a head-dress in protest, but no one paid any heed to him.

Wajid Ali Shah ascended the *masnad* upon the death of his father in 1847. It also enhanced the status of Iftkhar-ul-Nissa. She was now given the title of Hazrat Mahal, and it is by this name she is better known in history.

38

The Nawabs of Awadh

Awadh was the largest province when the Mughal dynasty was on the decline after the death of Aurangzeb in 1707. Its borders extended from the Ganga in the north to the Tapti in the south, and from Azimabad in the east to Shahabad in the west, covering an area of approx. 42,923 square miles. This fertile and rich province was divided into 12 major districts, with the capital at Faizabad. Its agricultural economy was enriched by 35,264 villages, of which 11,762 were under the direct rule of the Nawab, while the others were under *taluqdars* (landed nobles) and zamindars (landlords). Together, they were the sources of high revenues, making the province wealthy, which became an eyesore for the powers that had set their greedy eyes on Awadh.

As the central power weakened, several local chiefs raised their heads in revolt, and the province of Awadh was no exception. In lieu of this, in 1722, Saadat Khan, a Persian nobleman, was sent as the governor, called Nawab or assistant, to quell the uprisings, and he was successful in establishing peace. This Shiite Nawab

also worked to inculcate communal harmony between Shiite and Sunni factions of Muslims, and between Hindus and Muslims, laying a foundation of harmony for the province. Upon his death in 1739, his nephew, Safdar Jung became the governor, who continued with his uncle's policies, though he witnessed violent disturbances during his rule, which brought spectacular vicissitudes. Shuja-ud-Daula became the next governor in 1754 and continued with the same policies. These three governors allowed the traditional system of local self-government to continue in towns and villages as long as they deposited the revenue and abided by their edicts. Moreover, they worked for people's welfare, which made them popular.

The latter half of the eighteenth century witnessed volatile developments, especially after the British East India Company overtook Bengal following the Battle of Plassey in 1757. This created turbulence across India as the Marathas started expanding their territories and extending their influence to northern India. However, they could not withstand the invasion by Ahmed Shah Abdali and suffered a massive defeat at the second battle of Panipat in 1761. It was a massive shock for the Mughal Empire too.

This made the British all the more ambitious, as they saw this as their chance to expand their territories, leading to the Battle of Buxar in 1764, in which the combined forces of Awadh, Bengal, and the Mughal ruler were truncated. This brought Awadh under the atrocious and vicious influence of the British. On August 16, 1765, Shuja-ud-Daula buckled under pressure to enter the Allahabad treaty, as per which he had to pay 50 lakh rupees and hand over two districts to the British. The revenue of these two districts was assigned to the Mughal ruler in lieu of obtaining the right of Diwani to Bengal, Bihar, and Orissa. In addition, they obtained concessional trade rights in Awadh and forced it to garrison the British army at its expense.

Shuja-ud-Daula could not overcome this evil British influence. When he died in 1775, Asaf-ud-Daula became the next Nawab. It was he who shifted the capital from Faizabad to Lucknow. His suffering only worsened when the seat of Governor General was occupied by Warren Hastings. He first forced the new Nawab into another treaty, by which he snatched away the regions of Banaras, Ghazipur, and Jaunpur, among others, and also pressurized him to increase the army garrison at his expense. Apart from this, crossing all ethical limits, he even divested the Begums of their money, jewellery, clothing, and other assets. All this while, the Nawab undertook construction work to bring some relief to the unemployed masses.

This continued until his death in 1797, and after this, Wazir Ali ascended the throne only for four months, followed by Saadat Ali Khan, who remained the Nawab until 1814. It was he who ceded Rohilkhand, Doab, and Gorakhpur to the British and gave them the right to hold Durbar even against himself. The other Nawabs included Ghazi-ud-din Haider (1814–1819), Nasir-ud-din Haider (1819–1827), Muhammad Ali Shah (1837–1842), Amjad Ali Shah (1842–1847), and then came to the *masnad* Wajid Ali Shah, whose one wife was Hazrat Mahal. These nawabs surely contributed to Awadh's cultural enrichment, but lacked the qualities demanded of a ruler.

None of these Nawabs were able to take up the imperial challenge against the British. The British, on the other hand, availed every opportunity to harass and plunder wealth and rights. In return, they gave mere promises or played stratagems that the Nawabs failed to understand. These Nawabs were rulers only in name; the actual power now vested with the Company Bahadur. The British played them like fiddles, manipulating them to give into every pressure and tactic. For example, when the British declared Ghazi-ud-din the sovereign, he did not realize that it would only bring him into conflict with the Mughal ruler without gaining

anything. He, too, was happy to receive the title 'King' which, in effect, was meaningless as it did not go with privileges and rights, as the British resident came to have powers equal with him. Powerless and with little to do, the Nawabs were now more inclined towards debauchery. For instance, Nasir-ud-din spent most of his time in woman quarters and even dressed like a woman. While many of these Nawabs built magnificent buildings, they failed to organize the administration, while the British hold on Awadh turned into a vicious clutch from which there was little hope for deliverance.

The British faced little resistance from the Nawabs against their injudicious policies and unreasonable demands. This only encouraged them further, and without a care about what impact their covetous policies would bear on the common populace; they were like the greedy leeches that wanted to suck all the blood from the host.

When the young Wajid Ali Shah came to the masnad, he made a bid to take an interest in setting the affairs of the state right. Though he was divested of his power even to appoint or dismiss even a lowly servant without prior permission of the British Resident, he thought of ways to help his subjects, and Begum Hazrat Mahal seemed to be the driving force behind this thinking. He first took steps in the administration of justice and placed petition boxes in public pathways in which common people could drop in their grievances, and he dealt with these petitions in open durbar. He also undertook public works. For instance, it was he who constructed the road between Lucknow and Kanpur and ordered the metaling of the road from Lucknow to Faizabad. He even allotted funds for the maintenance of hospitals, and in the initial months, he even inspected his troops and oversaw their training at Husseinabad. Sadly, this did not last long.

The British threatened the new Nawab with dire consequences, and he was asked to remain limited to his passion for music and

dance. It is also rumored, as Amrit Lal Nagar claims in his book, that he was given some medicine to be overly occupied within the *zenankhana*.

With this, the civil administration broke down completely. While Wajid Ali Shah spent all his time writing poetry, singing thumri, and enacting dance-dramas, common people in the state were suffering in numerous ways. The Nawab has been projected as a great patron of fine arts, but let us not forget that he was not courageous enough to do what a ruler was supposed to do, i.e., he utterly failed in his duty to the masses. The Nawab was aware of the problems his subjects were facing, yet he had nothing but excuses to offer. He would say that he wanted to appoint more men, but he was powerless as he could not do it without the Governor General's permission.

The number of dancers and singers rose in his harem, and the relatives of all these ladies grew powerful. They divided the city into sectors among themselves to demand ransom from traders, shopkeepers, and other people. The powerful landlords and nobles snatched away the wealth from the weaker ones, just as the big fish swallows the smaller ones. The situation was so drastic that even the nawab's minister could be pulled out from his coach and robbed in the street. There was no security of life or property. Dignity was at stake, as handsome boys and pretty girls were the worst victims. The city that welcomes visitors with the tagline 'Smile because you are in Lucknow' was a hapless victim to the whims of all those who wielded some power.

39

The Serpentine Hairy Braid

As Wajid Ali Shah was fully occupied with debauchery, even in the name of exalted fine arts of poetry and dance, the presence of about three hundred begums and paris in his zenankhana did not suffice, and he desired more.

One day, on a visit to the Mother Queen, he happened to see a young attendant with lovely expressions, further intensified by the dimples on her cheeks. His insatiable desire for lust turned into a tempest in no time. Forgetting what he had come for, he requested, "I want her in my harem."

"No, there is a limit to everything. You've fully turned away from the administration, and you're doing nothing for the people," retorted the mother.

"I cannot live without her," said the Nawab, but his mother was not impressed.

He wanted to have her anyhow. When his request persisted over several days, his mother said, "She has an ominous feature

that can exacerbate your troubles—a serpentine, hairy braid on her back."

"Does that bring bad luck?"

"Yes, for sure," the mother quipped.

Listening to this, the Nawab sank deep into thought and grew anxious that there could be others in his harem with such a braid, causing his misfortunes. He returned to his palace immediately and ordered the chief eunuch, named Bashir-ud-Daula, to examine all the ladies, other than the chief Begum, for the sinister mark.

Bashir-ud-Daula saw in this command a golden opportunity to mint money. The wily eunuch knew who all could pay handsomely, and he pointed them out as the ones who had the braid. Now, none of the ladies wanted to be a blot on the Nawab's fortunes, so they entreated and pleaded not to be named on the unlucky list. With this, the eunuch's pockets grew deeper and fatter. He had gathered a fortune for himself, yet he knew he could not seek bribes from those who actually had the ominous feature on their backs. He included them in the list and handed them over to the Nawab. One of them was none other than Hazrat Mahal. All of them heard the words, "Talaq, Talaq, Talaq." To divorce a wife—eight wives—was as simple as that.

They were all ousted from the Kaisarbagh Palace but were given a place to stay in the Chaulakhi Kothi, which was a favor to them as they had not otherwise done anything against the Nawab.

The Nawab never wished to part company with any of his wives. He was disappointed but helpless. He missed Hazrat Mahal specifically, as he enjoyed her company the most. He liked her for her practical proposals on different aspects of life, including the kingdom and its administration.

The Begums who had bribed were afraid that the eunuch would exploit them further. They also realized that the Nawab found separation from Hazrat Mahal somewhat difficult. Therefore,

together, they planned and convinced him that the Hindu priests could profess remedies to do away with the evil effect of the ominous feature. And this was precisely what the Nawab wanted.

The Hindu priests were quickly summoned, and after consulting the texts and calculating the effect of stars, they proclaimed that the evil effects of the braid would be eliminated by offering a gold snake to fire.

This was promptly done, and satisfied with this, the Nawab himself invited the eight expelled begums to return to Kaisarbagh Palace. To his dismay, only two of them consented; the others, including Hazrat Mahal, declined the offer. She felt hurt after the whole predicament and continued to stay in Chaulakhi Kothi with her young son. The gentle Nawab respected her decision, and instead of forcing her to return, he would visit her himself every now and then.

The Nawab's eccentricities did not stop here. Once, he ordered all his employees to join in a three-day-long celebration in saffron-colored clothes, only to see how they looked together.

While the Nawab was busy with his amorous celebrations, composing poetry, and singing thumri, the entire Awadh was facing an acute breakdown of law and order. People were seething in anger and dissatisfaction, and with new developments taking place at a rapid rate, they were destined to see more difficult times not too distant in the future.

40

The Crown Is Lost

It was 11th of February in 1856. It was the day that would write a long tale encompassing victory, defeat, struggle, suffering, plunder, atrocity, sacrifice, torment, agony, courage, strategy, and tactic, entailing a vital lesson in history.

"What!" roared Nawab Wajid Ali Shah, springing up on his feet in his royal court. He began with a thunderous roar, but before the last syllable escaped his mouth, the ferocity melted away into a feeble scream, akin to the bewildered, frightened mewl of a defeated cat. Struggling to regain his composure, he wiped the winter sweat from his forehead with a trembling hand, then turned to Colonel Outram, the Resident, his voice tinged with disbelief. "Are you sure?" he managed to utter, his words hanging in the cold air.

"Yes, *Huzoor*," said Outram tauntingly, else he would normally address the Nawab with 'Your Excellency', "If you have any doubts, I can read it again." With this, he waved the letter up and down to ensure that everybody present could see it clearly.

The Nawab was unable to think of how to respond. Then he remembered the Treaty of 1837. "You can't do it to me, we have a treaty that you can't divest me of my sovereignty, though you have all the power to take over the administration."

"Forget about that treaty. It has no value for us," said Colonel Outram.

The Nawab was young and wanted to enjoy his life to the fullest. He had been doing so ever since he was an adolescent, and his amorous ways had only expanded ever since he ascended the throne. He had taken things for granted yet had not anticipated this massive shock, despite many indications from the British sources.

India was reeling under the autocratic pressure of Lord Dalhousie, who had become the Governor General on January 12, 1848. In the name of modernizing the country, he was using all authoritative tools, both legal and illegal, he could conceive. The Doctrine of Lapse was his brainchild, by which he had annexed a number of Indian native states on the pretext that their rulers did not have a natural heir. He first annexed the princely states of Satara in 1848, then Jaitpur and Sambalpur in 1849, followed by Jhansi and Nagpur in 1853. He also wanted to annex Karauli in 1849, but it was not approved. He had also annexed Baghat and Udaipur in 1851 and 1853, respectively, only to be restored to the native rulers. It may be pertinent to note that it was he who had annexed parts of Burma and had also seized the famous diamond Koh-i-noor from the twelve-year-old monarch, Duleep Singh of the Punjab.

While his policies were bringing the Indian psyche to a boil, Dalhousie now intently fixed his greedy gaze on Awadh, a large and prosperous state. It was his letter that was being read to the Nawab by Outram. It clearly stated that the state of Awadh now stood annexed to the Company and that he was being pensioned off. He had been laying the foundation of this decision ever since

he assumed the high post. He had appointed Colonel Sleeman as Resident to the Awadh Court in 1849 and asked him to write a detailed report focusing on the plight of people under the Nawab. In his report, published as *A Journey through the Kingdom of Oude*, in two volumes, he had written a voluminous account of how people suffered in Awadh. However, his prejudice is evident in his writing and it is clear that many of these woes were the result of British policies, and in many cases, the British troops were the robbers. G.W. Forrest notes in his book, "Thus the natural tendency of the introduction of an alien rule to embitter the feelings of the influential classes was increased by indiscreet and unwise measures."

Dalhousie was under pressure from the Board of Directors of the East India Company (EIC) to annex Awadh, so he wanted Sleeman to submit the recommendation with that 'spirit'. Sleeman, however, did not abide by his wish, and was of the opinion that the removal of the Nawab could result in an uprising of the common people, and even the native sepoys could join and lead them. Notwithstanding this, he had been reporting the Nawab in unfavorable colors. In one report from 1848, he wrote: "This systematic disregard of high duties and responsibilities still continues to be manifested by the King of Oude; and is observed, with feelings of indignation and abhorrence, by his well-disposed subjects of all classes and grades, who are thereby left to the mercy of men without any feeling of security in their tenure of office, any scruples of conscience, or feelings of humanity or of honor." This is only the tip of the iceberg of his writings about the Nawab's misgovernance. In his book, he states that the Nawab enjoyed great respect among the common masses, yet he paradoxically concludes that the change (into British rule) would be popular among people, including members of the royal family, the mercantile and manufacturing classes, and other common folks.

Meanwhile, Dalhousie was growing restless as he wanted to accomplish his objective quickly, so he replaced Sleeman with Outram. Initially, he too was not in favor of dislodging the Nawab but buckled under pressure. Consequently, he was now reading out the annexation letter to the Nawab.

When the Doctrine of Lapse was brought into existence, the Nawab was confident that at least he would not suffer on account of it, as he had four sons, the youngest being groomed under the careful watch of his favorite wife, Hazrat Mahal. He never knew that his kingdom could be appropriated on the flimsy ground of misgovernance, for which the British themselves were responsible.

It was through this letter that Outram materialized Dalhousie's ardent desire, which had also been the dream of many of his predecessors. The Nawab recalled his father and other elders, who narrated their woeful experiences of what their forefathers had suffered at the hands of the governors general but were lucky enough to somehow save the kingdom through giving some concessions, though they realized that the British hold on them was growing tauter.

Even after their victory over the combined forces of Bengal, Awadh, and Mughal emperor in 1764, the British continued to respect Awadh's independence as they saw it as a buffer state between themselves and the Marathas. When the Mughal ruler Shah Alam II put himself under the Maratha tutelage in 1770–71, the British garrisoned the Company's troops in Awadh for its protection, of course, at its expense. This brought Awadh into conflict with the Ruhellas, but the Company's forces joined him in annexing Rohilkhand to Awadh. Warren Hastings was the Governor General at this time. He was criticized for this act back home as he had unjustly put an independent state under another and, through this, opened a way for the Company to bring more and more territories under its control under one or the other pretext.

Hastings's conduct exceeded all limits when Asaf-ud-Daula became the Nawab in 1775! This time, his victims were the Begums, who resided in Faizabad and had some *jagirs* to their names. Hastings fleeced them of money from time to time and also compelled the new Nawab to seize their jagirs. This act was so atrocious that even the British called it 'an ignoble kind of undertaking'. When pressed by the Court of Directors to provide some relief to Awadh, he only increased the burden on the Begums and the Nawab in its name. He was sucking finances from Awadh to the extent that the Nawab was left with no money to put the administration back on track and save it from falling into disarray.

The Nawab earnestly hoped that he would be able to get some respite from the Company's financial burdens to find some ways to set the administration right during the tenures of the next governors general—Cornwallis (1786–93) and Shore (1793–98), but that was not about to happen. His petitions fell on deaf ears; on the contrary, more burdens were inflicted on Awadh.

The British greed was not yet quenched, they wanted the whole of Awadh for themselves, and this happened during the tenure of Wellesley (1798–1805). He wanted to accomplish this within the first year of his tenure, but the plan had to be postponed and revised in view of a sudden revolt of Wazir Ali in Benaras in early 1799. The British were somehow able to suppress this revolt, which had all the attributes of spreading across Bengal and Bihar; even the Shah of Kabul was invited for the invasion.

Wellesley's exploitation of the Nawab became so severe that he decided to abdicate, but when his sons were excluded from the throne, he withdrew his intention. This infuriated Wellesley, and he increased the burden on Awadh in numerous ways. Not only this, he, in 1801, ordered the occupation of Rohilkhand and Doab, which were the most fertile tracts and constituted more than one-half of the state's area. With this, the Company's

territories surrounded the remaining Awadh on all sides but the north. While this step was being criticized by his own peers, Wellesley was thinking of more ways to exploit the native states. His policies later laid the groundwork for Dalhousie's annexation of several states, including Awadh, on the pretext of 'the good of the governed', as the powerless rulers were made responsible for the failure of the administration. Thus, it was an unethical and unjust method by which the native rulers were accused of everything evil.

The British felt no shame when it came to not keeping their word. In 1837, Lord Auckland had entered into an agreement with the Nawab (Muhammad Ali Shah) that, in case the administrative reforms were not introduced, the Company could take over the administration while sovereignty would remain with him. Sleeman writes that this treaty was got finalized by putting the Nawab under duress as upon the death of his predecessor, he was not being allowed to sit on the throne. This treaty had also created much controversy in England.

And now, in 1856, Wajid Ali Shah was being forced to be pensioned off. He contended that the Treaty of 1837 was in force. To his dismay, he was informed that it was merely 'a dead letter'. This annexation essentially meant that the British could unleash any injustice on the rulers and people of India in the name of mere superficial ideas, only to tighten their clutches around their necks to meet their selfish ends.

As Outram marched out of the court, the Nawab felt dizzy and sank down on the masnad with his face hidden in his trembling hands and it was the last time that he had sat on the royal seat. He was being ousted on fictitious, frivolous grounds. The Nawab could not do anything but curse Outram. Only Heaven knows whether it was the impact of this curse that Outram fell sick so seriously that he had to sail back to England just two months later. He would, of

course, come back to play his part in the uprising that was about to unfold.

Charges of two types were alleged against the Nawab—personal and administrative. Outram described how the king remained in his harem day and night and lived merely for debauchery. Prior to him, Sleeman said that there did not exist a government in Awadh anymore, and the Nawab did not meet anyone but singers and dancers. The truth is that misgovernance had arisen more out of British interference in the administration, as the Nawab had all the responsibilities without any power.

Any conversation about Wajid Ali Shah would be incomplete without talking about his personal qualities. He was more of a simpleton, without any trace of wiliness, nor did he take part in any confrontation with anyone, including his family, nobles, or subjects. He was docile to a great extent, harboring cowardliness. He had all the 'soft' qualities that made him a good artist. The credit for evolving thumri goes to him. He was a good poet and writer, the proof of which we find in numerous books he wrote, many of which are available even today. The British have described him as 'almost always drunk, an insomniac who drove out at night with naked girls', yet such charges have been disputed as he is described as a teetotaler. The charge that he was surrounded by women all the time is correct, with the difference that he married a girl he liked with her consent rather than using force to get her. He had established the *Parikhana*, an establishment with numerous paris or damsels who were there for his entertainment, and if he happened to love one, he would marry her (under the tradition of *Mutah,* or temporary marriage) and raise her to the status of his Begum.

It is an important fact that all his Begums enjoyed an equal status. In those times, having a zenana was nothing extraordinary, even several British officials had one, who admitted *bibis* (native women) into the zenanas and expelled them from their harems at

their sweet will. He is said to be respectful to all the ladies, as he addressed even the servants with respectful terms. For instance, he addressed the broom-woman as Musfa Begum (a woman who keeps cleanliness) and the water-woman as Abarsan Begum (the source of water).

The Nawab gave in to the British atrocities without any protest, he only meekly said, as the newspaper *Kohinoor* reported on February 18, 1856, that the Nawab was willing to surrender his cannons of all types without raising a voice, only if he was allowed to retain the crown. How anguished the people were is described in the same paper the following week. One landlord went to the extent of sending a 'female dress' with the message that it looked befitting on him (Nawab). It is also reported that the force at Kanpur was asked to stand by while the local troops quelled the protesting people in several districts across Awadh. The local rulers, called *rajah*, and landed nobles, called taluqdars, across several districts were in league with the protestors. It was also reported that the king of Nepal was willing to help the Nawab. Such messages kept coming. Reports were also filtering that the native sepoys were ready to rise. This further validates the narrative that the Nawab was not like what the British were projecting him to be; he was popular with people. At some places, the Company troops had to even use force.

Pitiably, the Nawab himself laid down arms . . . nay, did not pick up arms at all! Had he confronted the unjust command, Dalhousie could have been compelled to take back his orders. But that was not to be!

Despite the cowering Nawab, people found means to protest. Many Hindus did not celebrate their festivals for a year. The hearth did not see light in several households across Awadh on this fateful day. The Nawab composed this poem to depict people's resistance:

Aa ke paas jo kahta tha koi iska yaar,
Na kiya abke baras aapne koi tyohar.
To wah kahta tha kisase kahen kis gam mein hain,
Apni Sarkar mit jaane ke maatam mein hain.

(When a friend came to intimate,
You did not celebrate any festival this year.
He then said whom to tell what sorrow inflicts him,
He is in mourning over the loss of his government.)

A contemporary Urdu poet, Hajju Sharaf describes the scene and resultant unemployment in these words:

Hua Shahar mein gul sawari chali,
Gulasta se bade bahari chali.
Jo darmanda the ranj unko rahe,
Hazaron ki aankhon se aansu bahe.
Madad kijiye Lucknow lut gaya,
Khabar lijiye Lucknow lut gaya.
Tabahi ko aabaadi hai napasand
Ghulamon ka Hazrat ke hai rizq band.

(A roar travelled across the town as the vehicle drives,
A spring wind started from the orchard.
The victims were anguished,
Thousands shed tears.
Help that Lucknow is plundered,
Be warned that Lucknow is plundered.
Destruction dislikes population (prosperity),
Employments of the Nawab's slaves have ceased.)

41

The Begum's Resolve

Nawab Wajid Ali Shah returned from the court and entered Begum Hazrat Mahal's chamber with a lusterless face. She had been residing in Chaulakhi Kothi ever since the whacky serpentine episode. As soon as she learned of the annexation, she returned to the palace. She knew the Nawab needed her more than anyone else right now. He loved her attitude toward life and any situation; he had asked her to return to Kaisarbagh Palace earlier, but she had declined. Now finding her husband in trouble, she returned on her own accord, proving her unwavering loyalty and love.

Seeing the Nawab's piteous face, she was afraid that he would break down miserably. Bowing down to salute him, she said, "Destiny tests everyone, and now it's your turn."

Sitting lifelessly on the couch, the desperate Nawab said, "I've lost everything. You know it's beyond my capacity. The British are very powerful. I can't see my people being massacred, can I?" He looked to her hoping that she would concur with him, however, the Begum disappointed him.

She pulled out her royal seal from her waist, walked near the Nawab, and said, "Look at this insignia. Interspersed among the exalted, noble words, you can see swords and daggers. This simply means that we believe in harmony yet will never hesitate to take up the sword if oppressed."

"I understand your sentiments, but you know I have never wielded a sword."

"You don't have to fight yourself, there are thousands who will sacrifice their lives for you. You just need to stand up," said the Begum in a resolute voice.

"I'm sorry, I can't do that," said the Nawab as his complexion faded further. A touch of offense crept into his voice as he continued, attempting to salvage his dignity. "I mean there are other ways to explore. This can well be done even peacefully."

The Begum remained silent, seated in the distance on a chair. Without uttering a single word, her gaze spoke volumes, conveying a silent message, 'You may be timid, but I am not.'

The Nawab continued, "I've faith in the British sense of justice. I ought to plead with them; they'll surely listen to me."

"Do you still think they'll listen to you? All the misery our people are facing is due to them. They have taken away all our powers, yet we are sitting like stooges," said the Begum a bit impatiently.

The Nawab pondered over the situation for some time, and then he said, "I think I must go to England and appeal to the Parliament and Queen Victoria against this injustice. What do you say?"

"The voyage to England is long and treacherous, and your health is not very sound. Moreover, justice is elusive with these wily people. They'll humiliate you and insult you. I won't advise you to go there yourself. I firmly believe you ought to be here and lead people."

The Nawab was unable to decide anything for sure. He had approached her, thinking that she would concur with him. He had no heart to confront the British. He was a great poet, but his demeanor now revealed how faint-hearted he was. He felt himself disgraced before the pretty Begum; he stood up and walked out to his chamber with unstable steps, while she looked at him intently.

On March 13, 1856, the Nawab left Lucknow for Calcutta in the company of his mother, the eldest Begum Khas Mahal, his brother, and two (second and third) sons, in addition to his attendants and Paris. He left behind Begum Hazrat Mahal, his youngest son, Birjis Qadr, and the remaining Begums. His eldest son, mentally deranged, stayed back as well.

As the Nawab appeared at the large door of the main building to take a seat in the palanquin, he could see a crowd at the main gate. He kept looking down; he lacked courage to look into their eyes, let alone face them. He had nothing to offer them; he had no heart to inspire them, soothe them, or stand by them in misery. Before he bowed to enter the palanquin, he waved to people. He could not even look at them from behind the thin screen.

Soon, his train marched off. He did not want to offend the British, who were otherwise generous enough to give him a pension of 12 lakh rupees. He did not want to lose that princely sum, with which he could continue to feel himself in the sublime, imaginary, fanciful world of poetry and drama, which had little to do with the hard realities of life or his subjects' misery. For his beloved Awadh, he composed a thumri on his way to Calcutta; this was all he could do. This song is, of course, popular even today. It depicts that he was fancying himself as a bride who was taking leave of her father to go to her beloved's place. Its opening five lines are:

Babul mora naihar chhuto hi jaye.
Char kahaar mil mori doliya uthayen.

Mora apna begana chhuto jaye.
Angana to parbat bhayo aur dehri bhayi bides.
Jaye babul ghar aapno main chali piya ke des.

(O Father, I'm forced to leave your home.
Four bearers carry away my palanquin.
I am forced to abandon those of mine and others.
The courtyard is like a hill and the threshold, an alien land.
I take your leave to head to my beloved's place.)

Begum Hazrat Mahal stood at the gate, looking at the departing train without even waving goodbye. Her one hand rested on Birjis Qadr's shoulder and pressed it when the party disappeared at the next turn outside the gate. It was only now that she raised her hand to wave to people with an erect head. She was trying to indicate to people that all was not yet lost.

Her fourteen-year-old son found her conduct strange as he looked at her with several questions in his eyes. He was an intelligent boy in whose qualities even Wajid Ali Shah expressed confidence.

The Begum mildly smiled and said to him, "When you bow down to injustice, you're sure to get more of it. The responsibility now falls on your shoulders, prince."

The other Begums looked at her in amazement, and one of them asked, "What do you intend to do?"

Begum Hazrat Mahal's eyes shone with resolve while the slender smile now extended to her cheeks, "Time will tell."

The Nawab had disappointed her; she will now have to take up the reins in her own hands. As she turned away to go to her chamber, she could hear one of the ladies hum the song that the Nawab had composed recently to describe his distress at abandoning Awadh:

Saare ab shahar se hota hai yah Akhtar rukhsat.
Aage bas ab nahin kahne ki hai mujhko fursat.
Ho na barbad mere mulk ki ya Rab khilkat.
Dar-o-diwar pe Hasrat se nazar karte hain.
Rukhsat-e ahle Watan ham to safar karte hain.

(Akhtar [Wajid Ali Shah's *non de plume*] now takes leave from the whole of town.

I'm left with little time to say a thing.

O Lord, the subjects of my country may not be ruined.

I look at the door and walls in hope.

Depart I, O countrymen, I set out on my journey.)

She was disappointed, but some of her faith in her exiled husband was restored when she received reports that, on his way to Kolkata, Wajid Ali Shah met revolutionaries in Kanpur and Patna. KK Dutta has quoted Subedar Hidayat Ali of the Native Sikh Infantry, who has written that "on the 24th March [1856], when the Nawab of Lucknow also arrived there, *en route* to Calcutta . . . The chief persons of the city, the *Vakeel* of the Raja of Bithur and the Officers and Sepoys from the regiments stationed there, used to pay visits to the *Vakeels* and servants of the Nawab." Similarly, he met Muslim leaders in Patna when he stopped there overnight. W. Tayler, Commissioner of Patna, has written: "It was previously within my knowledge that when the King of Oude passed through Patna, Mahdee Ali, the *Cotegusht* or patrol Daroga of this city who is a man of superior knowledge and attainments, resident of Lucknow, had been frequently admitted into the royal presence and was treated with the greatest consideration." The Nawab was also reported to be in touch with the revolutionary leaders during his sojourn in Calcutta, which is one of the reasons why he was detained when the uprising broke out. The Begum's resolve to rise in rebellion was now all the stronger.

42

Awadh Uprising

The native sepoys rose in revolution at Meerut on May 10, 1857. Walking all night, they reached Delhi and occupied it. The British tried their best to keep this news under wraps. If they informed their officers in Lucknow of the Meerut occurrence on the 13th, it was only to warn them of something likely occurring there too. The news of the happenings in Delhi reached there on the 14th. Despite their efforts, the news somehow filtered out, first among the sepoys and then among the civil populace. With this, tension mounted in Awadh.

Some signs of unrest had emerged even earlier in response to the Nawab's expulsion, like on April 18, when some people threw a ball of mud on the chief commissioner's convoy. The native sepoys confronting the white ones had become a common occurrence. The caste or faith was no longer a barrier among people and native sepoys, and its signs were becoming more manifest over time. Posters were also being put on the streets to incite people to rise. Challenges for the British were numerous and varied now.

With the arrival of the news, plans were being made; rumors spread far and wide, and somehow, it was a talk of the town in Lucknow that the revolution would occur at 9 p.m. on May 30. The British knew from their experience at Meerut what overlooking these rumors could mean. A perceptible change was visible in people's demeanor. The spies were out, but the source of all these rumors remained a mystery.

However, the British could not take these rumors lightly. Sir Henry Lawrence was appointed the chief commissioner of Awadh on March 20, 1857. He would soon be facing the initial heat of the uprising. Interestingly, as noted by Lt Gen McLeod Innes in his book, *Lucknow and Oudh in the Mutiny*, Lawrence had thirteen years ago forecasted that in case Delhi fell into hostile hands, the number of rebels would swell from hundreds to thousands in a day's time, and in a week, every ploughshare would be cast into a sword. The forecast could come true, and the signs for this were here, there, and everywhere.

Lawrence sat down with his officers and came to the conclusion that the nerve center of Awadh was Lucknow, so there was a need to strengthen its defenses. There was every chance that the city would rise if the sepoys mutinied. The discontent among the native sepoys was ripe, as it appeared from Lawrence's letters to Lord Canning. On April 18, he wrote that a clod (of mud) was thrown at him. He also wrote that the men of the 48th Regiment seldom, or never, saluted an officer not of their own corps and recommended that it should be moved out of Awadh to another province. In response, the Governor General wrote that "the 48th Regiment, or any other which you wish to get rid of, may be moved to Meerut." Lawrence had also received letters from junior officers; one of these said, "If the Sepoy is not speedily redressed, he will redress himself." They were aware that there were scores

of grievances of all kinds—social, economic, political, and most importantly, religious.

On May 4, 1857, Lawrence wrote to the Governor General: "... that on the 2nd instant, the 7th Oudh Regiment, stationed seven miles from the Lucknow Cantonments, refused to bite the cartridge when ordered by its own officers, and again by the Brigadier." This letter further informs us that the regiment rose in revolt but quietened when confronted with force, and a decision could be taken to disband it.

Lawrence, seemingly scared, held an open durbar in which he addressed the native sepoys, officers, and nobles in their 'vulgar' dialect. His words, as quoted by GW Forrest, were: "Mussulman rulers at Delhi have prosecuted Hindoos, Hindoo rulers at Lahore have prosecuted the Mussulmans; but the British Government has ever extended equal toleration of all. The history of a hundred years should teach them the falsehood of those who would now deceive them with assertions that the Government entertained designs against their caste."

We can see that tension prevailed even before the news about the Meerut uprising reached there; however, things turned really grave for them after it. Lawrence weighed his options. At this time, there were about 8,000 troops garrisoned at Lucknow—both Europeans and Indians. The European troops numbered about 1,700 (32nd Regiment of Foot and auxiliary British artillery), including loyal sepoys; while the native troops, numbering about 5,000 men, belonged to six regiments. In addition, there was also a military police platoon of native men.

Lawrence was not ready to trust the native sepoys, the very troops who were instrumental in expanding the British empire across India. An atmosphere of suspicion was created. He immediately started strengthening the fortification of

Machchhi Bhavan and some other buildings around; however, he was doubtful if this arrangement could withstand the artillery onslaught. He reached the conclusion that the Residency would prove the ultimate bastion for them, from where the final battle would be fought.

Lawrence ordered to garrison the Residency, which contained the treasury, and other important public offices, as it, due to its several favorable features, could be used as a fort. Located in a commanding position, it was surrounded by a deep ditch, with an opening to the Gomti River from which reinforcements could be procured. It had abundant open space with several buildings to house people, with the provision of water. Also, there was plenty of open area to the front, and the buildings on the flanks could be destroyed to prevent any attack from there. Moreover, it comprised adequate structures where cannons could be mounted.

On May 16, 130 men of the 32nd Regiment and four guns were sent to the Residency to start preparation for its fortification. The European sick, women, and children too accompanied them. The rest of the regiment reached the Residency the following day. Extra precautions were taken as there were rumors that the party could be attacked on its way. The entire movement was carried out very quietly by night so as not to arouse any suspicion among common people. An eyewitness, Mrs Case, has given a detailed account of what all occurred there in her book, *A Journal of the Siege of Lucknow*. She says that the English ladies reached the garrison at 6 a.m. Supplies, rations, and ammunition were stored in abundant quantities, which could last months.

Lawrence's choice of the Residency was not an ideal one, as criticized by Field Marshal Lord Roberts, but it was certainly the best available option as it could be defended even with a small force while it could shelter a large number of Europeans and their families.

As the days passed, rumors of varying nature intensified. Fires, shoot-outs, and attacks were often reported but were found to be false; however, they kept the inmates on their toes. The frightened souls expected a calamity any minute. Mrs Case narrates that the ladies always kept a bundle ready by their bedsides in case they had to flee in an emergency. As the families poured in from surrounding towns too, the living spaces became overcrowded to some extent. Inconvenience coupled with tension only made them desperate.

Lawrence did not believe in defensive posture much; he loved action rather than routine garrison life. His peer, G.W. Forrest says about him: ". . . he longed impatiently for the period when the irksome routine of garrison duty should be exchanged for the substantial delights of war." While his men were busy fortifying, he was planning brief attacks and sallies aimed at capturing all those people who could provide leadership to people, and these included the Nawab's brother Mustafa Ali Khan, former Nawab Saadat Ali Khan's son Ruknuddaula, former Vizir Sharafuddaula, and Amjad Ali Shah, among several other royal family members and nobles. Raids were also conducted to imprison the local rulers, like that of Tulsipur. He also set up an open 'hanging place' in the marketplace, and one or the other 'rebel' was regularly found hanging there without even a summary trial. It was being done to envelop the city in terror; however, time would show that such tricks did not work for long.

Lawrence was granted absolute military powers on the 18th. The Governor General's telegram to him declared: "You have full military powers: the Governor General will support you in everything you think necessary."

As the days passed, the daily dose of alarms and reports flooded in. For example, on the 29th, as noted by GW Forrest, there were reports of the murder of a *tehsildar* on one hand and the

rising green standard on the other, while reports of disaffection in three irregular regiments also came in. Everything was reported as quiet. But was it so in reality?

Mrs Case writes in her book that she went to visit the cantonment with Mrs. Inglis (wife of Colonel Inglis) on the evening of the 30th They were returning to the Residency after dark set in. She writes: ". . . and towards dusk, we felt uncomfortable, especially as we passed the Iron Bridge, a place very much crowded. We fancied the people we saw looked fierce and sullen . . . I cannot express how thankful we felt when we drew up at the door of the Residency, and alighted in safety. It is really surprising that we did so, for the mutiny in cantonments broke out that very evening, showing how rebellious the prevailing spirit must have been."

It was May 30, 1857. There had been a number of warnings earlier, and Lawrence seemed to have grown accustomed to them. There was a warning of rebellion at 9 p.m. that day, but he chose to overlook it as he invited his staff officers for dinner at the Government House in the Cantonment. As it was custom then, a gun was fired to indicate that it was 9 p.m.

With it, Lawrence mocked his staff officer with a laugh, "Your friends are not punctual."

Scarcely had these words been uttered when the loud rattle of the musketry was heard. Before he could overcome his surprise, the attendant rushed in and informed him that the sepoys were attacking and putting the houses in the cantonment on fire. The bugle of revolution had finally been sounded in Awadh. The lead was taken by the 71st Native Regiment, which was soon joined by the sepoys belonging to the 13th and 48th regiments. A large number of civilians, too, joined the fray. Their focus was on doing away with the British officers, putting the buildings on fire, and erasing any signs of the British. Violence continued late into the night,

and then quietness prevailed. A number of burning buildings could be seen from a distance. But the Residency was not yet attacked. The ladies and children staying there came out of their rooms. Mrs Case writes: "The sight of the burning bungalows was awful, and we could do nothing but watch the flames with beating hearts, and listen tremblingly to the booming of the cannons." It was only the beginning. On the first day to fall, there was Brigadier Hanscombe, among several other British officers. With this, Lawrence shifted his headquarters to the Residency.

On 1st of June, the civilians broke out in rebellion in a large crowd numbering about 6,000. The British were trying their best to defend the cantonment. They sallied out in a good number and chased them away, but not before both sides ended up losing several lives. Intermittent eruptions kept occurring across Lucknow, and they continued over several days.

As the news of the uprising spread, the parganas, too, rose. Sepoys and civilians came together to put an end to the British rule in all four divisions of Awadh. In the division of Khairabad, the 71st Native Regiment rose on June 3 at Sitapur, and then they were joined by their comrades from the 13th and 48th regiments. The 7th native platoon did not fall behind either.

With this, people rose in other divisions too. The division of Mohammadi saw the uprising on June 5, followed by similar occurrences in the division of Behraich. Faizabad rose in several towns on the 7th. While they forced the British to flee from there, the greatest achievement for them was that they rescued the imprisoned Maulvi Ahmadulla Shah, who would play an important role in the uprising that had just started.

Towns after towns were slipping out of British control as the native regiments and platoons, in cooperation with the civilians, were forcing the British to recede and flee. The imperialists found

it hard to tackle the developing situation, so they vented their ire against Nawab Wajid Ali Shah, who was now staying at Metiabruz in Calcutta. They charged him with conspiracy in the rebellion and put him under arrest in a quarter far below his dignity. Not only this, he was treated very shabbily. The sorrowful poet in the Nawab penned down a long poem. Here are the opening six lines:

Koi aankh hamse milata nahin.
Nazar janwar tak bhi aata nahin.
Fir us par gazab chaar sandas hain.
Ki mujh diljale ke woh sab paas hain.
Tapas mahaj hoti hai barsaat ki.
Yah fars jo hoti hai har raat ki.

(No one looks at me.
Not even animals can be seen around.
Still amazing is that there are four latrines.
All of these are in my vicinity.
There is only heat from rain.
This is how I pass each night.)

All this while, Begum Hazrat Mahal was keeping herself informed of the developments not only in Lucknow but across the whole province. She was actively doing her work, i.e., sending out her spies, keeping Birjis Qadr near her all the time, and speaking to him in silent whispers, while other ladies looked at her with strange looks, wondering what she was up to. She was sending her messengers to the leaders with information that they ought to learn from Kanpur and besiege the British, but few paid heed to her for now.

The Begum knew that it was not going to be easy, but she detested the British and wanted to do everything that was in her

power to chase them out of the country. She started collecting supplies in the empty chambers of the building, including grains, firewood, and also arms. The taluqdars were helping her with guns and gunpowder. As the place was ill-equipped for this purpose, she had to employ maids to protect the grains from mice and thieves. All this went on under strict confidentiality.

43

A Forgotten Battle

During the course of their rule in India, several British people wrote books on contemporary history. They have, however, focused more on those occurrences or aspects that depict them as civilized, victorious, brave, and powerful, while completely overlooking and undermining all other instances that could dent their *ikbal* (prestige). It was with this view that they dismissed the uprising at Meerut as only a 'sepoy mutiny', and even undermined the battle of Chinhat, merely making a passive reference to it as if it bore no substantial consequence. Its significance can be gauged from the fact that it led to the siege of the Residency, which lasted over months and compelled the British to make extraordinary efforts for relief, in the course of which they lost scores of lives.

The uprising at Lucknow started on May 30, 1857, and gradually spread to a large number of towns across the whole of Awadh. As chief commissioner of Awadh, Sir Henry Lawrence had responsibility for the whole of province, he had been

receiving distress calls from Kanpur, where General Wheeler was at the receiving end. In response to his letter written on June 24, Lawrence promised help from Allahabad but expressed his inability to spare even a single troop from Lucknow as he was under tremendous pressure due to continuous revolutionary attacks. He replied on the 27th of June: "Endeavors have been made to induce me to send 200 Europeans to Cawnpore, which would have been simply sacrificing the whole, and endangering Lucknow." He added a line in the end: "Would that we could succor Wheeler." This letter would not reach Wheeler, as the time for 'succoring' him had already passed.

The news of Nana Saheb's success at Kanpur motivated the rebels at Lucknow too. Until now, they had restricted themselves to relying on harassing tactics rather than fighting pitched battles with the British. On June 28, 1857, they started to gather at Nawabganj under the leadership of Barkat Ahmad; a large number of civilians too joined them. An advance guard reached Chinhat, a small town on Faizabad Road, just about 12 km from the Residency. In all probability, an attempt at the siege of Lucknow would be made.

After the fall of Kanpur, Lawrence would not have liked to pass through the terrible situation that the siege had brought there. Taking immediate action, he first ordered the withdrawal of all troops in the cantonment into the Residency and the Machchhi Bhavan. He realized that now the prestige of the Empire rested on Lucknow, so he braced himself for the occasion. He intended to go on the offensive; this could delay the siege till 'better times' as he called. His decision to attack the rebels was due to the incomplete intelligence reports that described the situation as: 'the rebel force was in no considerable number, and their delay in advancement led him to suppose that he had not an enemy with a sharp sword to fight'. He also supposed that the decision to attack could also test the loyalty of his native troops.

In the wee hours of June 30, 1857, Lawrence started with a force comprising about 540 infantrymen belonging to four native regiments and 120 horse-mounted men belonging to 1st, 2nd, and 3rd irregular cavalry regiments, in addition to 10 guns of field battery, supported by one 8-inch howitzer christened 'Turk'. The force reached the iron bridge and had to wait for more force from Machchhi Bhavan. The sun was growing hotter overhead when they crossed the Kokrail bridge, and they soon found themselves marching on the sandy embankment. Lawrence ordered breakfast to be served to the hungry troops, while he himself advanced ahead towards Chinhat with some cavalrymen and officers. Seeing no trace of the enemy anywhere, he asked one of his officers to ride back to the force with an order to countermarch. He, however, decided to go ahead himself and soon learned that the enemy's advance party was on the other side of the village. He immediately sent his *aide-de-camp* to order his troops to advance immediately.

The British force advanced and was bypassing Ismailganj on their left when their videttes were fired upon with muskets. At this, the Turk was turned to the source of fire to cannonade.

As if it were a signal, they soon sighted the revolutionaries drawn up in a battle line-up from the front and ready for an onslaught. The British writers have exaggerated their numbers only to explain their major defeat. GW Forrest notes: ". . . not four or five thousand, as the spies had reported, but numbering at least fifteen or sixteen thousand men, with not merely two batteries of field pieces, but six or seven, consisting of more than thirty-six cannons of various calibre."

However, the reality was far from this. The revolutionary force consisted about 6,000 infantrymen, 800 cavalrymen, and 16 guns. These troops belonged to a number of native regiments and police detachments. Several taluqdars had also joined them. This, of course, was true that the British force was greatly outnumbered.

The well-led revolutionaries opened the assault and fought well. The British force was confused and suffered substantial casualties. It was disheartening to see that many of its men overturned their rifles and hid themselves in pits. When the final cavalry charge was ordered, its Sikh troops turned their horses and fled. Under the intense bombardment, the elephant towing the Turk went berserk, and horses went out of control. The so-called hardy European soldiers turned tail, leaving behind their dead and wounded. To prevent total annihilation, Lawrence ordered a retreat, and the Turk had to be abandoned. The British suffered almost half of their force, with about 118 European officers and men killed, 182 natives killed and missing, 54 Europeans, and 11 native troops wounded.

During the retreat, the noble qualities of the Indian troops and civilians were clearly manifested in large measure. They saved and fed several wounded men, and often preferred to save the Europeans over the Indians.

It is estimated that the revolutionaries suffered close to 600 casualties. Despite such a heavy loss, Barkat Ahmad was able to keep them motivated. After darkness set in, he asked his troops what his next step should be. The troops cried in unison, "Attack, what else!"

Lawrence was right to suppose that the revolutionaries could besiege the Residency, so the guns at Machchhi Bhavan were directed towards the bridge so as to disallow the attackers from coming closer. In response, the revolutionaries mounted their guns on the other side of the river and fired at the Residency so accurately that the British were in awe. They advanced, crossed the river, seized the nearby houses, overtook the entrenchments, and besieged the Residency. With this began the memorable siege that was to last a few months and would earn a deserving place in the annals of Indian history.

Begum Hazrat Mahal was in her chamber when the report of the battle and siege of the Residency was brought to her. She had been waiting eagerly for today's developments.

"This ought to be the most opportune moment. Time has come when I must act," the Begum said in a tone as if she were addressing a great crowd. Birjis Qadr gave her a surprised look; he had seen a twinkle in her eyes after several months. He needed time to understand things, as he was still too young. He only said, "Ji, *Ammi Huzoor*." He wondered what role he would play in the coming days.

44

The Regent Begum

The siege of the Residency was strengthened on July 1, 1857. The first day began with a heavy musketry and cannon fire with adequate response from the defenders. The revolutionary force could not break through the defenses, so it moved back to plan its further strategy.

Sir Henry Lawrence understood, and rightly so, that it would be difficult to hold on to both Residency and Machchhi Bhavan, so he decided to vacate the latter. He sent messengers to Machchhi Bhavan, but they fell victim to the keen revolutionary fire. So, to communicate the message, an old semaphore, installed on the roof, was used. The besiegers did not miss it too, and brought it down thrice cutting its strings and poles with bullets; however, Lawrence succeeded in sending across the message: "Spike the guns well, blow up the Fort, and retire at midnight."

Colonel Palmer, commander at Machchhi Bhavan, prepared for the evacuation. At midnight, all his troops marched out of

its eastern gate and entered the Water Gate of the Residency in complete silence with treasury and two 9-pounder guns.

Surprisingly, funny things occurred even when so much tension prevailed. The troops approached the Water Gate and shouted, "Open the gates."

The artillerymen heard it as "Open with grape", so they rushed to their cannons and prepared to fire when their officer realized the folly, and the withdrawal was completed without any untoward occurrence. Of course, they had stored a large quantity of arms and ammunition that could not be carried in such haste. It contained 240 barrels of gunpowder, 60 lakh ball cartridges, several lakhs of percussion caps, and numerous boxes of ammunition and small arms, in addition to explosives. Such massive firepower could not be left to the revolutionaries. As soon as the evacuation was complete, there was a bomb report, followed by a massive fire flame rising from Machchhi Bhavan, coupled with a massive explosion, so terrible that the whole Lucknow shook, which many people took for an earthquake.

In this grave situation, another amusing incident occurred, for which Divine ought to be on your side. L.E.R. Rees has narrated this anecdote. A British troop in Machchhi Bhavan was so drunk that he could not wake up when the order to fall in was given at midnight. In the explosion, he was thrown in the air several feet but landed safely on the debris, and more funnily, he kept sleeping right into the daybreak when he realized what had happened. He walked all the way to the Residency without any protection and entered the gate. The guards welcomed him with a flurry of jokes and loud laughter. He was so lucky that not even a single bullet came his way from the revolutionary gunfire that had already started.

Now confined to the Residency, the British erected defenses in the buildings and elsewhere; guns were mounted and men posted. There were a total of 1,720 fighting men, both Europeans

and the native sepoys loyal to the British. The number of non-combatants, including women and children, was 1,280. Most of the posts were named after the officers or occupants, like Bailey Guard Gate, Redan Battery, Evans' Battery, Innes' Post, Gubbins' House, Sikh Square, Anderson's Post, and so on. Barring women and children, all of them took part in the defense. The Residency was thus prepared to bear the onslaught by a larger body of trained revolutionary sepoys in cooperation with civilians.

The first day of the siege, July 1, witnessed heavy cannonade and gunfire the whole day. The real challenge for the garrison was to prevent the revolutionaries from launching a ground attack. The sundown witnessed a little respite in the offensive. It was at this hour that a shell was shot into the room where Lawrence had retired for a rest. He was fatally wounded, and succumbed on the 4th. Now, Major Banks was appointed the chief commissioner, but he too did not live long—he was shot dead on the 21st. Now, no one was appointed to this post, but Lt Col John Inglis became the chief commander. While fighting went on unabated around the Residency, more important things were taking place elsewhere in Lucknow.

Begum Hazrat Mahal was keeping herself informed of each development ever since the Nawab was expelled to Calcutta. She was in constant touch with a number of taluqdars, nobles, military leaders, and others, including Mammu Khan, Barkat Ahmad, Raja Jailal Singh, Subedar Rajmand Tiwari, Ghamandi Singh, and others. They were all playing an active role in the struggle against the imperialist British.

As soon as the Begum learned of Lawrence's casualty, a new wave of energy was flowing in her veins. She sent out an oral invitation to all the native military leaders, taluqdars, local rulers, and nobles to meet her in secrecy. A general body meeting was convened on the 4th in which all of them participated.

With a confident demeanor, the Begum did not wait for the formalities to take place; she arrived in the assembly and said, "We are all aware of royal formalities, but this is not the time for them. So, please keep sitting. The situation is in our favor and we must take full advantage of it. Our people are getting the better of the *firangis*, and this is the time when they ought to be given leadership."

The Begum paused for a while and then continued, "The royal masnad must never be empty; this is our tradition, but sadly, this is what has happened. News has arrived from Calcutta that the Nawab has been imprisoned and thrown into undignified quarters. Let us have a king to rule us. Let our masnad be no more vacant."

Those present in the chamber looked to one another, and hushed voices started to float in the air. Instead of silencing them, the Begum chose to give them some time to discuss and then said, "All right, respected dignitaries. What do you say?"

All of them were in agreement that all fighters and people could be united under a Nawab. With Wajid Ali Shah away, there was need to appoint someone who could lead the revolution. The vital question was: Who could do justice to the position in such crucial times? All of them did not take long to consent that someone from the royal family ought to occupy the throne. Wajid Ali Shah's eldest son, being of unsound mind, was out of the question, while the second and third sons had gone to Calcutta with their father and were then in England to plead with the queen. The fourth son, Birjis Qadr, was too young.

All that transpired in the meeting is not known. It is conjectured that several other names were also discussed, including those of Nawab Saadat Ali Khan's son, the sons of two other living Begums, and Wajid Ali Shah's brother. They were all either found wanting or unwilling to take the bull by the horns. Ultimately, the choice fell upon Birjis Qadr. His name was approved when Begum Hazrat Mahal assented to be his regent. There is also hearsay that Hazrat

Mahal was not ready for this as it could put her son in trouble, but the military leaders forced her to assent; however, her subsequent conduct disproves this.

An important question that was raised in the assembly was: Should Awadh be declared an independent, sovereign state, as it had been recently, or a province under the overlordship of the Mughal emperor of Delhi, as it was earlier? A lively discussion took place. The final decision was postponed until the next morning, when the coronation ceremony would be conducted.

At midday on July 5, 1857, the royal court was held in the Baradari in its usual glory. There were present not only the military leaders, nobles, and taluqdars but also important traders and officials. Common folks thronged the open ground outside. Curiosity and eagerness to have the first glimpse of the new Nawab permeated the atmosphere.

Soon, the doorman announced the arrival of the ruler, and with this, the fourteen-year-old Birjis Qadr walked in with the Begum just a couple of steps behind him. As everybody stood to welcome him, he walked to the masnad and stood tall. Everybody bowed in salute. He shook his head in reply and with a motion of the hand asked everybody to take their seats, as he sat down on the masnad covered in blue satin. The Begum sat down on a chair just near him. The ladies of the royal household stood behind the screened windows above to watch the proceedings.

Raja Jailal Singh was supervising the ceremony. He took to his feet, bowed to the masnad, and then beckoned to the entrance. With it, a soldier and a civilian walked in, each with a silver platter. On one of them was the crown, and the other had a turban; the former was a mark of sovereignty, and the latter that of Mughal overlordship.

The previous night had seen several rounds of discussions among all those concerned. The Begum took to her feet and

inquired about their choice: the crown or the turban. A unanimous voice favored the turban, called *mandeel.* This decision would help boost the revolutionary war against the common enemy across the whole country.

Before the coronation ceremony, the following terms were presented and approved by the assembly: The Vizier will be appointed by the military. The military will have a complete say in the appointment of its officers. The troops' salaries will be doubled. The military will be fully empowered to decide how the traitors will be dealt with. More platoons will be recruited to strengthen the Awadh army, and civilian officers will be entrusted with the civil administration.

The Begum approved of all these conditions as she wanted full cooperation from all. Moreover, Awadh did not have any force of its own and the ongoing conflict was fully dependent on the revolutionary sepoys who were until now part of the British army. Of course, many civilians were joining the force in large numbers now, yet their enthusiasm could not substitute the professional training that the sepoys had received.

With the blazing sun heading westward gradually and losing its heat, the wind started to blow to provide much-needed succor to all living beings. At such an hour, Ahmed Hussain moved the resolution, which was seconded by Mammu Khan. All those present raised their hands in assent. With this, several nobles together placed the turban on Birjis Qadr's head. The officers saluted and presented the sword to the new ruler. A 21-gun salute was given. The proclamation was read out in public to the beat of drums:

Khalk Khuda ki,
Mulk Badshah Dilli ka,
Hukm Birjis Qadr ka.

(The world that of God,
The country that of Delhi emperor,
The command that of Birjis Qadr.)

With this, the masnad was occupied once again. While the nobles and military officers were presenting gifts to the new ruler, Begum Hazrat Mahal, the new regent, took some necessary steps immediately. She first ordered the immediate restoration of dismissed officers to their respective posts to run the administration smoothly. Two committees were immediately formed—a military committee comprising of 12 members, most of them being military or police personnel, and an administrative committee comprising of 14 members experienced in administration. The members were both Hindus and Muslims. Raja Jailal Singh was the link between and head of both committees, as he was also appointed the collector in the administrative committee. Other important members in it included Sharufuddaula (deputy collector), Mammu Khan (civil affairs), Mir Qasim Ali (armoury), Maharaja Balkishan (finance), and Ahmad Hussain (land revenue), among others. In the military committee, in addition to those in uniform, there were Mammu Khan, Muzaffar Ali Khan, Mir Ali Khan, and Sarju Singh.

The next important step that the Begum took was to send an emissary to the Mughal emperor with a present and a request to approve the overlordship. The Emperor did as was expected and issued a royal *firman* (declaration) instantly. It strengthened the new Nawab's position, especially among the non-Shiite Muslims.

Before the assembly was dismissed, the Begum appealed to all officials to do their duty earnestly and devotedly. She also called upon the common people to make adequate contributions to the war effort. To this effect, she issued a firman saying that the English were hostile to their faith, dignity, life, and property, and they must

not be misled by them. She also urged people to abide by the laws and troops not to plunder. They were promised double salary, but it could not be implemented for want of funds.

In the meetings until now, the Begum had appeared with a fine screen attached to her turban. In the subsequent meetings, she appeared without any screen. She noticed several eyebrows get crooked, so she explained in the very first meeting: "This is not the time to pay attention to trivial things; the entire nation is at stake. The British enmity is not limited to one or another section of our society, like Hindus or Muslims; they are against each Indian. I have to be proactive, and the veil can only be an impediment to our endeavors. I am the Nawab's mother, so I am mother to all my subjects. A mother doesn't cover her face when she meets her children, does she?" Her sentimental tone won hearts.

There was a need to undertake immediate steps to contribute to the ongoing war effort. Particularly, there was an acute need for arms and ammunition, so quick decisions were taken. A number of ammunition factories were set up, and the lack of workers was overcome by sourcing them from Delhi and elsewhere. Cannon balls were also produced, while a factory for cannon repair was set up in Faizabad.

Awadh had always been a place of harmony among people without discrimination between religions or sects. The uprising in 1857 brought them all together without distinction between Hindus and Muslims, between Sunnis and Shiites, between high and low, or between rich and poor. A large number of people were visiting the Begum and the new ruler, affectionately called Kanhaiya by them, to offer their presents and services. They were especially popular among the poor, who lined up for hours to have their glimpse.

The military officers had promised that they would not take any salary until the war was finally won, yet the Begum was aware that revenue was a critical factor in both military operations and civil

administration. A limiting factor was that the British had deprived the royal members of their personal assets when their private buildings had been dug out to plunder. Somehow, the Begum had succeeded in protecting her jewellery and other precious articles. R.A. Zafri, as quoted by K.C. Yadav, notes that these articles were all sold to jewelers for four lakh rupees. People were also asked to contribute. The coins were cast in the name of the new crown. In about two months' time, the treasury contained an amount of 3.2 million rupees.

The older system of administration was restored, and the divisions, divided into *chaklas* and *tehsils*, now functioned under officers, as they did during Wajid Ali Shah's time. Of course, lack of funds and resources could not allow a great administration, but a wave of confidence permeated the atmosphere.

The Begum took every possible measure for victory, ensuring people's welfare, and the restoration of Awadh's glory. She was available day and night. She would visit the fighting sites herself to motivate the troops. She also offered rewards for bravery and successful skirmishes. She announced a halving of the revenue for the taluqdars who would support the national cause. Despite heavy casualties, the war went on unabated. A breakin into the Residency was not yet achieved while ceaseless cannonade and sneak attacks continued. The situation could grow grim if the British reinforcements reached Lucknow, so the task needed to be accomplished quickly.

All this while, Awadh was not immune to palace conspiracies either. Some nobles nursed divisive tendencies. Several Begums wrote to Wajid Ali Shah about how Hazrat Mahal was misled by the revolutionary sepoys and how she was taking control of things in her hands. One Sarfaraz Begum wrote that it was a bad omen for Awadh, as Birjis Qadr had ascended the masnad when his father was still alive. Yet another wrote that the British could assassinate him (Wajid Ali Shah) in retaliation.

The Begum had no time to worry about these plots, and she undertook rapid tours to all divisions and important taluqdars to seek their support. She was able to create a stir against the British. With more people rising in her support, she felt that the goal could be achieved despite impediments. Raja Devibaksh Singh of Gonda arrived with 3,000 troops. The taluqdars of Gosainganj contributed 4,000 troops. Raja Shivdarshan Singh of Samrota-Chandapur contributed 10,000 troops, while one landlord came with 2,000 fighters and three cannons. Raja Lal Madho Singh of Amethi-Sultanpur came with four cannons, 200 cavalrymen, and 5000 footmen. Rana Benimadho Singh arrived with five cannons and 5,000 troops. Other important kings to contribute included Raghunath Singh of Khajurgaon (four cannons and 2,000 troops), Chaudhary Hashmat Ali of Sandila (4,000 fighters), and Mir Mansab Ali of Rasulabad (1,000 troops). Reinforcements also came from places such as Roiya, Katiyari, Rajpur, Taraul, and Kalakankar, among others.

Evidently, it did not take long for the troop strength to rise to about 40,000, and the number of problems rose in an equal proportion. The severest impediment was that such a massive force had failed to break through the Residency manned by a few hundred Europeans. The troops were promised double salary, but due to the shortage of funds, even normal salary could not be afforded. This affected many of them, some abandoned their posts, while others indulged themselves in plundering traders and travelers. Revenue was being collected from the countryside actively, but a large share of it was evaporating in corruption.

The Begum worked hard day and night. She had multiple duties to perform, right from ironing out differences to managing revenues to motivating the fighters. Holding the nerve amid so many monolithic challenges could not be easy for her, yet she was resolved to emerge victorious.

45

How the Saviors Were Besieged

The siege of the Residency continued, and now it was 20th of July. The British, despite heavy losses of life and the destruction of buildings, kept themselves in the fray. Not only this, they carried out brief sallies to burst targets, which could be dangerous to them. They were in dire need of reinforcement, which proved elusive time and again. With the passage of each day, their situation was growing more hopeless. It was this day that the first cheerful news arrived at the hand of a former soldier, now a pensioner, named Angad, who informed, "Havelock Saheb had beaten the Nana in three great *larais* (battles) and was now master of Cawnpore." The message that was sent out of the Residency in response was not so cheerful. It read, "Aid is what we want, and quickly. Our defenses are struggling and our numerical strength quite inadequate to man them. The artillery is weak and the casualties heavy." This letter was covered in a bird's feather so as to avoid any suspicion in case Angad was caught on the way.

The revolutionary force, on the other hand, mostly limited itself to cannonade and musketry fire, with some field attacks on the outposts. It also made many a bayonet charge, the first of such being on July 20, but without much success. It too faced a shortage of resources.

Begum Hazrat Mahal and other leaders found it hard to keep the fighters motivated without salaries and ammunition. The situation was so bad during the first phase of the siege that they often used wood and stone as cannon balls. The words from GW Forrest make for an interesting read: "The batteries of the enemy were not only well placed but their fire was generally precise. At the commencement of the siege the rebels were somewhat short of ammunition and masses of stone and wood bound with iron were hurled against our posts."

Interestingly, defenders and attackers came so close to each other on several occasions that they hurled abuse and bullets together. The native sepoys fighting on both sides often knew one another, and they tried to seek the opponents' defection.

Another roar of cheer was heard in the Residency five days later when Angad returned with the message that Havelock was coming on the 29th with a large force to relieve the Residency and destroy the enemy. But this proved to be false. The inmates kept looking for the relieving force all night on the appointed day and for days after it, but hope proved elusive as ever.

July passed, and each minute of the first week of August too ticked by. Messengers kept coming but not reinforcement, making the besieged desperate. One of them wrote, "We were so sanguine that the natural result of our disappointment is that we believe in evil tidings and doubt all good news." GW Forrest wrote: "Within the entrenchments the monotony of suffering, and the continued presence of death had produced its natural effect. The excitement had died down, the jests had become rare.

As the siege wore on, the condition of the atmosphere was day by day becoming more frightful . . . Everywhere wounded officers and men were lying on couches covered with blood and often with vermin. Everywhere cries of agony were heard; piteous exclamations for water and assistance."

The situation outside the Residency, on the contrary, was quite positive. The jealous GW Forrest notes, "Outside the walls the enemy kept high festival and from the houses around came each night sound of revelry, music and dancing which greatly roused the ire of the British soldier." Evidently, the efforts of the Begum and other leaders were in the right direction. The rise at Patna, Arrah, and other places in Bihar, under the leadership of the elderly Kunwar Singh, added to their joy.

When the revolutionary force found it hard to launch a ground attack, on August 6, they dug mines to reach underground. However, this effort did not prove to be very successful in view of the loose earth in addition to the alert defenders. On August 10 and 12 too, they launched multiple attacks, but without any substantial result.

The vital question is: Where was Havelock all this while?

Havelock was so confident of having mercilessly crushed the native people at Kanpur and then at Bithur that he thought he could reach Lucknow in 3–4 days, but the situation was not so rosy for him. He could not make it there on July 29 due to casualties and diseases. Finally, he started for Lucknow with his large column in early August 1857; however, he found that it was a daunting task. Every village on the route was like a big blockade. He was surprised that people in good numbers would rush out of the village wielding sticks and homemade swords to attack the troops without caring for their lives. At some places, the resistance was so stiff that he had to fight pitched battles.

Seeing the trend, Havelock thought that he would have to

fight a major battle at Unnao, so he marched cautiously, but to his surprise, there was not a soul in the place. It was the 4th of August. Proudly thinking that people must have fled upon the news of his arrival, he proceeded ahead. He reached Bashiratganj, and his confidence was shattered when he faced a massive attack. He busied himself in suppressing the strong uprisings. Several of his officers have praised the way people fought. Martin writes that each village seemed to be opposed to the British; the farmers had cast their ploughshare into swords and fighting. At one place, he says that those who fell the previous day were all farmers. The same story was being repeated village after village.

By now, it was the middle of August. Havelock himself was under so much stress, as reported by Martin, that he wrote to his wife on August 9 that there was little chance of his surviving such endless terrible skirmishes. He suffered a massive loss on August 11 further down the road to Lucknow. Three weeks he had been on the road, but without reaching anywhere, so he withdrew back to Kanpur.

At his ignoble retreat, Brigadier General Neill, his junior, wrote a harsh letter reprimanding him for the loss of guns and asking him to move ahead until he was in Lucknow. Look at the war of words between two high British officers. Neill admonished his senior Havelock: ". . . It has been most unfortunate you're not bringing back any of the guns captured from the enemy. The natives will not believe you captured one. The effect of your retrograde movement will be very injurious to our cause elsewhere…" How could his commander tolerate this? He shot back his letter admonishing him: ". . . I wrote to you confidentially on the state of affairs. You send me back a letter of censure of my measures, reproof and advice for the future. I do not want and will not receive any of them from an officer under my command, be his experience what it may." He was not only locked in jibes with the commanders of other armies,

but also was ignoring any advice that he did not want to listen to. This proved what John F. Kennedy (of the U.S.) said more than a century later: "There is an old saying that victory has a hundred fathers and defeat is an orphan."

The poor Havelock, however, had nowhere to go but Kanpur. Earlier, he had conquered Kanpur and destroyed Bithur, but in the meantime, Tantya Tope had gathered his forces to harass the British, so he was obliged to return on August 16 to assist Neill. It would take him some time before he could head to Lucknow to provide succor to the besieged Residency. Interestingly, despite his animosity with Neill, he had to trust him for command of a division, as he had few other viable options.

Havelock's return to Kanpur bore a positive result for Begum Hazrat Mahal. Until now, several taluqdars operated in disobedience. Now, thinking that the British were fully defeated, they fell in line. They sent tribute to her and also contributed their forces.

Havelock was duly reinforced at Kanpur and was ordered to relieve Lucknow in cooperation with Outram and Neill. With a massive force at their command, they set out to Lucknow on September 18, 1857, destroying everything that came their way. This day saw a partial solar eclipse, perhaps warning them of what lay in store for them. He had to fight battles even at places he had earlier won, like at Bashiratganj, and in these places the struggles were as stiff as before. Most of the British historians and soldiers have written that they attained victories in these battles, but they forget to mention that the revolutionary force adopted a tactic, that was, to hit and run—they would come, attack, cause a loss, and by the time the British force would respond, they would run to their secure hideouts.

Meanwhile the Residency was short on everything, right from rations to ammunition to rum to meat, while men were dying every day and the native sepoys supporting them now believed that the

reinforcement would never come. Inglis found it hard to keep his men motivated.

On the way, Havelock had to fight major battles on 21st, 23rd, and 25th. It rained on 21st and 22nd, and despite this fact, skirmishes took place in several villages. The battle at Alambagh took place on the 23rd. It was the day that the news came in that Delhi was under the British control once again. This enthused his troops. It rained on the 24th as well, so not much fighting took place. Alambagh remained under the revolutionary force.

On September 25, 1857, Havelock headed to the Residency with his heavy force from Alambagh. He wanted to follow the route, which was: Cawnpore Road → Char Bagh Bridge → Main city → Bailey Guard Gate. However, in view of his heavy guns and rain-wet ground, he followed: Char Bagh → Along the canal → Between Kaisarbagh and river → Residency.

It was in this battle that the Begum mounted a horse to inspire her men with a sword in hand. Mrs Case, noted in her journal on this day: "I have also heard that the young king (Birjis Qadr) who was placed at the throne a short time ago has been wounded." This shows that the Begum took part in the hostilities with her son. Havelock used all his resources to move through the route but had to fight severely, losing a large number of troops and officers. Neill fell to a great shot to the head by a sharpshooter near Khas Bazar. Both sides suffered a large number of casualties. His force was often confounded as each building and cabin, alley and parapet, balcony and pillar seemed to be fortified. On the side of the revolutionary force, it was Raja Jailal Singh who laid down his life fighting bravely.

Outram chose for himself narrow streets to advance to the Residency. He had to face bullets and bombs, but he was ready for these, although he was embarrassed when he found that there were many women and children on the roofs who spat and pelted stones

at them. He did not know how to deal with this hatred. He ordered his troops to shoot them down if need be.

Somehow, Havelock and Outram fought their way to the Residency, but before they could give out a loud shout of cheer to those besieged, they found, to their dismay, that they themselves were besieged with the very people they had come to relieve. It was the 87th day of the siege, and the situation was bound to remain as grim as it had ever been, with half of the fighting men dead. It, of course, goes to the credit of the besieged that they bore the brunt of repeated onslaughts for this long despite limitations of all sorts; they were not garrisoned in a fortress, they were sheltered in collapsing buildings. They lacked unhindered supplies of food and ammunition, yet they faced the enemy dauntlessly. Some respite was that they had added manpower to their posts.

The number of besieged now rose from a few hundred to over five thousand. Their confidence touched the lowest ebb now, as relief seemed like a pipedream. In a letter dated September 30, Havelock wrote: "The killed, wounded and missing, the latter being wounded soldiers who, I much fear, some or all have fallen into the hands of a merciless foe, mounted up to the evening of the 26th to 535 officers and men." Mrs Case noted in her diary: "Everyone was today out of spirits; in fact, we felt we were not relieved, but only reinforced."

Prior to September 25, 1857, the British troops were besieged within a smaller place and a few buildings, and the revolutionary troops being near caused them a large number of casualties. The arrival of Havelock and Outram, together with long-range firepower, forced the besieging troops to position themselves farther from where muskets could be used effectively. However, they now used their guns imaginatively. Praising them for this tactic, Malleson writes, "The plan was ingenious, and was so far well worked that the point of fire was constantly shifted."

More terrible was the fact that Havelock did not die a hero's death. He died of dysentery on November 24 when the battle of Lucknow was at its fag end. Not only that, his troops often went berserk, looting and raping. Maybe it was the way the Divine manifested wrath for the brutal, unjust punishments that he had accorded to the innocent at Kanpur and elsewhere.

46

Battles of Lucknow

Several historians have tried to emphasize that the incidents of the 1857 uprising at different places were unrelated to each other. However, if we look at the pattern, we find ample proof that such historians were mistaken, or rather, they tried to mislead intentionally in order to set a vested narrative. The sepoys who rose at Meerut marched to Delhi and caused the uprising there. When Lucknow was under attack, a large number of towns around it rose in revolt, including Faizabad, Sitapur, Kanpur, Unnao, Allahabad, Banaras, and so many others; so did the surrounding regions such as Rohilkhand and Bihar. Reinforcements kept flowing from one place to another. Every time Lucknow was in danger, Tantya Tope would attack Kanpur forcing the British force to move out of Lucknow. He fought at several places, including Jhansi and Gwalior, to help the revolution spread there. Babu Kunwar Singh led his march not only across Bihar but also across Madhya Pradesh and Awadh and fought to relieve stress in other places. After the defeat in Delhi, fighters joined the revolutionaries in Awadh and Bihar.

Cooperation might not have been adequately planned as the revolutionary force was confronted with a superior British force, yet it existed as the circumstances warranted. Otherwise, it could not have continued for about two years when the British were forced to commission troops from not only within India (like from Madras and Punjab) but also from abroad (like from England, China). They found the situation so hopeless that even the Commander-in-Chief (Sir Colin Campbell) was sourced from England.

Colin, known by his mother's surname (Campbell) rather than his father's (Macliver), was commissioned in 1808 when he was barely 15, and at this age he took part in the first battle and continued to fight a large number of battles in his life. When the British found it hard to tackle the 1857 Uprising, they looked for experience, and this was how Colin was asked to move to India. He arrived at Calcutta on August 13, but needed more than two months and a half to find courage and resources to move out to the seat of war. He utilized this period to cast more guns, manufacture more rifles and cartridges, and wait for more armies from the south and also from China and England.

Colin started on his mission on October 27. A few days later, he narrowly escaped being captured by the revolutionaries when he confronted the inattentive revolutionaries, who were moving away on elephants guarded by cavalrymen. Instead of striking at them, he chose to move away. Had he been captured, the entire scenario would have changed in favor of the revolutionaries. Malleson noted this incident in his book *History of the Indian Mutiny of 1857–58,* concluding: "But for the good look-out and prompt action of the drivers, the Commander-in-Chief could not have escaped capture—and worse."

Colin reached Allahabad on November 1 and started his operations. He had a very massive force under his command, with almost 180 cannons, including several 68-pounders, which even 12

horses found hard to draw. His force comprised close to one lakh men, and his animal baggage train was almost 25 miles long, being drawn by about 16,000 camels and 12,000 oxen. In addition, he had received two ships laden with cannon consignments and troops under Captain Peel. The railways helped him transport his men, material, and equipment quite comfortably.

On his way, Colin used his brute force to destroy whatever resistance he met. On November 3, he arrived in Kanpur, then faced a grave threat from Tantya Tope and his Gwalior force, but he preferred to relieve Lucknow first as the Residency was short on rations. He set out for Lucknow on the 8th and reached there the following day. Before him, his reinforcements were already there, including Hope Grant's column consisting of over 5,500 troops. As Delhi was captured by now, the force from there was at his disposal as well, which included the cavalry under Hodson, a British officer who had criminally murdered the Mughal princes whom he was supposed to arrest. To add to this, there was a force already garrisoned at the Residency. Such a massive army it was!

Begum Hazrat Mahal was in the thick of action. She knew that she would have to make extraordinary preparations to meet Colin. She issued a sentimental appeal to the citizens, which led to a favorable outcome. She exhorted them that the British would pretend non-interference with the native faiths but, on the contrary, would do everything to destroy them. They would be compelled to eat pigs and drink wine, to bite the greased cartridges, and to eat sweets mixed with pig fat. Moreover, they would destroy temples and mosques under the pretense of making roads, build churches, and would convert people to Christianity, and they would also establish English schools and pay a stipend to learn the English sciences. In conclusion, they would do all in their power to destroy everything native. She emphatically asked in the end, "How then can we protect our native faiths and institutions?"

She also appealed to the taluqdars for men, material, and money. The outcome was enthusiastic. The revolutionary army soon grew to over 53,000 strong. This strength included about 8,000 troops, about 5,600 Awadhi troops, about 7,700 cavalrymen, and over 32,000 taluqdars' troops. To add to this number was Bakht Khan, who arrived at the head of about 10,000 troops from Delhi, accompanied by prince Feroz Shah, and engineer Muhammad Ali.

Begum Hazrat Mahal was confident that she would now be in a position to confront the growing British army. Maulana Ahamadulla Khan, too, was there with his Ghazi contingent. In consultation with the commanders, she garrisoned the army across the city. Strong fortifications were brought into existence at Sikandar Bagh, Alambagh, Moti Mahal, Dilkusha Kothi, Hazratganj, Kaisarbagh, and other places. The heavy and field guns were positioned at vital points. The stone bridge across the Gomti was destroyed. With this, an anxious wait commenced for the British attack.

It may be pertinent to narrate an interesting episode. Outram in the Residency and Colin outside needed to communicate, which they did through an enterprising British clerk named Kavanagh, who stained his body and face black, cut his hair, and dressed like a native volunteer, complete with a turban and shoes, to sneak through native defenses to deliver messages. A two-pronged attack was planned with an aim of joining the two armies.

Hostilities began on November 14. The Begum once again issued an appeal to fight for "your *Deen*, your *Dharma* and your *Desh*."

Colin advanced towards the Residency while Havelock and Outram started their operations from their besieged position with a heavy cannonade and then made a bid to move to meet Colin's relief force midway. Severe fighting took place at each post. Both sides displayed several unique movements, suffering a large number of casualties. Colin was perplexed at the extent of garrisons in each building.

The most terrible battle was fought at Sikandar Bagh on the 16th. Here, the 3,000-strong native troops, under the command of Barkat Ahmad, reminded the attackers of the defeat they had suffered at Chinhat. However, he could not withstand the onslaught of heavy cannons and fell to the British. Malleson, describing the battle at Sikandar Bagh, writes, "The fight for the possession of the enclosure was bloody and desperate, the rebels fighting with all the energy of despair. Nor did the struggle end when our men forced their way inside. Every room, every staircase, every corner of the towers was contested. Quarter was neither given nor asked for, and when at last the assailants were masters of the place, more than two thousand rebel corpses lay heaped around them. It is said that, of all who garrisoned it, only four men escaped, but even the escape of four is doubtful." The revolutionary troops were fighting with such a missionary zeal that even when death was imminent, they faced the enemy bravely.

Despite a massive defeat at Sikandarbagh, the confrontation continued at other places. Much blood flowed at Dilkusha Bagh and Alambagh, but the most terrible encounter took place at Shah Najaf, a large Imambara with thick vegetation surrounded by high stone walls.

When Colin found it impossible to penetrate, he ordered a bayonet charge as he found himself squeezed in narrow lanes where the heavy guns could not be brought and from where he had little chance of deliverance. The experienced general never staked his life so badly. His expressions revealed how tense he was. While he was trying to motivate his troops to advance, he found it hard in the face of heavy casualties. He was lucky as the rocket launchers came to his rescue, which allowed the British troops to take shelter under the walls, from where they launched a desperate bayonet attack. The Awadh troops thought that they could not bear the two-pronged attack and retreated from there;

unfortunately, they did not realize that they had an upper hand here, and had they stayed put there for some more time, they could have won the day. A British officer, as quoted by Malleson, writes, "Panic-stricken apparently by the destruction caused by the rockets, and the sudden appearance of the assailants within the walls, they [defenders] fled from the place and gave up the struggle just when victory was secure."

Despite facing reverses, Begum's troops continued to harass the British advance. They were still 30,000 strong and had a strong base at several places, including Moti Mahal, Mess House, Begum Kothi, and Kaiserbagh, while the city in the background was their stronghold.

The fighting continued on the 17th and 18th. Despite being at the receiving end, the revolutionary force continued to attack the British positions and pickets all across Lucknow, yet they were gradually losing out to a superior strategy, cannonade, and force.

After Moti Mahal fell on the 19th, contact between Colin and Outram was established, but not without losing several officers to the musketry fire from the garrison at Kaiserbagh. Havelock established his base at Kothi Farhat Baksh, just adjacent to Chhatar Manzil, from where the revolutionaries had moved out by now.

The focus of fighting now shifts to Kaiserbagh on the 20th, with Colin using a menacing bombardment. Despite this, the revolutionary force dared to face him, and thus, fighting continued for two more days, and it was by noon on the 23rd that the British could gain a hold there. With a massive loss, the revolutionaries were trying their best to launch sporadic attacks. They did it with some measure of success on November 24 and 25, but could not sustain it. Their remaining resistance was wiped off from Lucknow on the 26th, allowing Colin much leeway to proceed to Kanpur on the 27th to take on Tantya Tope, as the sound of cannonade was heard from that direction, and the garrison under Windham was

reportedly overwhelmed. The British command at Lucknow was now with Outram.

Before we close this chapter, two points are quite worthy of attention. First, whichever palace or building the British occupied would be plundered. They would even dig out walls and floors to take out gems used in construction, along with other valuables that they could get there. It was due to this that a large quantity of gems, diamonds, ornaments, silken clothes, and artifacts, in addition to cash amounting to about 2,40,000 pounds, was collected in Dilkusha. Both officers and troops participated in this loot. Several of them were found hanging a bundle of the valuables to their waists in subsequent battles, which had an adverse effect on their liver too.

Second, when Colin receded from Lucknow, he was afraid that he could be besieged with his force, so he moved away, continuously cannonading Kaiserbagh in order to misguide the revolutionary force. Interestingly, the battle of Lucknow was far from over. More interestingly, at Kanpur, despite his best efforts, he could not harm Tantya Tope or Nana Saheb, both of whom were well out of his reach. In anguish, Colin ordered the destruction of Nana's palace at Bithur. Only after that did he turn back to Lucknow.

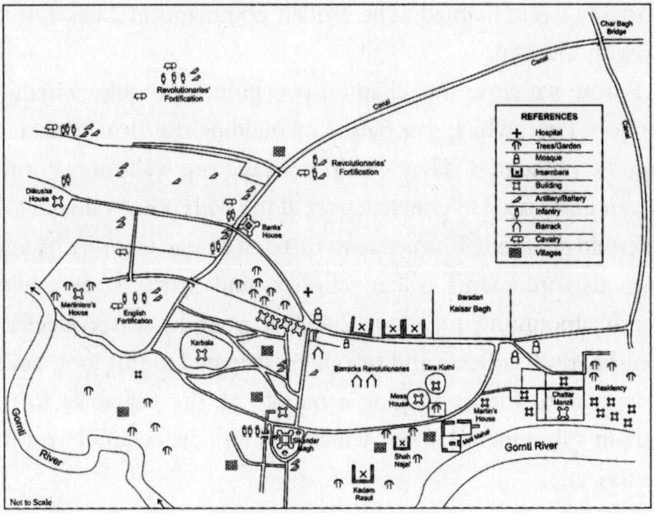

Lucknow in 1857

47

The Popular War

Colin's flight from Lucknow was an occasion of great jubilation for Begum Hazrat Mahal and her commanders, as it gave them an opportunity to reassemble the forces. The battle had assumed the nature of a popular war. The taluqdars forgot their differences, as did people from across different sections of society; they all came together to present a united front.

The Begum passed a written order to make preparations for the defense of Lucknow and the invasion of Banaras and Allahabad. She honored and issued a firman to Babu Kunwar Singh of Jagdishpur, Bihar, to occupy Azamgarh, while she herself established and strengthened garrisons around Lucknow. Thus, Outram's garrison at Alambagh was greatly threatened by the revolutionary force's garrison at Dilkusha Kothi.

Ahmadulla Shah led his troops to attack Outram on several occasions. On January 12, 1858, he attacked with about 30,000 troops, although he did not succeed. On the 16th, he took

measures to cut off any reinforcement that Outram could receive from Kanpur, where Colin was getting ready for his march to Lucknow. All this while, Outram was receiving reinforcements, so his garrison was growing stronger with each passing day. Despite intense fighting on successive days, the garrison could not be conquered.

When Hazrat Mahal saw that her troops were discouraged by repeated failures, she herself took to the battlefield. Malleson describes her in these words: "The despairing attack of the rebels was made with all the pomp and circumstance of war. For the first time the royal Begam, mounted on an elephant, attended by the Prime Minister and principal nobles, similarly mounted, accompanied the assailants." Outram's artillery, however, proved stronger and forced the revolutionary force to fall back. Despite this, they made repeated attacks right into the dark.

In the first week of December 1857, Colin Campbell was free to return to Lucknow to complete the unfinished task. He wanted to adopt all measures for his safety, so he waited at Kanpur to strengthen himself. In the meantime, he had to undertake minor missions because the revolutionaries had occupied a number of places and garrisons in the Doab, and the revolution was now expanding menacingly.

Finally, he set out for Lucknow on the 24th, but he would need much more time to cover this small distance. In fact, he wanted to first suppress the uprising in Rohilkhand, which was more reasonable from the military viewpoint, but he had to bow before Lord Canning's wish. At this time, he had a very strong force, almost 40,000 strong, which included 10,000 troops from Nepal. This force, also called the Second Awadh Army, was 'the most efficient European army, ever ranged in the plains of India'. It comprised 'engineers, artillery, horse, foot, commissariat wagons, camp-followers', and more. It counted seventeen battalions of

infantry, twenty-eight squadrons of cavalry, fifty-four light guns, and eighty heavy guns and mortars. The British officers and authors underreported and claimed this number to be about 20,000 in a bid to sing laurels of their bravery.

After the fall of Delhi, a large number of revolutionaries turned to Lucknow and joined the Begum's force. On January 17, Outram ascertained their strength at about 1,20,000, which included 37 trained regiments of sepoys, 14 other regiments, 106 Najib or irregular regiments, 26 regiments of cavalry, and a camel corps, in addition to the artillerymen and taluqdars' armed men. He seems to have exaggerated this number in order to discredit the revolutionaries' action and bravery.

The British were under great pressure. They had never taken the Nepal's prime minister, Jang Bahadur, very seriously, but now they addressed him with unduly respectful terms in a bid to woo him for his Gorkha troops. When the Begum came to know of this, she sought his cooperation too and offered to secede to Nepal the districts of Gorakhpur-Azamgarh. However, she did not succeed.

On his way, Colin faced stiff resistance at several places, including Fatehgarh. He also played a ruse to misguide the revolutionaries by putting up a façade that he was heading to Bareilly and not to Lucknow, but the trick was exposed. Finally, he reached Alambagh on March 1, 1858, and started his operations on the 2nd.

Learning from the past battle against Colin, the revolutionary force had worked hard to strengthen their defenses. Both flanks of the canal were secured by strong bastions. They created a three-line defense system. The first line of defense was garrisoned at Hazratganj, defended by cannons; the second one extended from Imambara to Moti Mahal; and the third line encircled Kaiserbagh. Overall, about one hundred cannons, both heavy and field guns, were positioned at crucial buildings, junctions, and entrances.

Colin chose to attack from the east and the north, where the revolutionaries had left a loophole—they had neglected the north where the Gomti flowed.

On the very first day's operation, Colin secured Dilkusha and installed his field batteries, which forced the revolutionary force to retreat. The battle intensified with each passing day and raged on until March 21, 1858. Severe fighting took place at every turn, every post, every building, and every chamber of every building. Blood flowed, and lives were sacrificed by the hundreds. Whichever building the British occupied was plundered, and this was one of the main reasons why the hostilities took so long. Hodson, the murderer of Mughal princes in Delhi, was killed at Begum Kothi, where he had gone to have a share of the loot.

The plunder that followed at many places has been vividly described by Dr. Russell: "The scene of plunder was indescribable… The soldiers had broken up several of the store-rooms, and pitched the contents into the court, which was lumbered with cases, with embroidered cloths, gold and silver brocade, silver vessels, arms, banners, drums, shawls, scarfs, musical instruments, mirrors, pictures, books, accounts, medicine bottles, gorgeous standards, shields, spears and a heap of things which would make this sheet of paper look like a catalogue of a broker's sale." He further writes that they smashed or burned things to take out gold and silver from them, and in the end, they destroyed or put to fire all those things that they did not find useful, including china stone, glass, jade, pictures, and furniture. This plundering went on in all chambers and courts without a care for the stinking dead bodies lying around.

Intense fighting and plundering went on until the 15th, after which smaller skirmishes continued to take place right until the 21st. The revolutionaries had crossed the Gomti, but Colin did not dare chase them. He suffered over 720 casualties, both wounded

and dead, while the revolutionaries' casualties numbered well over one thousand.

The revolutionaries had fought well. It goes to their credit that they were able to sustain before the mighty British for this long. Several British writers have praised the revolutionaries, saying that they took to the field with a missionary zeal, fought until the last bullet with a resolute determination to sacrifice everything they owned. Victory for the British was never easy. Often, they had to make multiple attacks at the same location to bring it under their control. Outram and Colin escaped death by hair's breadth on more than one occasion.

Many encounters were proof of how brutal the British were. In vengeance, they would bayonet the survivors and often throw them in fire alive. A British officer wrote in a letter that the nineteenth century, which ordains the high ideals of civilization and humanity, would be 'the saddest to witness the human being so roasted and killed.'

During the whole course, Begum Hazrat Mahal continued to fortify one place after another. She was at Chaulakhi Kothi when it was attacked. She was advised to leave for safety, but she was reluctant to abandon the place. She had to be convinced by the promise that the entire Awadh would convert into a battleground; only then did she leave with Birjis Qadr and nobles.

On March 11, 1858, the Begum first walked to Maulviganj, where she took a horse-drawn carriage, and then went via Hussainabad to Mirza Mandi, where she stopped for the night with Mohammad Ghulam Raza, a noble. The next day, she arrived at Moosabagh Palace, where Maulvi Ahmadulla Shah, General Bakht Khan, and other commanders joined her with about 15,000 troops. It was here that the last battle of Lucknow was fought. When she could no longer resist, a decision was taken to abandon the place,

dividing the force into two, one led by Ahmadulla Shah and the other under General Bakht Khan.

Contrary to what the British had thought, now the revolutionaries rose almost everywhere; there was scarcely a town that did not see the revolutionary activity. The entire Awadh in general and the region within about 50 miles around Lucknow in particular saw a very explosive situation as the rebellious forces under taluqdars and landlords raised their banners of revolution, which made Russell remark on April 3, 1858, that 'the entire Awadh should be taken as an alien country'. The Begum might have lost Lucknow, but Awadh was still under her control.

48

Flight or Fight

Facing pressure from the British, the Begum travelled from Moosabagh to Bharaon on her way to Kathwara, Danapur, and then to Khairabad, where she was welcomed by the local governor, Harprasad. She consulted her commanders here and decided on the next course of action. She was in favor of running the movement in cooperation with the revolutionaries of Rohilkhand, but she had to abandon the plan, as now she was forced to move to Mehmoodabad, where she stayed for some time before moving to Bitauli. The British force under Hope Grant went after her. She did not have adequate force here, so she moved to Baundi in Behraich district. The local ruler, Raja Hardutt Singh, welcomed her and assured her of all possible assistance. His son Mahesh Singh accorded Birjis Qadr the status of his elder brother, exchanging the turbans, which was a mark of collaboration. Her commanders joined her, and she decided to fight a battle from here; therefore, it was fortified with troops and cannons.

The Begum knew the importance of setting up an administration. She empowered the taluqdars to run the local administration and collect the revenue. She also authorized her other Awadh officers to look after the administration in the districts under her control. Kamaluddin Hyder has narrated in *Kaiser-ul-Twarikh*, the prevailing situation at Baundi at this time: "The buzz of activity in markets of Baundi reminded one of Lucknow."

Sometime in May 1858, her force under Maulvi Ahmadulla Shah launched a massive attack on Shahjahanpur, and gave the enemy jitters. He died in a bid to relieve Rohilkhand, but no British could lay his hands on him until the last; his death at Pawai on 5th of June was attributed to treason by the local ruler. Even his enemies have showered praise on him. Sir Thomas Seaton, a British military officer, has described him as 'a man of great abilities, of undaunted courage, of stern determination, and by far the best soldier among the rebels'. Malleson has written for him thus: "Of his capacity as a military leader, many proofs were given during the revolt, . . . No other man could boost that he had twice foiled Sir Colin Campbell in the field!"

As the Begum tried to accumulate her resources and supporters, she decided to punish the deserters and traitors. There were a number of landed people who had switched sides, and on the top of this list was Raja Man Singh of Shahganj. He was first ordered to deposit three lakh rupees in the royal treasury in addition to paying four months' pending salary to the troops. She also ordered him to bring his troops with 15 cannons to move against the British. When Man Singh did not appear to submit, she sent a 20,000-strong force to siege his fort. To assist him, Colin Campbell sent Hope Grant. To avoid the battle at this junction, the revolutionary force divided itself into two, one column moving to Sultanpur and the other to Faizabad. Noting this down in his diary, Colin wrote: "Fyzabad is now occupied, a body of about

20,000 rebels having broken upon his [Hope Grant's] approach from before Shahganj, the stronghold of Rajah Maun Singh, who had been besieged for some time."

The Begum took similar actions against several other taluqdars, such as Shankar Singh of Tiloi, and a landed zamindar named Rustam Shah of Rustampur in Sultanpur, among others.

The year 1858 was drawing to a close now, and the Begum was making every possible effort to accumulate her resources so that a final showdown could be held with the British.

The occasion arrived on November 1, 1858, when Queen Victoria of England issued a proclamation of general pardon. It was read out by Lord Canning in Allahabad. At the very outset, the proclamation declared the British crown's takeover of the territories in India from the East India Company. It appointed Canning as the Viceroy and Governor General as the representative of the British Crown. It accepted all the treaties and engagements that the EIC had entered into and promised that no more accession of territories would be undertaken. It gave equality of citizenship to all Indians at par with the British citizens. It, 'firmly relying ourselves on the truth of Christianity', declared that no prejudice would be meted out on grounds of religious faith or observances, nor they would be interfered with. Pardon will be given 'on certain terms' and declared that punishment 'will be inflicted on those whose crimes place them beyond the reach of forgiveness'. It specifically talked of giving clemency to all except those who have 'directly taken part in the murder of British subjects', but remained silent about those murders that the British had committed.

The Begum was quick to read between the lines of the proclamation and pointed out its shortcomings. In response, she issued her own proclamation. She termed the Queen's proclamation a 'gross lie and deception'. She asked if anyone had ever seen the British pardoning a person for an act, great or small, which they

considered a crime against themselves. She warned her subjects to be careful of what was said in it. She also pointed out that the change of government from under the EIC to the British crown would bring no perceptible change as the governor general, his officers, and courts would continue to function as they did before. Moreover, she revealed the true nature of the past treaties and engagements that were continued. She said that it was a trick on the people of India because the entire country was already under their control and no change was sought to be made over the status of the princely states, which they had occupied on fictitious grounds. She also said that the British crown had no intention of giving the princely states back to the rulers, though the people wanted so. She said, "If the Queen has assumed the government, why does her Majesty not restore our country to us when our people wish it?" She boldly questioned why a proclamation should speak of the 'truth of Christianity' when no favor is sought to be given to any faith. She pointed out how the British had been destroying faiths by several means, including mixing bones in wheat flour, destroying religious places, sending missionaries to convert people, and more such acts. They would never care for any religion other than Christianity but would interfere with it on every pretense. She said, "The very revolution has occurred because of our faith, because it was interfered with, it was molested, and was considered inferior." She also warned that the proclamation spoke of giving amnesty to all people other than those who had murdered or helped the murderers. It simply meant that all villages in which the revolutionaries sought refuge would be punished. She asked, "What kind of clemency is it?"

In the end, she called upon her nobles, officers, and taluqdars to present themselves in her audience before January 1, 1859. She decided that those who did appear would be pardoned and honored while their posts would be reverted to them.

The British were now trying to silence Awadh, but skirmishes kept taking place. A large number of loyal taluqdars and common people still supported the Begum's cause. When Baundi was pressed by the British force, she divided her force in order to carry out the guerilla warfare. Thus, her commanders like Benimadho Singh, Raja Balbhadra Singh, Raja Narpat Singh, Devi Baksh Singh, General Bakht Khan, Mammu Khan, Khan Bahadur Khan, Muhammad Hussain, Jyoti Singh, Khuda Bakhsh, Umrao Singh, Jwala Prasad, and others fought pitched battles against the imperialists at different places. She herself participated in several missions. Ultimately, she had to abandon Baundi on January 21, 1859.

It was in connection with this prolonged struggle that the *Times* quoted Martin's words on November 29, 1858, saying the Begum "like all the women who have turned up in the insurrection, has shown more sense and nerve than all her generals together."

The Begum knew that it would be very difficult to settle down now. She wrote a poem in anguish, whose first four lines are below:

Zameen ki aag bujhane yah ghata umadi thi,
Haan, magar ulti havaon ne thahrane na diya.
Bikhar chala woh kafila mukam Baundi se,
Chaal dushman ki kuchh aisi ki ubharane na diya.

(This storm had set out to put out the land's fire,
Yes, but the adverse winds did not allow it to settle down.
Dispersed is the caravan to move away from Baundi,
The enemy's trick was such as not to allow it to rise.)

She moved towards Nepal via remote, inaccessible places like Tulsipur and Devi Patan, where she kept playing the game of hide-and-seek with the British chasers, fighting minor skirmishes at times. She still had a large force with her but had exhausted

resources, arms, and ammunition. Some estimates of her force range from 15 to 30 thousand warriors, most of them armed with swords or brown-base muskets, while the number of Enfield rifles (which fired the controversial greased cartridges) was just 20 to 30, but she had not even one cannon. It was next to impossible to face an enemy with even one-fourth its strength. With this, the popular war gradually declined.

To better understand the role of Indian women in this struggle, let's compare them with their European counterparts. In the siege of Residency, there were a number of besieged European women too, but they never took part in an action. At best, a few of them nursed the wounded, while others kept looking for safe shelters for themselves. The Indian women, on the contrary, took to the battlefields across India. In the popular war of Awadh, they were conspicuous right from Begum Hazrat Mahal with her band of women, in addition to common women who had nothing at stake, yet they took an active part in the hostilities. Many women were found attired in men's clothes and fought shoulder-to-shoulder with men, while several others functioned as sharpshooters. There is a mention of firing at the British troops from the thick foliage of a peepal tree near the canal. When this tree was shot at, a dead body fell down. To their amazement, she was a woman in a man's dress, with her musket still in her hand. The women who could not take an active part were involved in pelting stones at the invading troops whenever they went through lanes. We find mention of a tawaif called Hyderibai who spied on British visitors and later joined the Begum's band of women fighters. The participation of women delineates how extensive the revolution in Awadh was.

The Begum then moved to Naya Kot in Sultanpur and stayed in Baradari. It was from here that she corresponded with Nepali Prime Minister Jang Bahadur Rana for refuge. Her letter, under

the name and seal of Birjis Qadr, was carried by Mohammad Sarfaraj Ali. At first, Jang Bahadur turned down her request. She wrote again and was threatened by him. Upon repeated entreaties, he agreed to give refuge to her, her son, and attendants, but not commanders and troops. The British did not want her to cross over to Nepal, but they could not detect how or when she did. Colin Campbell was unhappy with Nepal, but Jang Bahadur acted like a determined sovereign.

The situation was growing hopeless for her. By February 1859, she had little resources to resist the British. How long could she fight in the face of such adversities? One moonless night, she walked to the border, turned and bowed down in her last salute to the motherland, and crossed over to Nepal, never to return. She headed to Kathmandu while her reliable, loyal supporters and commanders moved to the Terai region only to taste a violent death or to become victims of the malarial mosquitoes in the dense jungles.

A crucial question lingers: Why did Jang Bahadur allow Begum Hazrat Mahal to settle down in Nepal? Historians differ in their opinions. In my view, he felt insulted at the hands of the British, as they were the ones who first sought his assistance, and when his troops had already marched away, he was asked to withdraw them. His troops had barely returned to their base when Canning sent another dispatch to demand his troops, together with a promise to return the territories due to him. The 3,000-troop-strong Nepali army played a crucial role in the relief of Lucknow and elsewhere. And when the task was accomplished, he was once again considered unnecessary and was asked to move away to Nepal.

As if this were not enough, a force was sent to guard his movement through the Indian territory. Not only this, but the promise to hand over territories to him was never honored. Jang Bahadur expressed his mental distress in a letter to one of his friends,

Hodgson, in these words: "You see how I am treated. How do you expect to keep India with such (*British*) rulers as these?" Martin too has written about this matter: "Jung Bahadur had formed high expectations of the reward to which he was personally entitled, in the form of territorial concessions. The British government postponed the consideration of that question . . . " This was the reason that he had disallowed the British troops into his territory to go after the revolutionaries.

Even in Nepal, the Begum wished to run a campaign against the British with help from the Nepalese prime minister, but that did not materialize. On the other hand, the Governor General sent her a proposal to enter into a treaty, by which she was promised honor and good conduct while retaining her post lifelong. Despite facing numerous difficulties, she was reluctant to accept any conditions put forth by the British. She settled down in Nepal under the following conditions: She would not be turned over to the British. She would be allowed to stay in the Nepalese capital with her family and attendants. The Nepalese government would pay for her subsistence. She would not be obliged to present herself before the Nepalese court or the English resident.

Jang Bahadur made arrangements for her stay in Kathmandu in a rented house, owned by his minister Bhimsen, and also approved a grant of ₹ 400 per month. Several British writers, including Sharer, have accused Jang Bahadur of doing this in lieu of her assets in gold and gems; while others have accused that only one-third of the price was given. But these allegations do not appear to be true. It was on the basis of these assets that she could stay in Nepal for 19 long years, during which she conducted several marriages in the family and celebrated festivals along with other occasions. In 1864, she even constructed a small but beautiful house called Barf Kothi, and the area came to be called Barf Bagh. It was here that her son, Birjis Qadr, was

married. Today, no trace of it is found. Her pastime activities mainly included prayers or caring for the family. She also took to poetry and wrote a large number of couplets (*sher*), though none of them can be traced.

Once again, towards the end of 1864, there was talk of her returning to India, but she did not want to engage herself with the English, so she rejected the offer adamantly. It is likely that Birjis Qadr was not comfortable with the lack of finances and even wrote to Jang Bahadur for a raise in the subsistence allowance.

The Begum, despite growing weak, nursed an ambition to fight with the British, even in 1877. She saw an opportunity when Jang Bahadur died, but this could not turn into reality.

On April 1, 1879, both mother and son fell ill. Medicine had no effect, and their condition worsened. Both of them lay in the same chamber, looking at each other in despair.

On April 7, Birjis Qadr looked at her when he saw her raising her weak hand. He asked if she wanted to say something. She opened her fingers and moved them to say something, but he could not make out anything, and then suddenly the hand fell down with a jerk. This was how this astute flame of independence flickered for the last time. The plan was to bury her in the Sunni graveyard, but it was disallowed, since she was a Shiite, so the Nepal government made due arrangements for her burial. History has meted out injustice to her, and this is a humble tribute to record her life and accomplishments.

In 1887, Wajid Ali Shah died. The Begum had asked Birjis Qadr not to seek the British favor as it would undermine their sacrifice, but his wife, Mehtab Begum, tried her best for entry into India on the ground of marrying her three daughters. She was allowed by the British to stay in India for a short duration on so-called humanitarian grounds, but only with one daughter. When she returned, the British government was criticized, and so they allowed

Birjis Qadr to return. He came back to India in 1893 in violation of his deceased mother's wish, but he could not survive long. He died of poisoning the same year, maybe due to a property dispute. The descendants of Wajid Ali Shah continue to live in Metiabruz, also called mini-Lucknow, where the exiled Nawab erected several buildings to revive his remembrance of Lucknow.

Part
VI

Dharman Bibi

49

The Lost Love

Dalip Singh, a tall and sturdy young man, was conspicuous in his simple kurta, covering his protruding biceps and dhoti, as he walked with long steps in the muddy passageways of the large ground, looking at the stalls selling a variety of wares in the Shivratri Fair, an annual affair at Jagdishpur. Just a few paces ahead of him, he could see a band of 7–8 mischievous young men who casually remarked and mocked almost everyone around, which only brought a thin smile on his face, puffing up his right cheek.

Suddenly, he saw one of them tug at the saree of a woman coming from the opposite direction. He could never tolerate someone playing with a woman's dignity. He paced up, caught him by the neck from behind, and was about to slap him when his accomplices turned and attacked him. Soon they realized that they had confronted the wrong man when he alone put down three of them like a professional wrestler. Despite the increasing number of attacks on him, he was in no mood to back off, though he could

be clearly seen losing the fight like a tiger surrounded by a pack of hyenas does.

Suddenly, like a divine intervention, one noble soul, equally ferocious, joined him. The amazing fact was that she was a woman, with her saree tugged between her legs. Together, they were more than enough for their rivals. When she picked up one of the rivals above her head to bring him down with a thud, the remaining ones fled the scene. The mesmerized Dalip Singh stood rooted to the ground, looking at her in awe and admiration, as did she.

Realizing that they were surrounded by onlookers, they started walking. We already know the man; the woman was Dharman Bibi, a tawaif, who was there to present her muzra. They soon departed, with a mutual feeling of love already sprouting between them. In glances, they promised to meet again, which they would do quite often. In the first meeting itself, Dharam Bibi had decided to take him as her patron.

Dharman Bibi lived in Arrah and was the disciple and niece of Zahooran, a tawaif who, in her early 40s, was still known for beauty and wisdom. When the aunt realized that her young niece was meeting a farmer often, she counselled her, "Look, a dignified tawaif has two options. One is being independent like I am, but I choose my clients very carefully. The other is to choose a patron, who is wealthy and powerful and remain committed to him for life. He fits in neither category."

When Dharman tried to protest insisting that their bond was love, the aunt said, "For us, love is merely physical attraction, and without money, you are sure to have a terrible old age."

Despite this, Dharman was reluctant to abandon her lover, but fate had different plans.

Dilip Singh came from a Rajput family; his forefathers possessed a large landholding, but owing to fragmentation among brothers over generations, the size of farms had become

uneconomical, further aggravated by the Permanent Settlement, an exploitative system of revenue that the British had introduced after the Battle of Buxar in 1764. This was the reason that all his elder brothers had joined the army. He found it hard to survive with such low earnings, so before the next Shivratri, he too followed in their footsteps and was gone.

It was a shock for Dharman, as she was looking forward to living with her young paramour for life. Abandoned, she underwent a trance for a couple of months before she could accept the reality. This episode unfolded a long time ago, in 1831.

50

Forced into Love

Next year, in 1832, Dharman Bibi attended the Shivratri fair at Jagdishpur again. She took the stage when the local zamindar arrived and took his seat. Zahooran looked at her and nodded her head softly with a meaningful gesture.

This fair was held each year with fanfare under the control of the landlord, Babu Kunwar Singh, then 55 years old. The previous year, he was away in Shahabad as he was entangled in a prolonged lawsuit over the title to the land that he had inherited from his father, Sahibzada Singh, in 1826. Moreover, ever since the British had introduced the new revenue system of Permanent Settlement, most farmers and landlords were running on arrears. In addition, he had inherited a large debt, mainly due to the revenue arrears, as the British were stoneheartedly reluctant to exempt people from paying the tax even when crops failed on account of floods or droughts. He had incurred a sizeable expenditure on these accounts, making things worse for him.

Despite these personal problems, Kunwar Singh was an ideal ruler for his subjects, which earned him loyalty and popularity. He had undertaken a number of projects for the well-being of his subjects. He built ponds, roads, and irrigation systems. He had foreseen the threat from the British, who seemed to him like devils gulping down the resources of the entire country. Sooner or later, there would be an armed struggle, he had said when no one could imagine something like the 1857 Uprising. He had gathered around him a band of loyal people, many of them armed with muskets and others with small weapons like swords and lances. His band included a number of cavaliers too. He ensured that they were trained well enough in the dense forest that he had planted around his place. In his fort, big but not strong, he had also established a foundry to produce small field cannons together with its shots.

Owing to lack of finances, it was not possible for him to build a strong fort and fortify it, so he thought out a novel, innovative way for defense—this was to plant saplings covering about one mile and a half in length and half a mile in width that would make it impossible for cannons to pass through. Over time, these saplings had grown into a dense plantation, mostly with thick-stemmed trees like peepal, jamun, and banyan, many of which can be seen even today. One of them stands in the Qila, or fort, to which, as Babu Kunwar Singh's direct descendent claimed in his interview with me, no less than 500 people were hanged.

While Dharman Bibi enthralled the audience with her skillful performance, she looked at Kunwar Singh more than once. She was looking for a patron now, but the landlord could not be a choice for her, as he was almost as old as her grandfather.

While she did not see any prospects in the landlord, the latter did. He had become interested in her just a few minutes before when his attendant informed him how she had fought with the

miscreants the previous year. Impressed by her past feat and present performance, Kunwar Singh proposed to her. She was stuck dumb and looked down, not knowing how to respond. Later at home, Zahooran stressed that she take him as her patron as he was the most influential of the landlords in the district of Shahabad, but she did not agree. This led to bitter arguments between the two that day and over the coming days.

Destiny had a role to play in her life again. It first separated her from the young paramour Dilip Singh, with whom she wanted to live, and now it forced her into choosing an old man as her patron.

Zahooran had earned a sizeable fortune in her profession. In her early 40s, she was still pretty and enthralled her audience with her skillful movements and expressive eyes, so she was one of the most sought-after tawaifs in the district. She had not taken a patron, leading a freelancer's life.

A sudden change came about in Zahooran's demeanor at this age, when most tawaifs tended to retire from the profession. She was charmed by a frequent visitor. He was new to the district and appeared quite rich from his clothing, jewellery, and manners. He rented a large mansion, in which he lived like a nawab. He introduced himself as a travelling merchant and won Zahooran's trust in a few days with the exquisite gifts that he brought her. She was now inclined to take him as her patron.

She, however, did not realize that he was a swindler. One night, when her niece was away for a performance, he poisoned her and took off with her jewellery, precious stones, and silken dresses, never to be seen again.

For Dharman, her aunt's death came as a massive shock. She could think of no one but Kunwar Singh for help. He, on his part, tried to do his best. He employed his men and coerced the police to do what was required, but to no avail. It was as if the culprit had vanished into thin air.

Despite his failure, Dharman found in Kunwar Singh a man she could trust—powerful, influential, and respectable. He did not try even once to exploit her, but rather helped her in earnest. She realized that it was due to his qualities that people were at his beck and call. So she finally took him as her lifelong patron. She continued to live in her house at Arrah but was available to the landlord whenever he wished. On his part, he looked after all her needs. It was at her wish that he even constructed a mosque for her at Arrah, as the *maulvis* did not allow women in other mosques. This mosque is known as Dharman Masjid after her. She was a strict adherent to her religious edicts; she is said to have never missed her *namaz* five times a day and would take a break if she was in the middle of a performance. She was known not only for her delicate singing and skilled dancing, but also for her prolonged performances over hours without a trace of fatigue. Her areas of perfection comprised a wide range of folk-based and improvised Dadra, Hori, Kajri, and Thumri, further glorified with her facial expressions. She could sing and dance simultaneously for long hours without a sign of breathlessness. She would cast her magical spell through her performances, and at times, she would repeat a particular line of the song umpteen times, each time with a different expression or dance movement, and this was what made most visitors shower their money on her. She is said to be the most adept at *Keherwa,* a type of song-dance involving extensive use of the belly and buttocks. Impressed by her skill, the ageing patron once said, "I can see myself growing young in your company."

51

Honor, Helplessness, and Crafty Elusion

Protecting her dignity was perhaps the trickiest task for a tawaif, particularly for those whose sole occupation was enveloped within the domains of mehfils and muzras, personal or public. There was a strict code of conduct for the ones who had taken a patron. One had to avoid any intimate relationships with any member of the audience, and this was the case with Dharman as well.

Prior to her engagement with Kunwar Singh, she had had sex with a chosen few, but now she was loyally *paband* to him. On his part, the septuagenarian landlord protected her, as she was widely known to be his mistress. He did not allow her to dance before strangers in his private mehfils held in his brick-and-mud fort, though he allowed her to perform elsewhere. There were instances when people transgressed their limits by attempting to touch her, hold her hand, or show indecent overtures, but she was trained

to tackle such situations. On more than one occasion, she used her physical power to emphasize her boundaries. She, however, did not know that there could be an occasion when even her patron's overbearing status would turn into helpless servitude.

The late 1840s were the times when the British were expanding their dominance across India, and it had become imperative for the native landlords and rulers to entertain the British officers with lavish parties, of which nautch was a usual component. Kunwar Singh, whose forefathers migrated from Ujjain to settle here, hence called an Ujjaniya Rajput, was no exception.

Keeping in with the racial tradition, he was a great host who treated the guests as gods. As a generous host, he often invited colonial officers to sumptuous feasts that ran late into the hours of the next morning. It was a sort of compulsion, too, as his rising debt could become an eyesore for the British superiors; he had seen several landlords evicted from their lands due to this. The lavish tawaif performances were the hallmark of such parties. The British guests often exploited their position and demanded that the prettiest tawaif share their beds. This was one reason why the hosts invited a few tawaifs who did not object to such demands.

This was the precise reason that the septuagenarian patron carefully excluded Dharman from the nautch performances in his personal parties, though it was she who managed these events from behind the curtain. She took an active part in deciding which dresses and jewellery were to be worn by the performers, which songs and dances were to be presented, and in what sequence.

One such occasion was at hand now. A senior British officer was the guest, so Kunwar Singh made special arrangements as he expected a special favor from him that was waiving off the interest on his pending revenue payment. He invited several well-known tawaifs to entertain him in his outhouse. Dharman did her part and withdrew from the scene.

The party started with lavish drinks and performances, yet the guest seated on the comfortable leather-bound chair seemed sulky, while the host reclining on the masnad looked at him uncomfortably and inquired if anything was lacking. He wanted what the landlord had until now prevented; he had heard of Dharman and wanted her to perform before him.

The noble tradition of Rajput hospitality and his helplessness before the British officer confounded him for a while; he knew he could not afford to say no. He sent across a message asking her to give a performance.

When Dharman received the message, she guessed what prompted his patron to do this and what was in the offing. As she dressed in her best clothing and jewellery, her mind was busy planning how to preserve her patron's honor. As she took the stage with a thumri, the loutish guest tried to hold her hand. In a glance, she realized this gesture made her patron restless. She found him trying to suppress his fury with his clenched fist and squeezed eyes.

With this, she decided to execute the plan that she had made to meet this contingency. With fascinating expressions and skillful movements, she again came near the guest and allowed him to touch her hand while she poured a heavier dose of wine into his glass. Her eyes concealed a seething anger arising from the sense of humiliation she felt. She cautiously hid her inner emotions and looked at her patron. He understood what she was up to. His forehead muscles relaxed, and a smile returned to his face.

Dharman performed with a mission. A few more songs, and the guest was so drunk that he found it hard to keep his eyes open, so in his uncontrolled voice, he demanded bed with her to accompany. He held her hand as he wanted to take her with him, but he was convinced that it would be utterly uncomfortable for him as she was in her heavy clothing and jewellery, and needed

a change. This incident is mentioned in *Tawaifnama,* authored by Saba Dewan.

In the barely lit room, when the heavily drunk British officer welcomed a lady and quenched his lust, he never knew that she was not whom he wanted but a common prostitute of the same build as Dharman's. The next morning, he departed with hazy memories of the previous night, little realizing how craftily he had been tricked. As for Dharman, were it not for his patron's comfort, she would not have consented to undergo the humiliation she did.

52

Tests of Resilience

"I want to be a mother," said Dharman, as her now over 70-year-old patron Kunwar Singh looked at her intently.

Dharman vehemently disliked the British for real or perceived causes. She felt they were oppressive, atrocious, arrogant, and leading a corrupt and immoral way of life. She missed Dilip Singh and felt that he would be by her side, if it were not for the debt he took to pay the land revenue. Whenever he came on leave, he would manage to have a glimpse of hers but kept away because his meagre salary did not allow him to have any luxury. He felt guilty that he was now a tool in the very foreigners' hands to enforce their unfair policies, of which he himself was a victim.

Dharman had felt insulted by the way the *gora* officer treated her at her patron's party as if she were an ordinary prostitute. As she heard more tales of British oppression and atrocity, her dislike for the white race was gradually becoming intense and more intense. As if this was not enough, yet another incident would further aggravate this intensity, and this was related to her motherhood.

What if a tawaif, Dharman, nursed womanly, motherly feelings within her? A woman without a child was traditionally considered incomplete in the Indian society, so she aspired to have one. It was popularly said that horses and Thakurs never grew old. This adage did not help her conceive, despite her septuagenarian patron being strong and active even at an old age. From his married wife, he had had a son Dalbhanjan Singh, who had died long ago.

Not many years ago, Kunwar Singh married his only grandson, Birbhanjan Singh, in a grand ceremony spread over three weeks. His marriage procession is still talked about, which went to Munger. It was like a large caravan complete with its own mobile market, a team of dancers and entertainers, and a team of 35 native medicine-men (both Unani and Ayurvedic) as it journeyed ten days each side and stayed at the bride's premises for five days, where it was treated lavishly. To celebrate this occasion, Kunwar Singh threw lavish parties for the English officers at Arrah and Patna, complete with nautch performances. Birbhanjan was by his side throughout, when after the 1857 Uprising, he set off on a march to Rewa, he died fighting later at Banda, unfortunately.

In some corner of his heart, Kunwar Singh too shared Dharman's wish, but it could not be realized somehow. Her wish could not be fulfilled for a few more years, and now it was 1856. She conjectured that it might no longer be possible for her to conceive, so she nursed a secret ambition of adopting a child.

As per the earlier personal laws, the Muslim women, whether married or single, could not adopt, but the tawaifs were an exception to this rule. They could adopt a child if they entered into a written bond with the parent(s). This law was changed after the British occupied this region, and now even the tawaifs could not adopt as it was argued that they bought or stole children for sex trade. The only exception to this rule was that they could adopt a child from a close relative. This ruling applied to both Muslim

and Hindu tawaifs. We have already discussed in the course of this book how the British never distinguished between tawaifs (nautch girls) and prostitutes. It would also be pertinent to mention that a Hindu woman at this time could adopt only with the consent of her husband.

With a patriarchal bent of mind, the Indians have always preferred a son over a daughter across all segments of society. However, a tawaif thought differently even so long ago. It was the daughter who inherited a tawaif's assets, as she was considered eligible to carry on with the mother's profession.

Having made up her mind, Dharman actively approached her relatives for adoption, but to no avail. As her ardent desire touched newer heights, she fasted, visited mosques and temples, prayed to gods and spirits, and even went after astrologers and *tantriks*, but nothing seemed to help her.

While her belief in all these was wavering, major changes were taking place in the estate, province, and country. When Kunwar Singh learned of her desire to adopt, he warned her about how hostile the British were to it.

By 1856, the British greed and oppression had crossed all bearable limits. They had occupied almost the whole of India by wars, or under false pretexts. They forced farmers to grow crops that could be used for commercial profits, which in no way benefited the former. On the contrary, high land revenues forced them to abandon their land and seek employment as landless laborers. For instance, the farmers in Shahabad were forced to grow opium, which the British sold in China illegally, earning a huge profit. Likewise, in several Bihar villages, farmers were forced to grow indigo, which was used for dyeing cloth in England. This one-crop system played havoc with the soil. Moreover, the British created a system of advance loans, which trapped the farmers in unending debt. The raw materials were sent to England, and from

there, the finished goods were imported back. Being machine-made, these goods were better in quality and cheaper in price, and this threw the native craftsmen out of trade, forcing them to look for livelihood elsewhere; this badly impacted them, among others, with the majority being weavers.

When they could no longer sustain their lives, they had little option but to work as landless farmers, or as an alternative, if age permitted, to join the British army. Even in uniform, they found they were discriminated against in salary, promotion, and other privileges, which dissatisfied them. The Indian society as a whole was growing poorer. The terrible situation led many men and women to migrate from villages to cities to work as daily wagers. The social life too faced a grim situation. Often, girls and women were sold off to influential people. The demand for regimental prostitutes was so high that many of them landed in brothels. The influential classes of traders and landlords too were under a great burden due to unreasonable taxes, and this had an adverse impact on the tawaifs, whom they could no longer support. The overall situation was hopeless.

Babu Kunwar Singh was going through a bad phase himself. He had inherited a large debt from his father in the form of arrears of land revenue, to pay which he sought loans from moneylenders, and compound interest on these two accounts had further aggravated his financial burden. He had incurred a large expenditure on fighting a legal case involving the title to his land. This was later sorted out through an agreement among the brothers, but the debt continued. His financial condition was assessed by Mr. Taylor, the Commissioner of Patna, in a letter to the Secretary, Board of Revenue dated December 19, 1856, as thus: "He is the scion of an ancient and noble family, the proprietor of a large and valuable estate in Shahabad, a generous and popular overlord, much beloved by his tenantry and respected throughout the District both by the

Europeans and natives... a liberal disposition and hereditary habits of extravagance involved him in profuse expenditure which was sustained only by borrowed funds . . . the necessity of meeting with punctuality the claims of Government with an empty purse placed him at the mercy of moneylenders, who exacted the most exorbitant terms for every advance . . ."

The "liberal disposition," which Taylor admitted, was on account of helping the poor and the needy who came to seek his favor and building different kinds of facilities such as dams, irrigation systems, ponds, wells, roads, markets, religious places, and public buildings, in addition to exempting people from paying any rent on the land. There were numerous instances of his giving lands to the poor in lieu of nothing, and many of these beneficiaries continue to till the land even today. To secure the favor of the British, he was spending large amounts on feasts to supplicate the British officers, which screwed up his finances further, while the relief coming through such favor only had a superficial effect, as his debt rose from 17 lakh in 1838 to more than 20 lakh in early 1857. He sought to borrow 13 lakh rupees from Narayan Rao and Madhav Rao, the descendants of Peshwa Raghoba Scindia, then settled at Banda through the government treasury at Arrah, but this attempt was thwarted by the local moneylenders. Dharman Bibi, too, helped Kunwar Singh with finances, but it was not enough. Meanwhile, he also took steps to improve his financial affairs through better management of his estate and succeeded to a great extent, yet the shortfall continued.

The worst came in early 1856 when the commissioner turned down his application for any concession in the revenue or interest thereupon; he was little interested in heeding whether the crops had failed or the revenue was unreasonably high. Now, Kunwar Singh was confronted with the possibility of losing his estate. To meet the impending situation, he called a meeting of

his trusted lieutenants. The British had appropriated Awadh on fictitious grounds just a couple of months ago, which caused restlessness among the native sepoys of the Bengal army, that mainly comprised sepoys belonging to Awadh and Bihar. They looked at this usurpation as the gravest attack on their sentiments as a nation. As it had thrown a large number of people out of their businesses, they too felt likewise.

In fact, Kunwar Singh had planned to overthrow the British as early as 1845–46 and had been securing the trust and support of several taluqdars within his estate as well as those belonging to adjoining estates and districts. Unfortunately, the plot was discovered by the British. Despite this fact, the Company could not gather the courage to go against him as it was then facing the 'stubborn and formidable resistance of the Sikh army, and all the resources of the Company's government were being drawn to the North-Western Frontier'. The book *The Mutiny of the Bengal Army* notes, "Even as lately as 1846, its [Shahabad's] Mahomeden nobility had endeavoured to take advantage of our balanced fortunes on the banks of the Sutlej. They had then succeeded in corrupting some of the native officers and Sepoys stationed at Dinapur [Danapur]."

Kunwar Singh chaired the meeting. The discussion opened with the mention of what he had succeeded in achieving in 1845–46 with the larger support of the taluqdars, both Hindu and Muslim. When the Company was engaged in fierce battles in the Punjab, its officers in Patna got wind that money was being distributed among the native officers and sepoys at Danapur, and Rahat Ali was arrested in this matter. In searches conducted across Bihar, it was revealed that a meeting of several influential persons, zamindars, and Rajahs (local rulers) was held at Haribar Chhattar on the occasion of Sonepur Fair, and it was decided to raise a force at several places, including Jagdishpur. Also, it was decided to seek help from the king of Nepal and King (Muhgal ruler) of Delhi.

Different participants were assigned the task of spreading disaffection among different native regiments in Bihar, including Danapur, Sigauli (Sugauli), Hazaribagh (now in Jharkhand), Doranda (now in Jharkhand), and others. The emissary sent to Nepal returned with a positive assurance, while other points of agreement finalized at Haribar Chhattar were being implemented, including, as KK Dutta writes, "recruitment for raising a force had already begun at Jagdishpur under Kunwar Singh."

Unfortunately, the plot was revealed to EC Rawenshaw, the then Commissioner of Patna, who took prompt action to caution the Governor General and also ordered investigations and raids. Searches were conducted at several places. In Patna, on the premises of Malik Kadam Ali, in one of the wells, a parcel was found in a piece of bamboo well secured by bricks and wrapped in a piece of carpet. Its contents were found wet. They were dried and read with the help of a magnifying glass. Among other papers, there were several letters, most of which were from Kunwar Singh to Khwaja Hussain Ali, Kadam Ali, Barkutalla, and others, and all of them bore the distinct impression of his seal. The Patna Magistrate already had proofs that the Jagdishpur zamindar was actively involved in the anti-British movement and was in communication with Rahat Ali, who had gone to Nepal as the emissary. It was also found that Kunwar Singh would proceed to Lahore with his force to assist the Sikhs in the Anglo-Sikh wars. In one of the letters, Kunwar Singh said that the money to be given to him was ready, but there was no confirmation whether he had received it. The Patna Magistrate wrote to the Magistrate of Shahabad (the district of which Jagdishpur was a part) to institute an inquiry and arrest Kunwar Singh.

Amazingly, the British, who took disastrous steps even on an iota of suspicion, did not even question Kunwar Singh, let alone arrest him. Why it so happened is revealed in the letter

that Elphinstone Jackson, Magistrate of Shahabad, wrote to the Secretary to the Government of Bengal on January 22, 1846. He noted that "the arrest of Baboo Kooer Singh will very likely be followed by a rising of the people, who are at his beck . . . lead to most serious results."

This was due to the fact that the British had come to know that dealing with Kunwar Singh was like dealing with the whole province, as they had found out that, in addition to the King of Nepal and people of Shahabad, the zamindars and Rajahs of Tikari, Gaya, Sasaram, Darbhanga, Bettiah, and Hutwa were also involved, and they were being aided by several government servants, powerful bankers, and merchants. The government found that Khwaja Hussain (or Hasan) Ali was the leader of the entire plot and went after him, but he proved elusive until he presented himself before the Patna magistrate, but had to be released on October 27, 1846. In the entire conspiracy, no one was arrested or sentenced. Only two native sepoys bore the brunt, and that too with light punishments. One was Durga Prasad Pandit, who was sentenced to three years' rigorous imprisonment, while one Jamadar Beekhan Khan was dismissed from service. Kaye, in his book, regarded it as "one of the presages of the coming storm." And in this 1856 meeting, a storm was being planned.

Kunwar Singh and his comrades recalled what they had achieved ten years ago, shared a number of anecdotes, and analyzed their shortcomings. He then concluded the events by saying, "It's high time we learn from the past events. Had our scheme not been revealed, we would have shaken the *gora log* (white people) then. Ever since, their interference in our religions has crossed all limits; discrimination is rampant, and corruption is eating away our resources. The sepoys once again appear to be disaffected. We must take advantage of this situation. But this uprising has to be achieved at the national level. One thing is for sure: the uprising can

start with the sepoys, but the common masses would have to join them as well to make it successful."

While the meeting was underway at Jagdishpur, at Arrah, Dharman Bibi was doing something that would unnerve him for a while. Despite her patron's warning to her, she continued to spread the word that she wanted to adopt a girl child. This also reached the middlemen who stole or bought children from hapless parents to sell off as slaves, prostitutes, or concubines. The pre-British era custom was cruel by nature, and these sold boys landed up doing menial work for the wealthy, while the girls had to live a shameful youth and a pitiable old age. Many of such children were even bought by the East India Company's officials to work in their private households.

The Indian Slavery Act, 1843, abolished any kind of sale or purchase of humans as slaves. This law also prohibited law courts from enforcing any decree or legal order that enslaved people. Despite such provisions, slavery in households, farms, and mills continued unabated, but the courts were harsh on any transactions by prostitutes or tawaifs.

53

Being a Mother

As we know, Dharman really wanted to adopt a child, preferably a girl child. All her efforts to get one from her acquaintances and relatives proved futile. Meanwhile, several middlemen had gotten wind of her intention and approached her, but she could not adopt a child on one or the other ground. She did not want to invite trouble for her patron or herself by buying a stolen child; her patron's warning was at the back of her mind at all times. Thus, a few more months passed, and the year was coming to a close now.

Kunwar Singh had to deal with several challenges at the same time. He was trying to settle his revenue records with the British and was clandestinely uniting the factors that could cooperate with him in the uprising against the British. And now he had to deal with something he would not otherwise like. His men brought information that Dharman was more actively seeking to find a child for adoption and was in contact with middlemen. It was a

crucial stage of his plan, so he did not want to appear on the wrong side of the law. Any suspicion about him could blow up the entire plan on which he had been working for over a decade, and now he was hopeful that something concrete could come about in the months to follow.

Moreover, surprise was the *sine qua non* for the entire uprising. Without it, the British would crush it brutally. Ten years ago, they were busy in wars with the Sikhs, but now they had emerged far stronger, with the very same Sikhs being loyal to them.

A few days after Diwali, the festival of meet and greet, Kunwar Singh came to visit Dharman Bibi with an expensive gift and advised her to keep off her plans, at least until the British had been beaten out of the country.

Dharman was, however, unwilling to do so. She said, "I cannot crush my innermost desire! I want a child somehow. Please respect the mother inside me."

Kunwar Singh felt helpless before her. He said, "All right, but be sure to adopt on a legal deed and keep it a secret for as long as you can."

Relaxed, Dharman looked for a child more actively, and in a week or so, she was approached by a middlewoman who had a two-year-old girl with her. All the terms were to her liking, but above all, she loved the girl at first glance. As she took the docile girl in her embrace, she felt her soft maternal emotions being manifested in a strange current flowing through her body. She knew she wanted that very girl, and no one else, as her daughter. Over the next week, she secured the sale deed. She sent for her patron, as she did not want to be seen outside the house with the child. The mother was ready to sacrifice her freedom.

Kunwar Singh came promptly. She expressed her joy with a dance performance depicting how Radha made Krishna go after her. Then she took a seat just near him with the adopted daughter.

Smiling softly, Kunwar Singh said, "After months, I feel that you are your normal self; you have regained the spontaneous expressions you are known for. What I like about you is how strong-willed you are. Be cautious and do your best to keep her within the house. Pray that we succeed in becoming a free nation in a year or two. Until then, if someone comes inquiring, just say that you have adopted her from a sister in relation."

"I don't think anything should happen in my case. You see, there are scores of sold girls working as prostitutes in the Lal Bazar," contended Dharman.

"You are yet to know the real face of the British! They apply the laws selectively. They will ignore anything that suits them, like the girls in Lal Bazar. So, don't think this will happen in your case. Be aware at all times, but I'll always be there should you face any problem."

Kunwar Singh took the girl into his lap and caressed her head in affection. He had brought clothes and silver bangles for her. He said, "This girl is really cute, bring her up tenderly."

Keeping quiet was not enough, as everybody in the trade already seemed to know about this. It did not take long for a policeman to come and knock at her door.

"You've bought a child, haven't you?" he said, rudely tapping the bamboo cane on the ground.

Dharman expected this. Suppressing her fear, she said, "Do you know who my patron is? He is none else than the zamindar of Jagdishpur."

The policeman's demeanor turned softer, but he still asked, "And the child, is that true?"

"I've adopted the child from a close relative and not bought her," she said confidently.

The policeman scowled his eyebrows in suspicion but departed, saying, "Daroga Saheb might like to see you some day."

Dharman was worried and uncomfortable now. She did not want to be a source of any trouble for her patron at this crucial stage.

In the middle of November 1856, the winter set in, with widespread rains lashing the region. The sudden dip in temperature put the girl down with a fever. She sent for the *hakim*, the Unani medicine man. Medication and nursing with cold strips did not seem to work as the fever aggravated further. She cursed the policeman; she believed that his evil glance had cast a bad omen, and did everything to ward it off. She burnt red chillis, washed her hands with salt and promised charity, but the girl's condition deteriorated over the week. She served the sick girl day and night, and herself vomited and grew weak.

When the hakim came for the check-up next, she complained about her retching too. He examined her and said the words she wished she heard two weeks earlier, "You have a child in the womb."

On second thought, Dharman felt she became pregnant only because the little girl had aroused her motherly feelings. The girl's condition gradually deteriorated and the hakim too declared his helplessness. She consulted other medicine men but this did not help as they had no clue what ailed her. There was a European doctor at Arrah, but she could not think of going to him. Vexed to the extreme, she did not know whether to feel happy or sad. The lovely frail girl now barely opened her eyes; her pretty face gradually grew lusterless. Finally, the girl succumbed to her mysterious illness.

When Kunwar Singh visited to share her grief, she said, "The little angel had come only to awaken my feelings, which are necessary to become a mother. She was the Goddess incarnate."

At least, the girl would no longer be a source of trouble for them, though this could not be said of Kunwar Singh's plans.

54

Simmering Discontent

Well before the 1857 Uprising broke out in Bihar, there were several instances that indicated simmering discontent among the people and sepoys. We have already discussed how Babu Kunwar Singh was at the helm of plotting against the British a decade before this, in 1845–46. Having conquered the Punjab, the British emerged as more powerful as a large number of the martial Sikhs joined their army, and with this, they experimented with some steps that could be called cunning. While the East India Company officially declared that it had nothing to do with missionaries' work, several of its officers, on record, have supported conversion as they saw India as a ripe ground for Christianity.

The Hindus and Muslims were equally peeved at this, and coupled with socio-economic problems, they were on the verge of an uprising. The province of Bihar was no exception. As early as 1848, Rev. William Buyers, a missionary, observed in his book *Recollections of North India*, that their work had made little

impression on the inhabitants "hostile to the English influences" and that the missionaries "had often met with virulent opposition and even personal violence in the City (of Patna), chiefly from the Muhammadans." Tayler, Commissioner of Patna Division, observed in a letter to the Government of Bengal on June 27, 1855: ". . . the minds of the people in those districts are at present in a very restless and disaffected state and they have generally conceived the idea that there is an intention on the part of the Government to commence and carry through a systematic interference with their religion, their caste and their social customs."

The Santhal rebellion occurred in 1855 in the Bengal and Bihar provinces, from Bhagalpur to Birbhum, in which tens of thousands of tribals sacrificed their lives for their religion and economic rights. People also perceived that the British were favoring the Indians with workable knowledge of English for jobs.

The British were wont to put people behind bars even on frivolous grounds, often without a proper hearing so common people felt sympathy for the prisoners. In Bihar jails, dissatisfaction was ripe in 1845–46 when the messing system was introduced, as people from different castes were not willing to eat together, and such feelings had aggravated over time. People were so sceptic of any British 'reforms' that they would oppose them, an instance of which was seen in Bihar jails in 1855. The prisoners used a brass *lota* or utensil which they used for diverse purposes, including drinking water, bathing, and washing etc. The British replaced it with an earthen pot.

The experiment with earthen vessels in the jails excited the subdued emotions, not only within the cells but outside too. In Arrah, prisoners were so vociferous that guards had to be ordered to fire directly at them, as was the case at Muzzaffarpur and Tirhut. Common people mobbed the prisons in their support. The Magistrate of Arrah described it as 'a furious and altogether

unexpected outbreak on the part of the people of the town and district in support and sympathy with the prisoners.' He further said that 'the rioters' included almost all inhabitants of the town and *ryots* (farmers), who openly declared that they would not go back until the lotas were restored.

Interestingly, when the Magistrate of Arrah found the situation hard to tackle, he invited Kunwar Singh to pacify the prisoners. He did visit the jail, and as if under a plan, the prisoners remained quiet until he was there, but soon after his departure, attacked the guards and other facilities. It was enough proof of his popularity among the people.

The Company officials regularly got intelligence reports about people's disaffection, so any disturbance could not be called a sudden outburst, as Kaye talks of "rash and misguided ignorance, but the deliberate work of some of the rich inhabitants of the town, and some of the higher native functionaries of our Civil Courts."

In spite of such occurrences, the British carried on with their usual ways and continued to work against the popular sentiments. Another instance when people rose in revolt was in 1855, when a Christian missionary circulated a pamphlet exhorting the native people to embrace Christianity.

The Rajahs and zamindars of the region were at the forefront, giving vent to people's sentiments. It was also reported that those of Muzaffarpur, Arrah, Chhapra, Azimabad, Sahebganj, and Bhagalpur were in league with the king of Patiala and the Emperor of Delhi in planning an insurrection.

Disturbances continued to occur on a minor scale all through 1856 and the first half of 1857, when the outbreak of revolution at Meerut on May 10, 1857, proved to be a flashpoint. The British tried to suppress its news, but without success. In the neighboring Awadh, Lucknow rose towards the end of May and Kanpur in

early June. Fierce battles were raging in several other places across North India.

Outbreaks were reported from within Bihar too. For example, in Deoghar subdivision, on June 12, the 32nd Native Infantry declared an open rebellion, killing Lieutenant Norman Lesley. The way the British dealt with the revolting sepoys spread discontent further. For instance, in Deoghar, Major MacDonald noticed that the revolutionary sepoys belonged to high castes, so he got them hanged by low-caste people in the presence of the entire regiment. Tayler, too, ordered, in each district, the recruitment of 50 low-caste policemen with clear instructions not to admit any high-caste people (Rajputs, Brahmins), and Muslims, and also ordered the termination of the services of any such high-caste people if they had already been recruited. Such cases of prejudice and injustice brought the entire province to a boil, including Chhapra, Muzaffarpur, and Patna.

As the outbreak reports poured in from more and more places, panic spread among the British officials in Bihar. Chhapra's commissioner left the charge of the district to a native officer and fled to Danapur (also spelled Dinapur), a fortified British cantonment on the outskirts of Patna. The residents of Arrah and Buxar too sought refuge here. The officials at Muzaffarpur issued distress calls, and the situation in Patna was volatile too. A rumor spread there of a likely uprising by the native sepoys at Danapur on 7th of June; therefore the British forces flocked to the Commissioner's fortified house. At this time, there were three native regiments stationed at Danapur: the 7th, 8th, and 40th. It is interesting to note that all these regiments had been raised from Shahabad, where Kunwar Singh was a popular hero. Dharman's first love, Dalip Singh, was posted here too.

Tayler, the commissioner, tried to be proactive and adopted repressive measures. On June 19, he invited several prestigious

people from Patna for a consultation; they included three Wahabi leaders named Muhammad Hussain, Ahamadullah, and Baijul Haque. When the meeting ended, Tayler ordered the detention of these three Muslim leaders, while others were allowed to go. It was an act that he himself described as 'most successful until now', though the Lieutenant Governor dismissed it as 'barbarous and dangerous,' This step was also criticized by his successor and by several writers, including his contemporary Forrest, who called it a 'betrayal'.

On July 3, there was a widespread outbreak against the Company government in Patna under the leadership of Pir Ali. As slogans rent the air and the crowd tended to destroy the British signs and facilities, the Deputy Opium Agent, Dr. Lyell, was sent to suppress the uprising but was killed. Tayler came down hard on the native policemen and officers and dismissed the *Daroga.* Search operations were conducted all across Patna. Pir Ali, along with several of his associates, was arrested on July 5.

In a brief kangaroo court trial, 16 people were sentenced to death and were hanged within 3 hours. Not only this, two days later, two more people were hanged, two others were sent to Kala Pani (Andaman), and 17 others were sentenced to varying terms of imprisonment. The property of many of these accused was destroyed or damaged extensively. Other British officers in Bihar were no less unjust. Major Holmes declared martial law in Sugauli. He caught any one he wished and hanged him without a trial. He ordered to hang any deserting sepoy. This prompted four sepoys of the 12th Irregular Cavalry under him to kill him and his wife on July 25, while others killed several other British officers. Elsewhere too, on the landing ghats of the landlords, there were orders to seize all boats so that the deserting sepoys could not use them.

Thus, we can see that widespread disturbances prevailed all over Bihar on the eve of the uprising at Danapur. A revolution

in Bihar could have meant a death knell for the Empire because both routes from Calcutta to the upper provinces (Ganga River and Grand Trunk Road) passed through it. In addition, they would have lost a large chunk of income from opium and indigo. To worsen the matter, there was not enough European force to tackle the revolutionaries. Naturally, there was panic among the British all across Bihar. To meet the probable contingency, they converted police battalions into active troops. Also, they sought help from native zamindars and Rajahs and were not disappointed. The more the British tried to quell the discontent, the more it flourished.

All this while, Kunwar Singh, with his astute silence, kept the Company officials guessing about his intentions. He did not wish to leave any loose ends until the final strike. He succeeded in this, the evidence of which is in W. Tayler's letter to the Secretary to the Government of Bengal on July 23, just two days prior to the Danapur Uprising. He wrote, "Letters, anonymous and authenticated, have frequently reached me charging Baboo Kooer Singh with disaffection and conspiracy . . . My own knowledge of the Baboo's honorable and straightforward character, of his loyalty towards the State, and his feeling of personal friendship for myself forbade the supposition . . . I am still strongly convinced of Kooer Singh's fealty and good faith."

55

Birth of Uprising

The iron chain jingled, and the door creaked. Seconds later, Dharman Bibi's ever active octogenarian patron walked into her chamber with his usual long strides and took his seat on the dewan reserved only for him. Seeing him, a spontaneous smile flowered on her cheeks. She rose to her feet carefully to bow and said, "How lucky I am to have you here, Babu Saheb."

Never before in their three-decade-old relationship had Kunwar Singh visited her on three consecutive days. His glance seemed to have fixed on her protruding belly. He said, "Hope you are all right."

"Yes, no harm can come to me when I'm under your care. I suppose you were at Arrah even last night?" she enquired.

He nodded, gently sipping from the glass of water that the attendant had brought. "Did you consult the *ayah* (village nurse)?"

"She came this morning and said my pains can start any time now."

"You are sure going to give birth to the revolution," he said with a loud laugh, tapping his fingers on the forehead in his trademark style.

Dharman, however, was earnest. She said, "You are starting a war with the *gora log*, aren't you?"

"Don't ask things that you shouldn't," said Kunwar Singh as his fingers combed his long mustaches blending into his beard. He knew he could not tell her that he had amassed enough provisions to last 20,000 men for six months at Jagdishpur, as he foresaw a prolonged struggle for freedom.

"You may think me aloof, but I want to be with you when you face the enemy."

"Don't think of terrible things. You are going to be a mother. Be a happy mother! I can promise that our child will toddle in a free land." He said in a light manner, and then his tone turned grave, "The land is rising against them, and now, it is our turn. I'm waiting for the Danapur warriors. They will be here in two days. We don't want to let up in our endeavor."

By this time, the musicians had taken their seats. Dharman started singing at a low pitch; her first song related to the exploits of the Ujjainiya Rajput clan. In view of the advanced stage of her pregnancy, dancing was out of the question.

Rumours were afloat right from the first week of June 1857 that the three native regiments stationed at Danapur, on the outskirts of Patna, were likely to rise, but they did not materialize into reality. There was evidence that the sepoys were in contact with the local Muslim leaders, like Ali Karim, and they were given money too. As more and more places in the country rose, the British were in no position to determine whom and what to trust. Patna's commissioner, Tayler, was finally instructed to disarm the Danapur regiments. He was, however, unsure, as no soldier would take it kindly. He thought of a way out.

The rumors were ripe even amongst the sepoys. They were ready to revolt, but they also knew that once they got into it, they would not be able to turn their backs, so they needed to find a vigorous and visionary person who could lead them ably. They discussed several names under the guidance of the senior sepoys in the 7th and 8th regiments, namely Harekrishan Singh and Nishan Singh. It was decided that these two would be their immediate bosses, while Kunwar Singh of Jagdishpur would be the overall leader. Harekrishan Singh intimated them that Kunwar Singh had already assented to be their leader. They all belonged to the district of Shahabad, where the old zamindar was well-known for his qualities. With this, they decided to rise in revolt, when an attempt to disarm them would be made. He also revealed a broad plan for the further course of action.

At 7 a.m. on July 25, instead of disarming the sepoys, Tayler issued an order enjoining the sepoys to deposit their percussion caps at 4 p.m., nine hours later. The sepoys, on the other hand, knew that their guns, without the percussion caps, were worse than ordinary sticks. It did not take long for the sepoys in the barracks of the 7th and 8th regiments to pack their bags and baggage. Until now, the 40th Regiment was tranquil, but on Dalip Singh's exhortation, its sepoys too joined their brothers-in-arms. In two hours', they were all marching towards the Son River on way to Arrah, the district headquarters of Shahabad, where Kunwar Singh waited for them.

It was about this time that Dharman gave birth to two little girls under the care of the old *ayah* at her house. Her joy was boundless; what more could a tawaif wish for? She would need several days' postpartum care before she could start looking after the tiny souls. She had not yet learned about the revolution. She earnestly wished that her patron was by her side to share her happiness. Little did she know that fate would not allow him to even see the girls.

The sepoys were in revolt but indulged in no violence or destruction. However, when the British regiments started firing round shots from the field guns, they retaliated. Yet the sepoys kept moving towards their goal. The British had no courage to chase them. The sepoys fired only in self-defense. They even helped several European men and women flee to safety and only fired at those who confronted them. Mocking at the British attitude, Travelyan writes, "When they had gone a mile or two on their way, a few round shots were sent after them, as a parting compliment, and then the General [Lloyd] had plenty of leisure to sit down and reflect on the probable result of his masterly combinations."

The British anticipated their movement, so they ordered seizure or destruction of the boats at the Koilwar Ghat, but before the officers at Arrah could react, the sepoys pre-empted any action and ensured their safe arrival in Arrah, crossing the Son on the morning of July 26.

The Europeans at Arrah panicked and disposed of their families in Danapur. Over the past few days, Boyle, the executive engineer of the East Indian Railway and resident at Arrah, had already secured the outhouse in the collectorate and fortified it, thinking that it could be used in case of an emergency. Over a course of days, he strengthened its walls and constructed loopholes to fire through.

Arrah's magistrate Wake and other Europeans only had a few hours to take refuge in this fortified building, now known as Boyle or the Arrah House. They stored rice and flour sufficient to last a few days, but water was scarce as there were not many pots and pans to store it, which was a potential weakness. They were short on meat and liquor too. But, of course, they had abundant ammunition to last months.

The revolutionary sepoys, numbering about two thousand, were welcomed at Koilwar and led straight to the Civil Lines.

On their way, they plundered the treasury of ₹ 85,000 (₹ 70,000 in some accounts), freed the prisoners, and sieged the outhouse where now they knew all Europeans had taken refuge. This was also the site where one of the most stirring episodes of the 1857 Uprising was to unfold.

At this time, it included 13 Europeans, including Wake and Boyle, occupying the first floor as a safeguard if the Sikhs revolted too, and 50 Sikh sepoys who remained loyal to the British throughout.

The revolutionaries thought that it would be just a walkover, which was a folly on their part. As they approached the building in over-enthusiasm, a spray of bullets put 18 of them down, and only then did they realize that it was not going to be an easy game. They immediately withdrew and took shelter behind the thick foliage around. It was at this time that Kunwar Singh came and took over the command. Travelyan has described him as follows: " . . . he was not a devil at all, but the high-souled chief of a warlike tribe, who had been reduced to a nonentity by the yoke of a foreign invader."

At his age of just below 80, most would dream of a retired life. But Kunwar Singh had thrown himself in the midst of action. For now, he preferred a policy of 'wait and watch' as food and water inside the little fort would not last long. He asked the sepoys to fire from behind the trees only if they could aim at the inmates. He did not want more than necessary casualties at this time. He believed that it was more important to have the Sikhs on his side, which would ensure an easy victory for them.

The sepoys loudly beckoned the Sikhs to join their ranks, promising safe passage and five hundred rupees as inducement. In a clever ruse, the Sikhs feigned inaudibility, luring the sepoys closer. Then, with swift precision, they opened fire. Despite this, the Sikhs found themselves in a dire and hopeless situation.

56

The First Battle of Bihar

To lift the siege at Arrah, a force was sent from Patna under the command of Captain Dunbar. This force, consisting of 350 men of the 37th Queen's Regiment, 66 Sikhs, and some volunteers, set off by steamer. Near Arrah, they changed over to boats as they had to sail in the narrow canal to reach closer to their destination.

It was dark by now. The young Dunbar overlooked the advice that the tired souls should be rested for the night, as entering an unknown territory swarming with foes in the dark could be dangerous. He, however, was in a hurry to rescue his European brethren, so he ordered his troops to march. He was confident that the enemy would have no courage to face his brute force. His inexperience did not allow him to perceive the danger that lingered over his small force, as the revolutionary force had by now swelled to ten thousand and was eagerly waiting to ambush him.

With the Sikhs as the vanguard, the British force marched towards the Collectorate. The day-long journey, followed by a

rough walk on the pebbly road below only added to their fatigue and hunger. There was a thick plantation lining both sides of the road near the siege site, but the advance guard crossed it safely. As the British troops straggled past it, they were in for a surprise. From both sides came crashing musket fire. Many of them, including Dunbar, went down in the first attack, while the remaining struggled to load their weapons and find a safe place to hide. The party broke into disarray, running where it could find refuge. The revolutionaries chased and brought down several of them. In pitch darkness, their white summer uniforms made them easy targets. They regrouped near a tank but continued to face the onslaught of the incoming bullets.

At daybreak, several surviving Europeans managed to reach the boats, yet their escape was met with renewed gunfire. Remarkably, it was the Sikhs alone who showcased their exceptional battle prowess; they skillfully fought their way back to the boats in one piece. About one-half of the Europeans could reach back to Patna, and amongst them, not more than fifty were unwounded. The dead Captain Dunbar was ultimately blamed for the rout. General Lloyd telegraphed to the Commander-in-Chief, saying, "The result of the expedition to Arrah has been, I regret to say, very disastrous, owing entirely to the mismanagement of the Officer in command, the late Captain Dunbar. . . ."

Of this party, two were awarded the coveted Victoria Cross for their acts of bravery. Ross Mangles of the Indian Civil Service carried a wounded soldier on his shoulder for the last five miles, despite the extreme danger to his life. His colleague, McDonell, put his wounded self in peril by climbing onto the roof of the boat when the bullets came like rainfall to separate the rudder from the ropes allowing the boat to sail, and thus helped in saving several lives.

When the besieged inmates at Arrah House heard the fire, they hoped that their rescue was at hand, so they, too, started firing. As

the time passed, they realized, to their dismay, that the intensity of gunfire had diminished and finally ceased with no rescue in sight. However, distress only made them bolder to face the challenges.

High humidity caused much sweating, so more water was needed, but all of it had been drunk already. At this time, the besiegers were digging a tunnel into Arrah House near the back wall. The Sikh defenders, in the darkness of midnight, stole these tools and, with them, dug out a well in just 12 hours. Their ingenuity made up for the lack of meat as well when they stole some goats and sheep grazing in the nearby field. All these days, Wake had been recording the occurrences on the walls. Still, all was not well with them. Four of their horses had been shot dead, and their stinking carcasses made living there all the more difficult.

In ingenuity, the besiegers did not lag behind as well. They acquired more tools to continue to dig the tunnel, which the besieged knew could be the greatest threat to them. During an untoward hour of rest, they would start shouting as if they were attacking, keeping the inmates awake and confused. And one day, they burned chilies under the walls, whose smoke caused severe irritation, but in effect, this did not smoke out the inmates. They also offered the besieged to hand over Magistrate Wake and Deputy Collector Syed Azimuddin in return for a safe passage for all, but without a result.

On the morning of the 27th, Kunwar Singh declared to the excited followers that the British had been beaten away and that Arrah was a free country now. Immediately, he set down to form his government. He divided the town into two *thanas* (police stations), under the overall charge of Sheikh Ghulam Yahya. Other officers included Sheikh Azimuddin, Turab Ali, and Khadim Ali, among others. He himself sat in court to listen to people's grievances. People now believed that his Raj was firmly established. Samuell, Tayler's successor, noted later that the title of Maharaj had been bestowed on Kunwar Singh.

As if by providential intervention, Major Vincent Eyre of the Bengal Artillery was navigating the Ganges to Allahabad with his force and artillery guns. When he was steaming near Arrah, he learned about the siege. He, of his own accord, without waiting for any aid or instruction from Patna or elsewhere, decided to rescue his people. He was an experienced military officer who had scored several victories in Afghanistan.

At the moment, Eyre had with him 154 British infantrymen, 12 mounted cavaliers, and 3 field guns with 34 artillerymen. From his landing point in Arrah, he needed to traverse 50 miles, but the flooding rivers in the region had made the entire landscape watery, and this, coupled with the hostile populace, made the path zigzag and the journey challenging. The field pieces had to be drawn by bullocks which he snatched from farmers. He heard on the way that the revolutionaries had cut to pieces the force more than twice as large as his, yet his resolve was clear that Arrah must be relieved.

Eyre set up his camp at Gajrajganj on August 2, 1857. The next day, he set out towards Bibiganj on way to Arrah. Skirmishes took place all along the 6 km. route. When he finally made it to Bibiganj, he found the bridge destroyed, so he took a detour. On this route stood a deep wood where Kunwar Singh had set up ambushes. His force at this time included 2,500 sepoys and common people armed with domestic weapons, numbering about 8,000.

Eyre strategically positioned his artillery at the front and advanced, prompting Kunwar Singh's sepoys to launch relentless frontal assaults, resulting in substantial casualties. Undeterred, the sepoys regrouped, dividing into two flanks, and executed a point-blank musketry attack, putting the enemy in imminent peril. Eyre's forces were on the verge of defeat, disheartened by the relentless onslaught. However, his innovative tactic proved successful, turning the tide of the battle.

He ordered his officers to the front with naked swords and rushed at the advancing enemy in hand-to-hand do-or-die combat, forcing the besiegers to turn back and run, leaving more than 600 dead behind them. With this, Arrah fell back into British hands, ending an eight-day-long siege.

Kunwar Singh realized that he was short on supplies and bringing them from Jagdishpur at such time could not be accomplished, so he decided to shift his headquarters to his old fort in his hometown. He retained his grand posture while retreating. Though age did not favor him, he was determined to struggle hard. G.O. Travelyan, in his book *The Competition Wallah* (1866), writes, "Two facts may be deduced from the story of these operations: first, that the besiegers of the house at Arrah were neither cowards, nor bunglers; and next, that it was uncommonly lucky for us that Coer [Kunwar] Singh was not forty years younger."

All this while, Dharman was busy looking after the twin girls she had given birth to. When she came to know of her patron's defeat, she looked at the little souls. She sat motionless for minutes trying to decide what meant more to her: children or patron, but could not decide. Her informer brought news that her patron had fortified his fort at Jagdishpur; there he would be too strong for the English to even dream of attacking him. This pacified her.

Like her informant, many native people believed that despite his defeat, Kunwar Singh was formidable in his fort. This opinion was not Eyre's. He wanted to finish with him, who had all the potential to put the very empire at stake. He first disarmed citizens and presided over several court martial proceedings to give hanging orders for people without considering how serious the 'crime' was. Finally, on August 11, he set off on his mission to Jagdishpur to take exemplary vengeance. In the meantime, he had been reinforced too.

Kunwar Singh knew about the enemy's approach, so he strengthened entrenchments at Dulour, a village about 6 km from his fort. It was here that the two forces clashed.

Kunwar Singh fought valiantly at the head of 3,000 men, one-half of them being sepoys and other common people with domestic weapons. His field guns were manufactured in his own foundry, but they were primitive in nature and were no comparison with the enemy's.

Eyre, on the other hand, had at his disposal modern weaponry and artillery. He suffered losses, but emerged victorious. Kunwar Singh sustained minor wounds and was forced to withdraw towards his fort. The plantation helped him sustain the attack for some time, but the day was not in his favor. Finally, Eyre occupied his fort and residence. This battle was fought on August 12.

All this while, Eyre was busy destroying everything in Jagdishpur that he came across. He himself has reported: "I am destroying the town and preparing to blow up the palace and principal buildings around it. Today I partially destroyed a new Hindu temple on which Koer (Kunwar) Singh had lavished large sums. I did this because it is known that Brahmins have instigated him to rebellion." Kaye noted in his book: "All the principal buildings within Kunwar Singh's premises were soon heaps of blackened ruins, and a Hindu temple on the Raja's estate shared the fate of other edifices."

Eyre also found a gun foundry in the fort, which he destroyed too. His other officers destroyed buildings elsewhere, including Kunwar Singh's palace at Jitowara and the residences of Amar Singh and Dayal Singh (his two brothers).

The martial law was imposed, which superseded the ordinary law in force. The battle's details can also be gauged from the letter that Patna Commissioner wrote to Shahabad Magistrate on August 21, 1857, which instructed confiscation of the property of Kunwar Singh and of others in that district who had joined the movement

under Act XXV of 1857. Again, on August 27, he ordered to "take immediate steps to discover and punish the villagers who fired on Captain Dunbar's party . . . and the persons who tied up the rudders of the boats to prevent the returning troops from using them." The British hostility against villagers is evident from several communications which clearly order to 'adopt retributive measures' against those who did not help the British, who showed hostility towards the British, and who aided the rebels.

In response to this bitter vengeance, a large number of places in Bihar rose. Its repercussions were felt in scores of villages and towns across the province and adjoining Awadh. Gaya, Muzaffarpur, Patna, Shahabad, Sugauli, Chhapra, Mirzapur, Chunar, Munger, Deoghar, Hazaribagh, Chotanagpur, Palamu, Manbhum, Singhbhum, Ramgarh, Ranchi, and Doranga are only a few places to name. Bengal too was not untouched; it felt tremors in several towns, including Raniganj, Jalpaiguri, and Purulia. Both sepoys and civilians fought shoulder to shoulder.

When an informer brought Dharman the news of her patron's defeat at Jagdishpur, she was massaging the girls. Without hearing the complete message, she stood up, leaving the infants on the bare floor, and stared at them as if she did not know them. Tears rolled down her cheeks, which she wiped and then roared like a tigress, "My lord can be defeated only after I am dead. I must be with him now, but I don't know what to do of these girls. Ma Mundeshwari, give me strength!" She rushed to her wooden chest and took out the long dagger that Kunwar Singh had gifted her a few years ago. Standing over the crying infants, she breathed heavily, clutching the weapon hard as her heavy bosom heaved up and down. The attendant and the informant stood alarmed at seeing her menacing posture while her pretty face looked ugly in heightened sentiments. 'Is she going to kill them for whom she yearned and rubbed her nose before all deities?' was writ large on their anxiously frightened faces.

57

In Pursuit of the Patron

"Bibi, you haven't heard the entire news," said the informant.

"Speak," said Dharman intrigued.

"Babu has lost only a battle, but he is not beaten. He has just withdrawn to the jungles in Kaimur; he is safe."

This information had a cooling effect on her furious emotions. She threw down the dagger and knelt over her daughters. She picked them both, putting them to her breasts each, and started crying. Seeing her break down, the informant departed, while the attendant sat down near her. She said comforting words caressing her back.

"You don't know he needs me, I've to be beside him," said Dharman.

"Your first duty is towards these innocent infants."

"Babu promised that these infants would toddle in the free land, and I must stand by him to realize this dream," said Dharman. "Do you know any tawaif whom I can hand over these children . . . for the time being? I'll take them back when I return."

The attendant knew that her mistress would not listen once she had made up her mind. She nodded and started walking away, but turned when Dharman called her, "And ask the *sais* (horse caretaker) to exercise the horse. Also, send for the tailor, I need some new clothes."

"You are midway postpartum rest! Your body hasn't recovered enough to undertake this kind of exertion," the attendant protested before walking away helplessly; her wet eyes denoted how deeply she loved her mistress.

When the old tailor came, he was confused as to why she needed a man's dress, that too so urgently.

Two days later, Dharman breastfed her twin daughters for the last time, caressed them for a long time, kissed them scores of times, and then delivered them to the care of a distant cousin in Arrah. It is said that one of these girls grew to be a well-known tawaif, patronized by the Rajah of a nearby estate, and the other led the life of a homemaker. There are, however, no facts to confirm these stories.

Back at home, Dharman changed into the newly stitched man's dress. Then she gathered money, jewellery, and other things that she thought would be necessary and climbed up her horse to set out on an arduous journey towards Kaimur. She was aware of her delicate physical condition, so she rode the horse at a rhythmic canter.

Dharman circled around Jagdishpur to reach Kaimur three days later. She first headed to Ma Mundeswari Temple, a second-century temple. She was a Muslim yet had unfettered devotion in the goddess. She had visited this temple on several occasions in the past. She prayed for the safety and success of her patron.

On enquiry from the priest, she was informed that Kunwar Singh had already abandoned the area. He had possibly headed towards Sasaram with his remaining force. Immediately, she took

the road to the new destination and reached there two days later, only to be informed that he had proceeded ahead towards Rewa, now in Madhya Pradesh.

With her steadfast resolve, mere weeks after giving birth to twins, she braved the challenging journey across the rugged wooded plateau, uncertain of food and shelter. Despite the odds, Dharman pressed on towards the new destination, nearly four hundred kilometers away. Facing the rains, wind, and flooded regions, she went after her patron for another six days, and took a sigh of relief when she found his camp about 20 km from Rewa. A glance gave her an idea that there were about 2,000 fighters there, both sepoys and other armed men.

Her manly appearance did not give any room for the guard to doubt, though she had to wait for a couple of hours as Kunwar Singh was in a meeting. When he walked out, he did not take long to identify who the stranger was. He took her into the tent. Alone in his company, she broke down. She was happy to find him healthy and as high-spirited as ever. She raised her hands to thank the heavens.

"Why should you be here? Where is the child?" Kunwar Singh had several questions to ask.

"Not child, children. Two daughters were born," a faint smile emerged on her lips.

"I think they need you. Take rest and tomorrow, go back to them," said he.

"Your war is mine too. I will fight with you," insisted she.

"Have you seen a woman here? I know you are brave, but this mission is going to be very bloody. You have no business being here."

Dharman did not give in and Kunwar Singh felt helpless how to convince her. Finally, he allowed her to be part of the contingent. She was to remain in the male attire. She also handed over all the money, jewellery, and other valuables that she had brought.

During her stay, she was proud to learn about the exploits of her elderly but youthful patron. Despite the losses at Arrah and Jagdishpur, he had succeeded in spreading the flame of revolution throughout the eastern region. He knew that it was not enough to confront the British in one place. To spread revolution, he assigned the mission at Shahabad to his brother Amar Singh, and he himself was now on the road to realize his objective. Fighting small battles during the course of this treacherous journey at his age, he was now at Rewa.

A large number of people had joined his force, so he had to divide his army into several brigades under the command of his comrades. He was getting all types of reinforcement in the form of men and material from each place he had marched through, but he was short on ammunition for his field guns. More sepoys had risen in revolution and joined his force, like the Ramgarh battalion and the 5th Irregulars from Bhagalpur. The mighty British could not be defeated with mere swords and lances; he had muskets and field guns, but they could not be enough to face the enemy, even one-fourth in strength. The British informers reported that Kunwar Singh was 'with upwards of one thousand men, four elephants, fourteen camels, a lot of horses but no ammunition'. The British attempt to impede his march had so far proved to be futile.

In all the towns on his way and around, Kunwar Singh declared that the Company Raj had come to an end. He also deputed officials like Kanungo to realize and deposit revenue to him. He passed specific instructions that no Company official should be able to operate. He appointed his own officers wherever needed.

Kunwar Singh was now moving to Rewa as he was hopeful of getting ammunition there; its Raja Raghuraj Singh was his distant relative, who was in fact loyal to the British. He tried to obstruct the revolutionary force in Rewa but could not, so he fled from the fort. The British force under Lieutenant Osborne tried to launch

an attack but had to retreat when his place was surrounded by the hostile locals.

From Rewa, Kunwar Singh marched to Banda to join forces with the well-known Tantya Tope. A battle was fought here on October 8. It was the first battle in which Dharman took part. In the successful bid to capture the fort at Nimnipar, Kunwar Singh's grandson was killed when a shell burst near him. His grandeur was displayed when he himself laid him on the pyre. He is believed to have said on this occasion, "This sacrifice might be shattering personally, but the goal is so exalted that we ought not grieve over the loss."

He concealed his heavy heart and ordered the march to the next destination: Kalpi.

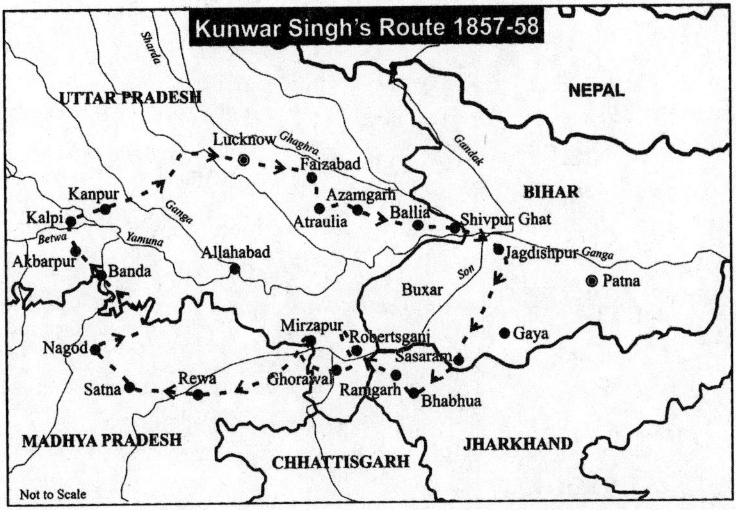

A sketch of the route taken by Kunwar Singh and his army

58

The Sacrifice

Having established his influence at Banda, Kunwar Singh marched on to Kalpi on October 20, 1857, with the 40th Native Infantry and irregular troops, with the intention of attacking Kanpur. He arrived five days later. Two other native infantries (7th and 8th) were directed to move to Chilla Tara on October 25 to cover the region around the Ken and Betwa rivers. They would rejoin Kunwar Singh's force at Azamgarh on their way to Jagdishpur.

At Kalpi, Kunwar Singh received an intimation from the Gwalior forces that they would join him soon. So, he decided to make good use of his stay there and capture Shiv Ram Tantia, a British protégé and eldest son of the British-supported zamindar of Kalpi and Atta.

On November 3, Kunwar Singh himself led a small party to undertake this mission he thought was small; Dharman was part of his horse-mounted contingent. He did not know that the enemy possessed field guns. He was about to launch the attack when he

came to know about the same. Instead of turning away, he decided to go forward.

No reward could be greater for the enemy than Kunwar Singh, who had a reward of five thousand rupees, a very high amount in those days, especially when he himself was giving so easy an opportunity. He was conspicuous in his white dress and a flowing turban of the matching color moving swiftly on his brown horse. Dharman was on his side. As he moved ahead, the defenders pointed the small field gun towards him and fired a round shot.

Dharman had sensed the danger to her patron from this. As the cannon roared, she instinctively grasped the peril unfolding. Without a moment's hesitation, she spurred her horse towards him, shielding him with her own body. It struck her torso and exploded. She fell down the horse, which too went down wounded.

Kunwar Singh, with his usual ferocity, did not take long to liquidate the defenders and take Shiv Ram Tantia captive. Then he went where Dharman lay on the ground breathing her last while he looked on helplessly. She moved her lips but could not say the parting words. It was at this time that her identity was revealed.

The patron oversaw her burial in the nearby ground. He stayed at Kalpi for four more days, and each day, he did not forget to visit her burial site. Now, no trace of her grave is found. She sacrificed herself, but her memory gradually faded. Even the *maulvi* at Dharman Masjid, located near Dharman Chowk in Arrah, claimed he did not know about her, for whom Kunwar Singh had built it. Many people in Arrah pretended to not know her, and those who talked about her did so in an embarrassing tone. Maybe people are wont to think that her being a tawaif could be a blot on her patron's exalted name, so her memory has been swept under the carpet. The only respite for her loving soul may be that people continue to offer prayers at this mosque even today.

On November 7, Kunwar Singh was joined by the Gwalior contingent, and then he moved on to Kanpur. The Gwalior army, 40th NI under Kunwar Singh, and Nana Saheb's army put up a combined front in the battle of Kanpur on December 4. However, they were no match for the British's superior arms and ammunition, under the command of Sir Colin Campbell.

Kunwar Singh decided to move on to Lucknow. At this time, Begum Hazrat Mahal was struggling against their common enemy. In the name of her son and Nawab, Birjis Qadr, she sent the champion of freedom a *khil'at* (robe of honor), money, and a *firman* (royal order) authorizing him to occupy Azamgarh.

Kunwar Singh had over 2,000 troops with him, in addition to irregular fighters. He first camped at Ayodhya, where the Gwalior contingent joined him again. By February 1858, he had received more reinforcements in the form of troops and guns. In the middle of March, he moved to Atraulia, and on March 22, he launched a massive attack on Colonel Millman's defenses and defeated them.

Emerging victorious in the massive battle fought on the 26th, he hoisted the Awadh and his own flags at Azamgarh. The British launched a retaliatory attack the following day, but he proved formidable. This firmed up his control over the district. How worried the British were can be gauged by what Mallesan writes in Kunwar Singh's praise: "But when he saw how British troops were being hurried up from every quarter to take part in the attack on Lakhnao, when he heard that the Nipalese and Franks had pushed on for that city, leaving the western frontier of the British provinces bordering Oudh comparatively denuded of troops, then he saw his opportunity, then he resolved to make a push for eastern Oudh, and combining with the numberless rebels still at large in that part, to make a dash on Azamgarh, and successful there, to avenge the storming of Jagdispur by a dash on Allahabad or Banaras."

It was at this stage that Kunwar Singh expressed his intention to return to his base in Jagdishpur. This sent a wave of terror through the British in Bihar. RV Boyle, the railway engineer at Arrah, wrote to the Governor General on March 31, 1858: "It is Koer Singh's intention to return to Shahabad. He has made his intention widely known, the people are expecting him and large numbers are prepared to join him and his force." In this letter, he also intimated that no other part of the lower provinces was more violently disturbed than Shahabad. The Patna Commissioner too sent letters of warning in this regard. He thought that Kunwar Singh had occupied Azamgarh in a bid to cross the Ganga and cross over to Shahabad. In his words, ". . . if he reappeared [in Shahabad] many Rajpoots and dismissed sepoys would join him and that great confusion would for a time be the inevitable result." At this time, the British were gathering troops from wherever it was possible to take on the impending march of the elderly but youthful warrior. The terror was so widespread that British officers in several towns around were unwilling to spare their troops to confront him. The Patna Commissioner himself planned to fall back to Gaya in case Kunwar Singh started the offensive. To make matters worse for them, the sepoys of the Bengal army, who had remained loyal to them until now, threatened to rebel in case they were deployed against Kunwar Singh.

At this time, Governor General Lord Canning was in Allahabad. He was very anxious as this offensive on the part of the Bihar chieftain could seize Banaras and thus 'sever the communications between Calcutta on the one side and the Governor General of India at Allahabad and the Commander-in-Chief of the army at Lucknow on the other.' Seeing the unwillingness of the officers in Bihar to confront Kunwar Singh, he ordered Lord Mark Kerr, then at Allahabad, to march to Azamgarh at once with his full force. He reached Azamgarh on April 6, but could not muster the courage to

launch an attack and wanted more reinforcement. The Governor General now ordered Sir E. Lugard to reinforce the Azamgarh force. This was an unprecedented mobilization of the British force at Azamgarh.

With all this happening simultaneously, Kunwar Singh relooked at his strategy. He deployed at Azamgarh about 2,000 troops under Nishan Singh, a trusted commander who had been on the battlefield all through, and himself moved towards Ghazipur with a smaller force. From this movement, it was evident that he wished to return to Jagdishpur with the intention of intensifying the revolution. Lugard reached Azamgarh on April 15 and had to struggle hard against the revolutionary force. However, Nishan Singh decided to withdraw under the pressure of a better-equipped force.

Lugard sent a force under Brigadier Douglas to go after Kunwar Singh and capture him. By this time, the reward money on him had been increased to ₹ 25,000. Lugard has himself admitted that the superior strategy employed by Kunwar Singh and his men outwitted his force, including cavaliers and guns. Kunwar Singh proved to be a better tactician when he marched from Ghazipur to Ghosee, Nagra, and Sikandarpur to cross the Ghaghra River and continue his march to Maniar. At each one of these places, he continued to get people's support, rations, and men, which shows how people adored him. To add to that, Mallesan notes that "he was well served by his spies."

The hot chase continued over the next two months. Brigadier Douglas, on July 21, moved ahead for a massive attack but was bewildered to find that the entire force had vanished into thin air. Mallesan notes in his book: "And although, by greatly daring, the British force succeeded in cutting off three of the enemy's guns, they found it useless to continue the pursuit. They therefore halted at Nathupur where they had fought, watched the enemy disappear in the direction of the Ganges…" In fact, in the evening, they broke

into small parties to reassemble at Santiwar, a thickly wooded area. They then proceeded to Shivpur Ghat (now in Ballia) to attempt crossing the Ganga into Bihar.

By this time, Kunwar Singh was wounded in the battle that he fought at Bansdih against Brigadier Douglas. Yet he supervised the crossing of all his troops across the Ganga, when he was under attack. Praising him, Mallesan writes, "But again Kunwar Singh did display great tactical ability. He kept Douglas at bay till he had secured two lines of retreat for his main columns, which he had divided. He then fell back leisurely . . ."

This was despite the fact that the British army and civil officials had invested their varied assets and manpower to check his movements and sinking of the boats. On this maneuver, the British intelligence reports said: "The villagers on the right bank assisted the rebels, many boats were raised from the places where they had been sunk." Kunwar Singh had planned his retreat aptly; when Douglas could locate his position, all but 200 had crossed the river.

Kunwar Singh was not like a commander who would think of his own safety first. He ensured that each of his troops and horses had sailed across, and only then did he himself take the last boat with a few men with him. Mid-stream in the sacred river, Douglas's artillery fired a shot that struck his right arm. He was also wounded in the thigh, yet the level of this great old man's courage and determination had not sunken an iota.

There is a popular legend about this incident. When the cannon ball struck his arm, wounding it badly, he looked at it with a sarcastic glance and said, "I don't want to die of a British bomb." With these words, he drew his sword, amputated his right arm from the elbow, and then cast it into the Ganga as his offering. And then he proceeded to tie a cloth around his profusely bleeding arm.

Kunwar Singh was back in Jagdishpur on July 22. Here, he was welcomed by his brother, Amar Singh, with several thousand-

armed villagers ready to support his cause. He formed a garrison with his men in the thick jungles around his fort.

On the very next day, a force under Captain Le Grand attacked his fort, but it had to retreat with a massive loss— as much as 90 percent of its strength. With this, Kunwar Singh firmly established his rule over Jagdishpur. Prolonged journey, intense fatigue, numerous battles, several wounds, and loss of blood took their toll on this exemplary man. He died three days later, on July 26, satisfied that he was breathing his last in a free land.

Kunwar Singh has died, but his name remains immortal. Not only Indians, but also many Europeans have praised him for his qualities of head and heart; no other leader seems to have earned people's love over such a large area as he had. His tactics baffled his rivals. Unlike the British, who indiscriminately handed out punishments to the native populace, he kept his prisoners safe from any harm. Travelyan wrote in his praise: "Kunwar Singh, a tall, noble-looking Rajput, was determined in character, and in spite of suffering from neuralgia, very active for a man of seventy-five . . . he was a worthy antagonist, for he kept in safety a large number of native Christians who were in his power." Once, when his men captured a European lady, he ensured her safe return. Mallesan has described him as "one of the three natives of India thrown up to the surface by the mutiny, who showed any pretensions to the character of a strategist, the others being Tantia Topi and the Oudh Moulvi [Ahmadulla Shah]." There are numerous folksongs dedicated to him, and many of these are sung on diverse religious and traditional occasions like festivals, fairs, weddings, and the birth of children. The fair of Shivratri continues to adore him and his comrades. Here are four of its lines:

"Luta dihal praan je, mita dihal nisaan je.
Chadha ke sees des ke, bana dihal mahan je.

Jane-jane jaga gail, naya nasa pila gail.
Jala-jala sarir ke, swades jagmaga gail."

(He sacrificed his life and wiped out his entity.
He offered his head to the motherland, and made it great.
He aroused each person, infused new motivation in them.
He burnt his body to enlighten the motherland.)

After him, his brother, Amar Singh, and comrades kept the flame of the freedom struggle burning until December 1859, much after the revolution had pacified at all other places. The British admitted that the campaign against the two brothers and their comrades was the toughest of all those 'which are counted more glorious in their results'. They could be overcome only when Havelock employed mounted infantry armed with Enfield rifles, for which the revolutionaries had no answer.

Dharman is talked about in hushed tones and is admired for her sacrifice as she wished to realize her patriotic patron's dream of 'free land' in which her daughters could toddle. Time has come when the names and exploits of such unsung and unknown fighters like hers are cherished as an integral part of our history.

Bibliography

Books (English)

1. Nevile, Pran, *Nautch Girls of the Raj*, Penguin Books, 2009.
2. Dewan, Saba, *Tawaifnama*, Context, 2019.
3. Dalrymple, William, *The Last Mughal*, Penguin Books, 2006.
4. Sampath, Vikram, *My Name Is Gauhar Jaan*, Rupa Pub., 2010.
5. Black, George, *On the Ganges*, St Martin's Press, 2018.
6. Gandhi, Mahatma, *Hind Swaraj*.
7. *Mahatma Gandhi: His Life, Writings and Speeches*, compiled by Ganesh & Co. (Year not given).
8. Gandhi, Mahatma, *Young India 1924-1926*, S. Ganeshan Pub, 1927.
9. *Great Works of Mahatma Gandhi*, compiled by Jainco Pub, Delhi.
10. Chandra, Satish, *History of Medieval India*, Orient BlackSwan, 2007.
11. *The Great Rebellion in India*, Edited by Biswamoy Pati, Routlege Studies in South Asian History, 2010.

12. Sen, Surendra Nath, *Eighteen Fifty-Seven*, Pub. Div., Min. of Information and Broadcasting, Government of India, 1957.
13. Innes, Arthur D., *A Short History of the British in India*, Metheun & Co., 1902.
14. Kaye, John William, *A History of the Sepoy War in India 1857–58*, Vol. II, 1888.
15. Banerji, Brajendranath, *Begams of Bengal*, M/s SK Mitra & Bros, 1942.
16. Wheeler, Sir Hugh Massey, Maj. Gen., *A Personal Narrative of the Outbreak and Massacre at Cawnpore*, London Printing Press, 1879.
17. Sharma, M.N., *Life and Times of Begam Samru*, Vibhu Pub, 1985.
18. Devsare, Harikrishna, *Tatya Tope*, Pub. Div., Ministry of Information and Broadcasting, Government of India, 2011.
19. Devsare, Harikrishna, *Nana Saheb Peshwa*, Pub. Div., Ministry of Information and Broadcasting, Government of India, 2011.
20. Shorey, Indumati, *Tatya Tope*, National Book Trust, India, 1973.
21. Kumari, Rashmi, *Maulavi Ahmad Ullah Shah and Great Revolt of 1857*, National Book Trust, India, 2016.
22. Nehru and Azad, *Nehru and Azad on 1857*, National Book Trust, India, 2008.
23. *Gazetteer of India Uttar Pradesh District Kanpur*, 1989.
24. *Gurgaon District Gazetteer.*
25. Francklin, William, *Military Memoirs of George Thomas*, , Reprinted for John Stockdale, Piccadilly, 1805.
26. Sleeman, Sir W.H., Maj. Gen., *A Journey Through the Kingdom of Oude*, Richard Bentley, London, 1858.

27. Banerji, Brajendranath, *Begam Samru*, MC Sarkar & Sons, 1925.
28. Qanungo, Prof. K.R., *History of the Jats*, M.C. Sarkar & Sons (Year not given).
29. Sharma, M.M., *Begum Samru* (A thesis with Agra University).
30. Sarkar, Jadunath, *Fall of the Mughal Empire*, 4 Vols.
31. Sarkar, Jadunath, *Anecdotes of Aurangzib.*
32. Bertlett, D.W., *The Heroes of the Indian Rebellion*, Follett, Foster & Co., 1859.
33. Roberts, P.E., *History of British India Under the Company and the Crown*, Clarendon Press, 1938.
34. Ansari, Tahir Hussain, *Mughal Administration and the Zamindars of Bihar*, Aligarh Muslim University, 2008.
35. Russell, W.H., *My Diary in India 1858-59*, 2 Vols., Routledge, Warne and Routledge, 1860.
36. Fraser, J. Baille, *Military Memoir of Lt Col J. Skinner*, Smith Elder & Co., 1851.
37. *Sardhana*, edited by Fr. Patrick, 2009.
38. Ray, Santimoy, *Freedom Movement and Indian Muslims*, National Book Trust, India, 1979.
39. Chandra, Bipan; Tripathi, Amales & De, Barun, *Freedom Struggle*, National Book Trust, India, 1972.
40. Majumdar, R.C., Raychaudhuri, H.C. & Datta, Kalikinkar, *An Advanced History of India,* Macmillan, 1946.
41. Chandra, Bipan, *History of Modern India,* Orient BlackSwan, 2009.
42. Sharma, L.P., *History of Modern India*, Konark Pub, 1987.
43. Mahajan, V.D., *History of Medieval India*, S. Chand, 1991.
44. Mahajan, V.D., *Modern Indian History*, S. Chand, 1990.
45. Aitchison, Sir Charles, *Rulers of India: Lord Lawrence*, Clarendon Press, 1892.

46. Martin, R. Montogomery, *The Indian Empire*, Vol. I, The London Printing and Publishing Co. (Year not mentioned).
47. Mill, James, *The History of British India*, 1858.
48. Malleson, Col. G.B., *History of the Indian Mutiny 1857-58*, Vol. II, W.H. Allen & Co., 1879.
49. Malleson, Col. G.B., *History of the Indian Mutiny 1857-58*, Vol. V, Longmans Green & Co., 1897.
50. Mead, Henry, *The Sepoy Revolt*, John Murray, 1857.
51. *The Mutiny of the Bengal Army*, (Writer not mentioned), Bosworth & Harrison, 1858.
52. Shadwell, Lt. Gen., *The Life of Colin Campbell, Lord Clyde*, Vol. II, William Blackwood & Sons, 1881.
53. Thomson, Capt. Mowbray, *The Story of Cawnpore*, Richard Bentley, 1859.
54. Newell, Lt. Col. Newell, *Lucknow*, H.A. Newell Bombay (Year not mentioned).
55. Case, Mrs. (wife of Col. Case), *Day by Day at Lucknow: A Journal of the Siege of Lucknow*, Richard Bentley, 1858.
56. Alli, Daroga Ubbas, *The Lucknow Album*, G.H. Rouse Baptist Mission Press, 1874.
57. *Selections from the Letters, Despatches and Other State Papers Preserved in the Military Department of the Government of India, 1857-58*, (Edited by) G.W. Forrest, Vol. II, 1902.
58. *Gazetteer of the Province of Oudh.*
59. Nevill, H.R., *Fyzabad: A Gazetteer*, Vol. XLIII, Government Press United Provinces, 1905.
60. Datta, Dr. K.K., *Biography of Kunwar Singh and Amar Singh*, K.P. Jayaswal Research Institute, Patna, 1957.
61. O'Malley, L.S.S., *Bihar and Orissa District Gazetteers: Shahabad*, Bihar and Orissa Government Printing, 1924.
62. Datta, Dr. K.K., *Unrest Against the British Rule in Bihar 1831-1859*, Secretariat Press Patna, 1917.

63. Travelyan, G.O., *The Competition Wallah*, MacMillan & Co., 1866.
64. Gathia, Joseph, *Child Prostitution in India*, Concept Publishing Company, New Delhi (1999)
65. *Journal of Francis Buchanan*, Ed. V.H. Jackson, Superintendent Government Printing, Bihar and Orissa, Patna, 1925.
66. *Letters Despatches and Other State Papers*, Ed. G.W. Forrest, Military Dept Press, Calcutta, 1902.

Books (Hindi)

1. Savarkar, Vinayak Damodar, *1857 Ka Swatantrya Samar*, Prabhat Pub., 2013.
2. Premchand, *Sewa Sadan* (*Courtesan Quarters*), Hans Prakashan (Year not given).
3. Nagar, Amritlal, *Ye Kothewalian*, Lokbharati Pub. (Year not given).
4. Chandra, Usha, *San Sattavan Ke Bhule-Bisare Shaheed*, National Book Trust, 1986.
5. *Inquilab 1857*, Ed., PC Joshi, National Book Trust, 2007.
6. Kant, Surendra, *Begum Hazrat Mahal*, Panchsheel Pub. Jaipur, 1989.
7. Singh, Veena Vatsal, *Begum Hazrat Mahal*, Rajpal Pub., 2023.
8. Ghosh, Pradeep Kumar & Chakravarti, Dr. Arup, *1857 Ki Kranti*, 2 Vols, Hindi Wangmay Nidhi, 2007.
9. Taqi, Raushan, *Begum Hazrat Mahal*, Hindi Wangmay Nidhi, 2007.
10. Yadav, K.C., *Begum Hazrat Mahal*, Pub. Div., Ministry of Information and Broadcasting, Government of India, 2008.
11. Sharma, Prof. Ashok Kumar, *Begum Hazrat Mahal*, GenNext Pub.

12. Nagar, Amritlal, *1857 Ki Do Viranganayen*, Uttar Pradesh Hindi Sansthan, 2007.
13. Sharma, Subhash; Singh, Anant Kumar & Pandey, Jawahar, *Kunwar Singh aur 1857 ki Kranti*, National Book Trust, India, 2007.
14. Bajpayee, Ram Kishor, *Lucknow ki Tawaifen*, Hindi Wangmay Nidhi, 2015.
15. Rizvi, Dr. Syed Atahar Abbas, *Swatantra Dilli*, Uttar Pradesh Hindi Sansthan, 1968.
16. Verma, Raj Gopal Singh, *Begum Samru Ka Sach* (Hindi) by Samvad Pub, 2019.
17. Mathur, Akash, *Umeda Ek Yoddha Nartaki*, Shivna Pub., 2022.
18. Gandhi, A.K., *1857 Kranti Va Krantidhara*, National Book Trust, India, 2016.
19. Ayachi, Pt. Rakesh, *Orchha Ka Itihas*, 2015.

Papers/Articles

1. "The Alpha Songbirds: Independent and Vibrant" by Kumud Diwan Jha, as compiled in the *Interrogating Women's Leadership and Empowerment*, as edited by Omita Goyal.
2. "*Only One Word Properly Altered: Gandhi and the Question of Prostitute*" by Ajay Skaria.
3. "*Courtesan Culture in India: The Transition from the Devadasi to the Tawaif or Baijee*" by Mekhala Sengupta.
4. "*Gandhi's 'Fallen' Sisters: Difference and the National Body Politic*" by Ashwini Tambe.
5. "*Lifestyle as Resistance: The Case of the Courtesans of Lucknow*" by Veena Talwar Oldenburg.
6. "*Prostitution in Northern Central India: an ethnographical study*

of Bedia Community" by U. Rana, D. Sharma and D. ghosh, *International Journal Anthropol. Ethnol*, 4, 2 (2020).

7. *Mayalee: The Story of an Indian dancing girl who stood up to the British Raj*, Katherine Butler Schofield, 2019.
8. "Gandhi and the Question of the Prostitute," Ajay Skaria, *Economic and Political Weekly*, Dec. 9, 2006.
9. *7 Courtesans and the 1857 Rebellion: The Role of Azeezun in Kanpur*, Prof. Lata Singh.
10. *Embodying War: British Women and Domestic Defilement in the Indian 'Mutiny' 1857-58*, Alison Blunt, *Journal of Historical Geography*, 2000.
11. "Revolt of 1857 in Awadh with Special Reference of Lucknow," Dr. Amit Wardhan, *Intl Journal of Scientific & Innovative Research Studies.*
12. *From Nautch Girl to Tawaif: The Lucknow Courtesan in Transition*, Vijay Prakash Singh, University of Lucknow.
13. "Prostitution in Northern Central India: An Ethnographical Study of Bedia Community," Usha Rana, *Intl Journal of Anthropology and Ethnology*, 2020.

Miscellaneous Online Resources

1. Video on YouTube "*Vidyadhari Bai: Chun chun ke phool le lo, Arman rah na jaaye*".
2. Video on YouTube "*Husna Jan or Husna Bai: Banaras Gharane Ki 'Sarkar-e-Thumri*"

About the Author

A.K. Gandhi is a historian, author, and translator. He writes in both Hindi and English and has several books to his credit, published by prestigious publishers including the National Book Trust (*1857 Kranti Va Krantidhara*), Madhya Pradesh Hindi Granth Akademi, Bhopal (*Pratap, Shivaji aur Chhatrasal*), Kitabghar Pub. (*Bharatiya Thal Sena: Badhate Kadam*), Prabhat Pub. (*APJ Abdul Kalam: A Saintly Scientist*), and others. The book *Pratap, Shivaji aur Chhatrasal* busted several myths about the three legendary

leaders, impressed by which the Madhya Pradesh Govt rewarded it by including it in the state education syllabus as supplementary study for class XI for two academic sessions (2016–17, 2017–18). His articles and stories have appeared in several prestigious newspapers and magazines, including the *Hindu*, *Times of India*, *Reader's Digest*, *Competition Success Review*, *Amar Ujala*, *Janwani,* and *Dainik Jagran.*

As a translator, he has several published books, including *Gond*, *Komagata Maru* (both Eng-Hindi, National Book Trust), *The Battle of Rezang La* (Penguin, NBT) and Narendra Modi's *Jyotipunj* (Hindi-English, Prabhat Publication).

An ex-IAF language specialist, presently A.K. Gandhi, is also a mentor under the Prime Minister Yuva Mentorship Scheme (for young authors) as part of the Azadi Ka Amrit Mahotsav program.

An inside view of Mastani Mahal at Dhubela, built by King Chhatrasal of Orchha

Azizan Bai's painting in Bithur Museum, near Kanpur

The Memorial erected over the Bibighar Well, the site of massacre, in 1858, has now been shifted to Memorial Church in Kanpur

Sri Krishna Dharmashala, Banaras

Nana Saheb Peshwa's sword, as displayed
in the Red Fort Museum, Delhi

Sri Radha Krishna Temple, Banaras.
It is in dire need of renovation

The Church (Basilica of Our Lady of Graces) that Begum Samru built at Sardhana

Salimgarh Fort, Delhi where Mughal Emperor Shah Alam II and other royal members were incarcerated in small dingy cells

The palace that Begum Samru built for herself at Sardhana, now an Inter College

Begum Samru's statue in marble, erected over her tomb in the Sardhana Cathedral

Sombre's and his son Zafaryab Khan's graves at Roman Catholic Cemetery, Agra

An inside view of Sardhana church

A view of Chhatar Manzil, the palace where Wajid Ali Shah lived with his Paris and Begums, from across the Gomti River

Tomb of Shuja-ud-Daula at Faizabad (Ayodhya), built by himself

Begum Hazrat Mahal's painting displayed at 1857 Memorial Museum, Residency, Lucknow

Baradari in Lucknow where Birjis Qadr was crowned

A building in the Residency in Lucknow bearing marks from musket fire

Sikandar Bagh in Lucknow which witnessed a fierce battle

Shah Najaf Imambara in Lucknow, a site of battle

Kothi Farhat Baksh in Lucknow, to the right side can be seen the famed dome of the Chhatar Manzil

Nana Saheb's destroyed palace at Bithur stands surrounded by thick woods

Dilkusha Kothi, a site of fierce battle in Lucknow, in the ground near which Wajid Ali Shah trained his troops

Hodson's tombstone

A painting depicting Kunwar Singh at Jagdishpur Museum dedicated to him

A field gun manufactured in Kunwar Singh's foundry

An inside view of Dharman Masjid at Arrah

MORE FROM FINGERPRINT

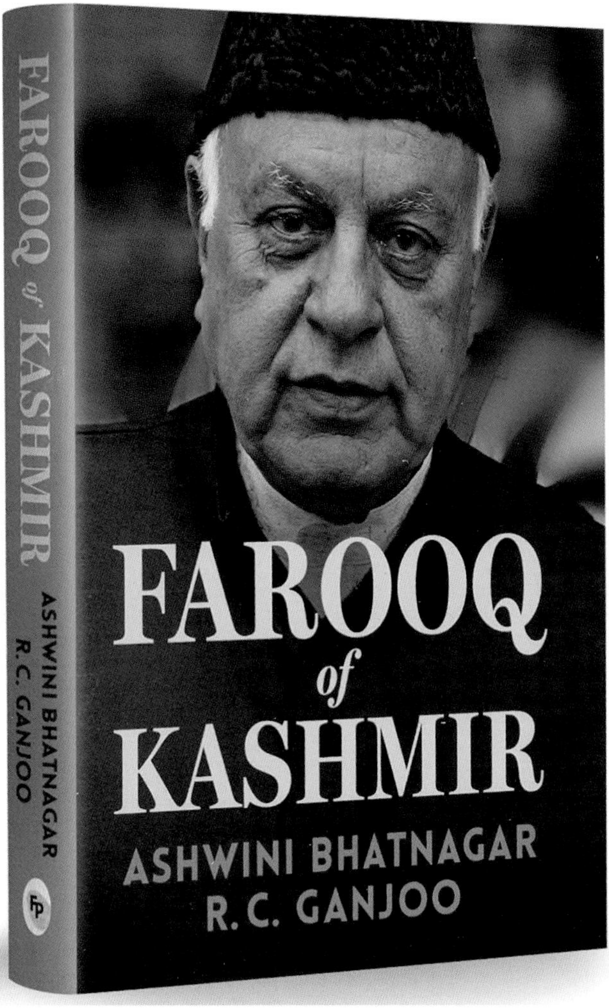
FAROOQ of KASHMIR
ASHWINI BHATNAGAR
R.C. GANJOO
FAROOQ
of
KASHMIR
ASHWINI BHATNAGAR
R. C. GANJOO

सर्वश्रेष्ठ कहानियां
मुंशी प्रेमचंद
रवींद्रनाथ टैगोर
शरत्चंद्र चट्टोपाध्याय
सर्वश्रेष्ठ कहानियां
मुंशी प्रेमचंद, रवींद्रनाथ टैगोर
शरत्चंद्र चट्टोपाध्याय